The International Faith

For

Stephen Bird

The International Faith

Labour's Attitudes to European Socialism, 1918-39

CHRISTINE COLLETTE

Ashgate

Aldershot • Brookfield USA
Singapore • Sydney

Published by
Ashgate Publishing Limited
Gower House, Croft Road
Aldershot, Hants
GU11 3HR, England

Ashgate Publishing Company
Old Post Road
Brookfield
Vermont 05036-9704, USA

The author has asserted her moral right under the Copyright, Designs and Patents Act, 1998, to be identified as the author of this work.

British Library Cataloguing in Publication Data
Collette, Christine
    The International Faith: Labour's Attitudes to European Socialism,
    1918-39. (Studies in Labour History)
    1. Labour Party (Great Britain)--History--20th century.
    2. Socialism--Europe--History--20th century.
    I. Title.
    320.5'31'094'09041
    ISBN 1-85928-385-3

Library of Congress Cataloging-in-Publication Data
Collette, Christine
    The international faith: labour's attitudes to European socialism,
    1918-39/Christine Collette.
        p. cm.
    Includes bibliographical references and index.
    ISBN 1-85928-385-3 (hc)
    1. International labour activities. 2. Socialism--Europe--History--20th
century. 3. Trade unions--Great Britain--History. 4. Internationalism.
5. Labour Party (Great Britain)--History. 6. Europe--Politics and
government--1918-45. I. Title.
HD6475.AIC53   1998   97-42174
331.88'094--dc21   CIP

ISBN 1 85928 385 3

This book is printed on acid free paper

Printed in Great Britain by Galliard (Printers) Ltd, Great Yarmouth

Contents

List of Figures, Plates and Music Examples   ix

List of Tables   x

Acknowledgements   xi

List of Abbreviations   xii

Introduction   1

1   Strike for Peace: The British Labour Movement and the International
    Federation of Trades Unions   12

2   Paths of European Unity, 1918-33: The Labour Party and the Labour
    and Socialist International   46

3   The Fascist Challenge, 1933-39: The Labour Party and the Labour
    and Socialist International   76

4   The International Faith: Subject and Special Interest Groups   99

5   'Arise ye Starvelings': The Language of Internationalism   124

6   'Matters affecting Women': International Contacts between Women,
    Young People and Cooperators   150

Conclusion   185

Bibliography   192

Index   204

Studies in Labour History
General Editor's Preface

Labour history has often been a fertile area of history. Since the Second World War its best practitioners - such as E.P. Thompson and E.J. Hobsbawm, both Presidents of the British Society for the Study of Labour History - have written works which have provoked fruitful and wide-ranging debates and further research, and which have influenced not only social history but history generally. These historians, and many others, have helped to widen labour history beyond the study of organised labour to labour generally, sometimes to industrial relations in particular, and most frequently to society and culture in national and comparative dimensions.

The assumptions and ideologies underpinning much of the older labour history have been challenged by feminist and later by post-modernist and anti-Marxist thinking. These challenges have often led to thoughtful reappraisals, perhaps intellectual equivalents of coming to terms with a new post-Cold War political landscape.

By the end of the twentieth century, labour history had emerged reinvigorated and positive from much introspection and external criticism. Very few would wish to confine its scope to the study of organised labour. Yet, equally, few would wish now to write the existence and influence of organised labour out of nations' histories, any more than they would wish to ignore working-class lives and focus only on the upper echelons.

This series of books provides reassessments of broad themes of labour history as well as some more detailed studies arising from recent research. Most books are single-authored but there are also volumes of essays centred on important themes or periods, arising from major conferences organised by the Society for the Study of Labour History. The series also includes studies of labour organisations, including international ones, as many of these are much in need of a modern reassessment.

Chris Wrigley
British Society for the Study of Labour History
University of Nottingham

List of Figures, Plates and Music Examples

Figures

1.1 Labour Movement international organisation, 1918-39   44
1.2 Labour Party international department   45

4.1 Workers' Travel Association annual turnover, 1921-39   123
4.2 Workers' Travel Association overseas bookings, 1921-39   123

Plates and music examples

Between pages 98 and 99

1 LSI Congress, 1923, postcard
2 LSI Congress, 1925, advertisement
3 LSI Secretariat, on balcony of a hotel in Paris, 1933
4 International Brigade Meeting, 1939, advertisement
5 *Sennacieca Asocio Tutmonda*, postcard
6 Labour League of Youth, 1930s, advertisement

7 The Red Flag
8 The International
9 March Song of the Red Army
10 The Soviet Airmen's Song
11 The Red Army March
12 The Mothers' International

List of Tables

1.1 British representation at the LSI   42
1.2 LSI conferences and congresses   43

2.1 Münzenberg's 'front' organisations   75

6.1 Women's representation at the LSI   183

Acknowledgements

Thanks are due to Chris Wrigley, for editing; Nicky Rippon, for preparing camera-ready copy; Caroline Cornish, desk editor at Ashgate; Peter Manasse, Sound and Vision Department, International Institute of Social History, Amsterdam, for photographs; Ms Ishbel Lochhead for permission to quote from Ramsay MacDonald's diaries; Nicky Rippon and Nicole Fraser for French translation. Edge Hill University College and the Dee Foundation supplied research and scholarship grants. Archivists at the National Museum of Labour History, Manchester, International Institute of Social History, Amsterdam, Esperanto Centre, London, Tate Gallery, London, Women's Art Library, London, the Ruth and Eddie Frow Centre, Manchester, Public Records Office, Kew, Churchill College, Cambridge, British Library of Political and Economic Science, London, Ruskin College, Oxford, Modern Records Centre, Warwick, Trades Union Congress, London, and the Bodleian Library staff should also be thanked for their patience and assistance.

List of Abbreviations

AFofL	American Federation of Labour
AIA	Artists' International Association
ASLEF	Associated Society of Locomotive Engineers and Firemen
BLES	British League of Esperantist Socialists
BWSF	British Workers' Sports International
CPGB	Communist Party of Great Britain
EWI	Education Workers' International
ICA	International Cooperative Alliance
IFTU	International Federation of Trades Unions
IFWW	International Federation of Working Women
IISH	International Institute of Social History
ILO	International Labour Office
ILP	Independent Labour Party
ISS	International Socialist Students
ITT	International Tramping Tours
ITWF	International Transport Workers' Federation
IWW	International Workers of the World
LRD	Labour Research Department
LSI	Labour and Socialist International
NCL	National Council of Labour
NMM	National Minority Movement
RILU	Red International of Labour Unions
SAT	*Sennacieca Asocia Tutmonda*
SDP	Social Democratic Party
SEI	Socialist Education International
SI	Sports International
SJC	Standing Joint Committee of Industrial Women's Organisations
SYI	Socialist Youth International
TUC	Trades Union Congress
WEA	Workers' Educational Association
WIPLF	Women's International League for Peace and Freedom
WIR	Workers' International Relief
WTA	Workers' Travel Association

Introduction

As major components of this title: internationalism; the Labour Movement are ideological constructs, it seems to me more than ordinarily important to explain my own position before defining terms and outlining the philosophical background and structure of the book. This study has been evolving for many years, stage posts including Ruskin College work on appeasement written for Victor Treadwell, who has nurtured many Labour Movement historians; my M.Litt. thesis under the supervision, at various times, of Victor, John Rowett and Raphael Samuel; the conference on the Second International organised by Chris Wrigley at Birkbeck College (1993), the North American Labor Conference, Wayne State University (1994) and that on Alternative Futures at Manchester Metropolitan University (1995). These people and events are among the many who have contributed inspiration but all involved are absolved from responsibility for the final outcome. My feminist approach, the need to address issues of gender and ethnicity stem from twenty years involvement in the Women's Movement; meetings of the Oxford Women's Studies group in the 1980s; my friendship with African historian Lindi Mhdluli, which makes me define myself as a white, Western woman; and teaching Women's Studies, with the rigorous questioning of gender, class and ethnic stereotypes which this discipline necessarily entails.

I came to academia from a trade union and political background. The initial and underlying commitment to this project stems from my past affiliation to the International Socialist tendency and the Socialist Workers' Party. I share this past history with many another politically conscious academic who has since moderated her opinions, but my belief in the inherently internationalist basis of socialism has remained unchanged. I use the word 'belief' advisedly. Like Arthur Henderson, inter-war Labour Party secretary, I think that: 'the international faith ... is the soul of socialism'.[1] Henderson, of course, was no revolutionary and this book seeks to show that, between the wars, internationalism was not the dogma of the revolutionary few, but commonly understood as the basis of socialism by the mainstream of the Labour Movement, its revolutionary and evolutionary wings, its leadership and its membership. While my political past explains my initial interest in internationalism, I think that it is relevant to assert this history today, as connections with Europe are again considered. We grapple with the problem of national, political and personal identity in our relationships to Europe, to Ireland; with the consequences of the break up of the Soviet Union; with racism, sexism and classism in our own society.

I have been concerned to write not just about the leaders but about the ordinary membership of the Labour Movement since, like Harry Gosling, president of the Transport and General Workers Union between the wars, I am strongly of the opinion that the membership must be 'at the back of' the formal international conferences if these are to succeed. This means dealing with the broad Labour Movement, but I have taken the perspective of its majority Labour Party and trades union element. This is partly because the other major ideological component, the Communist Party of Great Britain (CPGB), was relatively small and, more importantly, affiliated to and directed by the Third International. One expects the Communist Party to be internationalist; 'discovering' such CPGB principle and practice is redundant. The case I have to make is finding internationalism in the Labour Movement mainstream where expectations are of a less cosmopolitan orientation. The position of the Independent Labour Party was somewhat different; it was part of the Labour Party for the majority of the inter-war period and its disaffiliation and engagement in the London Bureau in the 1930s, despite disclaimers, helped pave the way for the Fourth International. My own particular background has, perhaps, heightened my interest in the ILP but the latter's loss of membership after disaffiliation make it peripheral to the main narrative of this book. The composition of the Labour Movement is more fully dealt with later, but first, the context of activity between the wars is outlined.

Context

The British had a long history of international involvement from the creation of Marx's First International, when the only large trades unions affiliated were from Britain. They had continued to participate in the Second International. In 1918, the British Labour Movement was in a position to take a lead in Europe. The Labour Party had not split during the war, enhancing its strength in comparison to that of other European parties.[2] The trades unions had grown in confidence. The British Labour Movement was situated in a victorious country whose structure of government was unaltered, but where the franchise had been greatly extended to include the working classes.

The 1990s re-emergence of Eastern European countries from a newsroom twilight has enhanced our view of the Europe perceptible to the British Labour Movement after 1918. Then, experience of war, the presence of reactionary forces, the rise of fascism meant a changing international situation calling for continual reassessment of policies; while rival principles and practices in European socialism, reformist social democracy *versus* communism, had to be addressed. Faced with such severe economic, social and political problems between the wars, the management of international organisations changed considerably. Not the least problem, from the point of view of the hegemony of the British Labour Movement's attitude to European socialism, was the division of international organisations into industrial, political, and consumer spheres of interest. Nevertheless, the separate wings of the Labour Movement made large contributions to rebuilding their respective Internationals.

In taking the lead in the recreation of the Labour and Socialist International, the organisation representing European social democratic parties, the Labour Party chose the reformist road. Trades Union Congress affiliation to the International Federation of Trades Unions also implied acceptance of reformism. Some energy was initially spent on a futile search for unity between the reformists and the revolutionaries; this search engaged the trades unions until the late 1920s, the Independent Labour Party into the 1930s and the Socialist League during its brief existence (1932 to 1937). Some trades unionists joined the CPGB. The historian should resist the temptation to impose political tidiness upon the inter-war Labour Movement. Abroad, the Labour and Socialist International maintained friendly relations with the International Federation of Trades Unions and the International Cooperative Alliance; it was, at times, inclined to negotiate with the communists and, at others, hostile to any collaboration. As Stefan Berger has written, European left ideological identities were not fixed: 'workers and their organisations could switch from one ideology to the other'.[3]

Labour Movement

The Labour Party and trades unions were often referred to, and referred to themselves as 'The Labour Movement', sometimes 'The Movement', or 'The whole Movement'. The balance of power swung between the Labour Party and the trades unions. However, on closer inspection the Labour Movement appears more diverse; there was interaction with cooperators and with socialist societies. Most unions were Party affiliates most of the time and provided the bulk of the Party's funds, but individual trades unionists were not necessarily Labour Party members; many voted Conservative or Liberal.

The term commonly used as a collective noun to describe the mass membership of the Labour Movement, the fee paying members of trades unions and political parties is 'rank and file'. This nomenclature suffers from a convenient vagueness about which parties, unions and groups are included and whether to count people who attended meetings and engaged in activity but paid no fees. The introduction, in the 1918 Labour Party constitution of individual membership substantiated the concept of a rank and file. It was between the wars that the Trades Union Congress and Labour Party consolidated their organisation and collected, defined, prescribed and proscribed a membership. As far as the leadership was concerned, the Independent Labour Party counted until 1932, the Communist Party of Great Britain until 1924, the National Unemployed Workers Movement never, trades councils if they behaved themselves. The 1935 decision to allow local parties directly to elect the constituency section of the National Executive was a small empowerment of the rank and file; the Women's Section was still elected by conference block voting.

Internationalism and Nationalism

The Labour Movement was named 'British' in contrast to 'The International' or 'The International Movement'. This designation was a product of its history; ideas of nation and class were roughly contemporaneous, and interconnected responses to the economic and socio-political forces of industrialisation. The emergence of the British Labour Movement, in order to represent the class interest of the nation's working people, was a corollary. Jean Jaurès, leader of the French socialist party before 1914, wrote of the link between ideas of class and of nation: 'the workers have no country as long as they are not a class ... and the more the workers have a class, the more they have a country'.[4] Two products of the Labour Movement's development as a national body were apparent; it was ethnically distinct (the first Aliens Act came onto the statute book in 1905); and it was gendered. Recent work associates 'nation-ness' with male bonding, defining nation as an imagined space men fought for. Idealisation of 'the English woman' followed, informing a social construction of sexuality which privileged heterosexuality and male sexual appetite while demanding female fidelity in order to perpetuate the English 'race'.[5] The white, masculine image of the Labour Movement was also a function of the labour market: ethnic minority and women workers were less likely to be trade union or Labour Party fee-payers.[6]

Acknowledging the Labour Movement's national identity, however, may obscure both its continuing regional diversification on the one hand and its international philosophy on the other. The first point, about regional differences, is generally accepted;[7] it was in the Labour Movement's interest when constructing national bargaining bases and a party capable of winning general elections to minimise these. The point about the Labour Movement's international philosophy is less often addressed.

It is sometimes asserted that Labour Movement internationalism existed in the nineteenth century (participation in the First and Second International gave evidence) but was damaged irretrievably by the experience of the First World War. This book takes issue with that assertion. Against the fact that workers fought against each other from 1914 to 1918 must be posed their lack of knowledge of modern welfare and invidious familiarity with domestic poverty. It was not easy to resist conscription from 1916. Experience of war, for nationalists, may have caused disenchantment. In his book of that title, C.E. Montague wrote that: 'soldiers are the most determined peace party that ever existed in Britain'.[8] One of the lessons of war had been the opportunity it gave revolutionary socialists to assist the discovery by workers of their class interests. This was illustrated, for example, by the revolutions of Russia and Germany. The destruction of European empires allowed social democratic parties to seize state power, notably in Germany. Ben Spoor (later Member of Parliament for Bishop Auckland) said with some justice at the 1919 Labour Party conference: 'the war, far from destroying internationalism, seems to have rediscovered it'.[9]

4

An example of the way internationalism changed course after the First World War, rather than collapsed, was implied in the international objectives of the 1918 Labour Party constitution. The first objective was given as cooperation with socialist and Labour organisations of other countries, addressing the need to collaborate against war and assuming the existence of organised class parties. The second objective was similar, assisting in the creation of a federation of nations for the maintenance of peace. The third spoke of a political programme for peace, the establishment of machinery for resolving international disputes by conciliation and arbitration.[10] The quest for peace was natural in a constitution written in 1918, but the Labour Party was not pacifist. Certainly, it found war repugnant and the antithesis of socialism, but was prepared, if necessary, to take up arms in defence against an aggressor or in defence of nation.

Admittedly, the idea of nation flourished after the First World War and, as E. J. Hobsbawm wrote, 1918 to 1939 was the time when it became an organising principle for defining territorial boundaries, creating 'a jig-saw puzzle of states', and therefore providing 'an exceptionally good opportunity for assessing the limitations and potential of nationalism and nation states'. It has since informed our history: Hobsbawm cites Renan, who wrote that 'getting the history wrong is part of being a nation'. National working classes can be more easily identified after 1918; however, it would be poor logic (as well as poor history) to assert that workers and their representatives must therefore be chauvinists.[11]

If class and nation were interconnected concepts, so were nationalism and internationalism. As Eduard Bernstein (German Social Democratic party) wrote in the Independent Labour Party organ *New Leader* (27 April 1925):

> the international idea ... presupposes the existence of nations; it could not arise until the nomadic tribes had settled and formed political units, held together by common laws and common language.

The point that workers' movements had both nationalist and internationalist perspectives has been noted by historians, for instance Georges Haupt, in his study of the Second International on the eve of the First World War.[12] Jaurès had warned that European war could result in either revolution or 'exaggerated nationalism'.[13] The historian Halévy argued in 1929 that state monopoly and collaboration with workers' organisations in the First World War would cause both revolution and reaction, socialism and fascism.[14] In language which indicated the fluidity of the concepts, James Middleton, Labour Party Assistant Secretary, wrote in 1929: 'the socialist does not substitute internationalism for nationalism, but building on a genuine nationalism stretches out to socialists in other lands and seeks to build up a wider policy of internationalism'.[15] The tensions implicit in the complex relationship of class, nationalism and internationalism did stress the fabric of international organisations. Between the wars, the Labour Movement was aware of both national and international responsibilities and devoted much energy to finding a satisfactory balance. What it meant to be internationalist in outlook was much debated. The diversity of the Labour Movement allowed a variety of definitions; internationalism was a kaleidoscopic vision.

Structure

As internationalism was such a varied philosophy, its practice differed. Broadly, it was the leadership which created, and had access to formal organisations. This book deals consecutively with the international practices of the trades unions and the Labour Party leadership, less formal contacts made by a broader range of the Labour Movement membership and those of women and young people. Chapter five addresses some of the imaginative media of contact used by the Labour Movement; different matter required a different style of communication. Of course, these contacts overlapped and people moved from one group to another; for instance, Vandervelde, President of the Labour and Socialist International, attended the 1934 Sports International meeting.

Separate trades union and Labour Party contact was a function of the twin power bases of the Labour Movement and its bureaucratisation. International contact initially devolved on to William Gillies, Labour Party International Secretary. Soon, he was managing contact with the Labour and Socialist International, while the Trades Union Congress dealt with the International Federation of Trades Unions. Conferences of the Labour and Socialist International were rarely held (a fact much deplored by its secretary) and British representation on its bureau and executive was increasingly dominated by William Gillies.[16]

At first, when internationalism was expressed as a commitment to peace, it was a unifying force within the Labour Movement. Later, leadership policies of resistance to communist advances and rearmament were more controversial and were defied by rebels. A person's international outlook came to define his or her place to the right or the left, within or without the Labour Movement; support of the official view was one of the tests used to maintain control and discipline. The International Department which Gillies headed was deeply involved in the disciplinary process. As Gillies was fervently and obsessively anti-communist, his omnipresence added to leadership caution about communist involvement. Gillies was the Labour Party policeman and his patch was the Labour Movement.

In tracing the less formal international contacts of the broader Labour Movement this book illuminates some of the people and groups which comprised the rank and file. Some people, relatively well known to contemporaries have since been forgotten (for instance, Tom Groom of the Clarion Cycling Club and Sports International) while others of roughly equal contemporary influence have been accorded posthumous fame (John Cornford, poet, of the Socialist Students). To find themes of rank and file interests and

6

philosophies, an approach is needed which discovers mass involvement. Manuscript sources tend to reflect leadership interests. Oral history is important but remains, inevitably, the recollections of a relatively small group of people. It also runs the risk of recording the memories of a vanguard, rather than a rank and file. Rank and file interests may, however, be inferred from activity and from the channels of communication by which such activity was promoted.

It has been sometimes argued that the actions and beliefs of the rank and file are those of the working class as a whole. An assumption of working class chauvinism has then been extended to the rank and file. There are problems with both parts of this xenophobic worker assumption. First, the evidence of working class chauvinism is far from overwhelming; the motives, wishes and culture of British workers at any point in history are open to doubt. Second, the rank and file was a distinct social grouping because it was characterised by some degree of political awareness and, if en-gendered and ethnicised, was from a range of social classes.[17]

Zeitlin has argued, controversially, that the term rank and file has been misused to describe a left vanguard, distinct from officialdom. Vanguards, from 1918 to 1939, often based their distinction on differences in international outlook: the Communist Party of Great Britain was the prime example, followed by those groups committed to a united front of socialists and communists, the Independent Labour Party, the Revolutionary Policy Committee formed within it (1931); the united front oriented Socialist League (1932) and the Peace Alliance (1939) of Liberal, Cooperative and Communist parties. All of these groups had leaders, many of whom left written records, particularly of their interaction with the Labour Movement leadership. The Communist Party and the Independent Labour Party had their own formal channels of international communication, respectively the Third International and the London Bureau (the latter was variously titled and its organisation formalised from 1934). It is accepted that the leadership of these groups, attracting press attention, organising a more or less substantial membership, do not constitute a rank and file; but the ordinary membership ought to be included. The debate is a useful reminder that including groups beyond the trades unions and Labour Party broadens the social mix of the rank and file; although working class interests were finding expression, they were not, necessarily, expressed by workers.[18]

En-gendering the concept of the rank and file has the advantage of clarifying that it is not merely one of alternative leadership, as women so rarely won leading positions; the same comments apply to ethnicising the rank and file. The study of these areas is illuminating: for instance, perceptions of sexuality inform the ideology of gender within the rank and file; sex was one of the social activities that built comradeship. The extent to which resistance to fascism was class based is remarkable; chapter six assesses the evidence for a distinct gendered politics. It is noticeable that women's groups acted rather as members of the rank and file than as leaders, keeping low individual profiles and taking a

7

fairly relaxed approach to Labour leadership prohibition of work with communists.[19]

There is some evidence of failure throughout the Labour Movement to challenge racist views, which were invariably expressed when Black troops were used; for instance, no comment was made on a particularly repugnant cartoon in *New Leader* (10 March 1923) which showed two stereotyped Black soldiers walking away from a woman on the ground at the time of the Rhineland occupation; the caption was 'what feeble folk the French are. They must always call us to finish their work for them'. The British Committee for Refugees from Spain wrote of 'Senegalese negroes' in French camps: 'the situation became more ugly when the Loyalist troops saw their women being roughly handled by the black soldiers'. Racism and sexism interact here, so that national space is perceived as female.[20] Derogatory language was, on occasion, directly used; for example, of American strike-breakers: 'they are branded as "blacklegs" in addition to being black by nature, which was reproof enough'. This view of White proletarian as opposed to Black worker was noted by Ramdin amongst the seamen's unions in Cardiff.[21] Racism was not universal. There were examples of anti-racist groups and of rejection of anti-semitism; a local Co-operative newspaper, for instance, wrote that 'Down with the Jews' was the start of fascism and that 'race persecution, like religious persecution, is un-British - and always wrong'; the British Non-Sectarian Anti-Nazi League Council joined the International Federation of the League against Anti-Semitism. Some of these groups, including communists, were amongst those proscribed by the Labour Movement leadership.[22]

Sometimes sexist and racist, the rank and file cannot be prejudged nationalistic on the grounds that they were working class. This is because evidence of working class chauvinism is not beyond challenge and because the rank and file was drawn from a larger social group. The distinguishing characteristic of the rank and file is a degree of political awareness. Between the Wars was a time when political thinking was bound to involve reflection on nationalism and internationalism, because nation had become an organising principle of the composition of political units exploited by militant fascism. To the socialist, internationalism was a necessity, for peace and disarmament and to promote working class interests. Arthur Henderson made his statement of faith at the 1933 Labour Party conference: 'Never shall we surrender our international faith - that faith is the soul of socialism'.[23]

Notes

1.   Henderson, Arthur, *Labour Party Conference Report*, 1933, p. 191, reproduced as *Labour Outlaws War*.

2.   Berger, Stefan (1995), 'European Labour Movements and the European Working Class in Comparative Perspective', in Berger, Stefan and Broughton,

David (eds), *The Force of Labour: the Western European Labour Movement and the Working Class in the Twentieth Century,* Berg, Oxford, p. 247 outlines the different effects of the war on political development.

3.   Berger, Stefan (1995), op. cit., p. 248. See also Williams, Chris (1995), 'Britain' in Berger, Stefan and Broughton, David (eds) (1995), op. cit., p. 128, note 2.

4.   Jean Jaurès, cited, Cahm, E. and Fisera, V.C. (eds) (1986), *Socialism and Nationalism,* Spokesman, London, p. 69. See Smith, Anthony (1986), *The Ethnic Origins of Nations,* Blackwell, Oxford, *passim,* for the classic exposition of the argument that Western ideas of nation are bound up with the formation of political units and that common recognition amongst people, the growth of class consciousness is a pre-requisite for class formation and contributes to the development of an *ethnie* into a nation.

5.   Kofosky Sedgwick, Eve (1992), 'Nationalisms and Sexualities in the age of Wilde' in Parker, Andrew et al. (eds), *Nationalisms and Sexualities,* Routledge, London, p. 239ff. See also Katrak, Ketu H. (1992), 'Indian Nationalisms, Ghandian "Satyragraha" and Representations of Female Sexuality' in Parker, *idem,* for assertion of traditional gender roles to empower the Indian Nationalist Movement with skills of passive resistance. For the export of the idea of Englishwomen, see Davin, Anna (1978), 'Imperialism and Motherhood', *History Workshop Journal,* 5, Spring. For discussion of the interaction of class, gender and national identity, see Bourke, Joanna (1994), *Working Class Culture in Britain 1890-1960,* Routledge, London, chapter 6.

6.   See Kirk, Neville (1994), *Labour and Society in Britain and the USA,* vol. 2, Scolar Press, Hampshire, pp. 291-294 for discussion of operation of labour market to exclude women and ethnic minorities from the labour market. Williams, Chris (1995), op. cit., p. 115ff. notes the regionally specific nature of labour market gender relations and that where women were marginalised in terms of employment, they were also politically marginalised.

7.   Williams, Chris (1995), op. cit., p. 129 stresses the regional perspective of British Labour and that a national perspective 'may not be the best framework for any analysis of European ... Labour Movements'.

8.   For working class participation in war, see Breuilly, John (1993), *Nationalism and the State,* Manchester University Press, p. 36ff.; Breuilly examines the basis for working class support for war, concluding that 'class and national loyalty ... conflicted with prevailing national sentiment'. Cf. Silvermann, Victor (1993), 'Popular Bases of the International Labour Movement in the US and Britain, 1939-1945', *International Review of Social History,* 38 (3) for the opinion that workers fought in the Second World War because they wanted a new world order and joined the Labour Party as an alternative to Conservative nationalism. Montague, C.E., (1922), *Disenchantment,* Chatto and Windus, p. 228. See also Oldfield, Sybil (1989), *Women against the Iron Fist,* Blackwell, Oxford, p. 208, citing Emmeline Pethwick Lawrence, pacifist candidate 1918: 'My supporters were the soldiers themselves'.

9.   Spoor, Ben, *Labour Party Conference Report,* 1919, p. 101.

10.   *Labour Party Conference Report,* 1918, p. 7.

11.   Hobsbawm, E. J. (1991), *Nations and Nationalisms,* Cambridge; jigsaw states, pp. 31-132; citing Renan, p. 12. See also Buxton, Noel and Evans, Conwil (1922), *Oppressed Peoples and the League of Nations,* London and Toronto,

pp. 8-9. Noel Buxton, one of the Liberal MPs attracted into the ranks of Labour by its foreign policy, was amongst those contemporaries enumerating the difficulties of the 'jigsaw' approach: 'the allies overreached themselves by including far too large groups of racial minorities ... How these minorities can be democratically governed, and their rights and interests safeguarded, are questions which cannot be easily answered'.

12.   Haupt, Georges (1972), *Socialism and the Great War,* Oxford, p. 228.

13.   Ibid., p. 227.

14.   Halévy, Élie (1967), *The Era of Tyrannies,* Allen Lane, London, pp. 161-170, 204-223. See also Berger, Stefan (1995), op. cit., p. 246.

15.   *James and Lucy Middleton Papers, the Ruskin Collection,* Ruskin College, Oxford, Middleton to John Irving, 'an ex-Tory voter', 18 April 1929, MID 23/11.

16.   *Labour and Socialist International Papers,* National Museum of Labour History, secretary (Adler's) report August 1939, LSI /22/2/4.

17.   See Kirk, Neville, op. cit., pp. 49-57 for discussion of homogenisation of working class at work and in the wider cultural sense and a challenge to the revisionist account of working class apoliticism and apathy. On working class gender and ethnicity, see Oldfield, Sybil (1994), *This Working Day World,* Taylor and Francis, London; Joanna Bourke (1994), op. cit.; Fryer, Peter (1984), *Staying Power: the History of Black People in Britain,* Pluto, London; Gilroy, Paul (1987), *There Ain't No Black in the Union Jack,* Hutchinson; Ramdin, Ron (1987), *The Making of the Black Working Class in Britain,* Wildwood House.

18.   Zeitlin, Jonathan (1989), 'Rank and filism in the British Labour Movement', reply Price, Richard, '"What's in a Name"', Cronin, James, 'The "Rank and File" and the Social History of the Working Class', *International Review of Social History,* xxxiv, part 1; see also Ely, Geoff (1989), 'Labour History and Social History', review essay, *Journal of Modern History,* vol. 61, no. 2, June. See also Berger, Stefan (1992), 'The British and German Labour Movements before the Second World War: the *Sonderweg* revisited', *Twentieth Century British History,* 3 (3) for the opinion that middle class people were not attracted at ward level; however, none of his examples are drawn from London. Berger (1995), op. cit., p. 253 notes that Labour Movements always require support beyond that of working people.

19.   The process of en-gendering the concept of the rank and file lags behind that of en-gendering the working class; see Thane, Pat (1990a), 'Women and Labour Politics', *Labour History Review,* 55 (3); Thane Pat (1990b), 'The Feminism of Women in the British Labour Party' in Smith, H. (ed.), *Twentieth Century British Feminism,* Elgar Press, London; Collette, C. (1991), 'New Realism, Old Traditions', *Labour History Review,* 56 (1); Collette, C. (1989), *For Labour and For Women,* Manchester University Press; Graves, Pamela (1994), *Labour Women,* Cambridge University Press. On sexuality, see Chambers, Colin (1989), *The Story of Unity Theatre,* Lawrence and Wishart, London, p. 159; Libmann, Brigitte (1994), 'British Women Surrealists - Deviants from Deviance?' in Oldfield, Sybil (1994), op. cit. See also Phillips, Eileen (1983), *The Left and the Erotic,* Lawrence and Wishart, London, *passim* and p. 11: 'An attempt to talk a politics of sex, to explore possible connections between desires, fantasies, pleasures and the kind of

10

transformation in social relations which socialist convictions involve pursuing'. Westphal, Max (1924), 'Youth takes the Helm', *Labour Magazine,* vol. iii, no. 7, November, pp. 320-322. Alberti, Johanna (1994), 'British Feminists and Anti-Fascism in the 1930s' in Oldfield, Sybil, (1994), op. cit., has written of the class based resistance to fascism. See also Collette, Christine (1993), 'Gender and Class in the Labour and Socialist International, 1923-1939' in Hauch, Gabriella (ed.), *Geschlecht, Klasse, Ethnizitat,* Vienna. Rose, Sonia (1993) reminds us: 'To make gender a core analytical concept in Labour History, we need to begin by rethinking and then revising the foundational assumptions', 'Gender and Labour History' in *International Review of Social History,* 38 supplement 1.

20.   British Committee for Refugees from Spain, (n.d.), *A Nation in Retreat* London. The link between racism and sexism is a common theme; for recent examples in post-Soviet Russia see Shreeves, Rosamund (1992), 'Sexual Revolution or Sexploitation' in Rai, Shirin et al. (eds) *Women in the Face of Change,* Routledge, London, p. 141, citing *Pravda:* 'can we really be surprised that young boys are going to "serve" foreign homosexuals'; and see Parker, Andrew et al. (eds) (1992), op. cit., p. 6 discussion of the 'Rape of Kuwait' and American *matériel* marked 'Bend Over, Sadaam'.

21.   Lee, H.W. (1923), 'White and Black Labour in the US', *Labour Magazine,* vol. ii, no. 8, December, p. 353; Ramdin (1987), op. cit., p. 75 and p. 81; Tabili, Laura (1994), 'The construction of Racial Difference in 20C Britain: the Special Restrictions (Coloured and Alien Seamen) Order 1925', *Journal of British Studies,* 33 (1), January is of the opinion that Ramdin overestimates the racism of local trades unionists and police and underestimates institutional racism.

22.   *Deptford Citizen* (February 1937); proscribed groups, see *Labour Party Conference Report,* 1933, p. 30 and listings thereafter in subsequent years; anti-semitic groups, see *William Gillies Correspondence,* National Museum of Labour History, Manchester WG 20/6.

23.   Henderson, Arthur (1933), op. cit.

11

Strike for Peace: The British Labour Movement and the International Federation of Trades Unions

British trades unionists and Labour Party leaders were to the forefront in recreating international organisations after the First World War. This process was inevitably tortuous after war and revolution but trades unionists were able to achieve the reformation of the International Federation of Trades Unions by 1919. The creation of the Third International in early 1918 made progress in the political wing more problematic. This chapter first, outlines the preliminary steps towards revival of international Labour. Second, it considers British participation in and changing attitudes to the International Federation of Trades Unions.

First steps: the people's peace

The rump of the Second International continued to meet during the war. The parliamentary committee of the Trades Union Congress and the Labour Party executive were instrumental in arranging meetings in London in August 1917, February and September 1918. One of the leading participants in these meetings was Arthur Henderson, who from 1912, as Labour Party secretary, had been secretary to the British section of the International. Typically, Henderson had echoed consensus trade union opinion in supporting the war effort and seeking gain from this cooperation. He had served in the wartime government from 1915 and the five man War Cabinet from 1916 to 1917. Henderson had understood his Cabinet appointment to include the right to represent Labour at the Peace Treaty conference. However, his position became untenable because he decided to support the Stockholm Conference arranged by Dutch and Scandinavian Socialists, to which delegates from the Petrograd Soviet had been invited. British Labour leaders in general were motivated in hosting International meetings by the desire for a people's peace, sharing with Henderson the aim of the inclusion in the treaty negotiations of the workers who had volunteered or been conscripted as soldiers. A special conference in December 1917 had agreed Labour Party war aims, including a people's peace, and referred these to the 1918 International meeting.[1]

The American Federation of Labour (AFofL, the umbrella organisation representing American craft unions) proposed that a world Labour and Socialist meeting be held at the same time as government negotiations to end the war. The September 1918 International meeting decided to persuade governments to include at least one national Labour representative in official meetings and to organise concurrent Labour and Socialist meetings. Emile Vandervelde of the Belgian Socialist Party and Albert Thomas of the French Socialist Party, both leading figures of the Second International who had served in their home cabinets, together with Henderson, were given the task of approaching their respective governments. The British Prime Minister was duly notified on 11 November 1918. Henderson wrote to French socialist Frossard: 'International Labour had the right, and should have the opportunity of ratifying the official peace treaty'.[2]

The claim to ratify the peace treaty dictated speed, as did the proposed creation of the League of Nations. Although it differed from the League of Peoples that had been one of the Labour Party's war aims, the League of Nations was seen as 'the best capitalist alternative and might be open to influence from an effective, international Labour organisation. In addition, in view of the appearance of the Third (revolutionary) International, principles and practices needed to be clearly formulated.

Jealousies over determining who should take the lead, nevertheless, delayed the first peace-time meeting of the reformist International. Henderson's own commission had failed to meet, Vandervelde and Thomas having to give priority to cabinet meetings, while the seamen's unions refused Henderson the passage he needed to attend meetings abroad. The Dutch/Scandinavian parties and the American Federation of Labour had lost enthusiasm; the pre-war International bureau (policy making body between conferences) took no action. Henderson finally took matters into his own hands, assisted by William Gillies, then of the Labour Party research department who was deputed to arrange visas, passports, journeys and hotels. British motives for participation were given at the 1919 Labour Party conference:

> Really an invitation to the working class movement to formulate their ideas of the foundation of a Peace treaty and resume International relations ... the decision of the conference would have the greatest influence on the work of the official representatives at Paris.[3]

There were early indications of difference in approach. While the British envisaged a consultative forum, some sections of French socialists sought definitive decisions on policy. The French and Belgians were reluctant to welcome German delegates to Paris. Indeed, Vandervelde resigned from the commission over the proposed attendance of German delegates. Berne, in neutral Switzerland was finally chosen as the venue. Those who had attended the London 1918 meeting were notified and Hjalmar Branting helped by inviting, in his own right as Swedish Prime Minister, neutral and Central European delegates. The American Federation of Labour declined its invitation, doubtless aware of President Wilson's inability to win support at home for the

13

League of Nations. Former members of the British section of the International from the Independent Labour Party and British Socialist Party, whom Henderson tried to exclude from separate representation, attempted to sabotage his efforts. These delays meant that the meeting started a few days after the commencement of the Paris Peace Treaty negotiations in January 1919.[4]

Eight delegates from 21 countries met at the International and by the conclusion of proceedings 102 delegates represented 26 countries. A French resolution to exclude the belligerents was avoided by welcoming the new, revolutionary Germany. Branting was elected President and Henderson was to serve on the bureau. Immediate British aims were satisfied by agreeing that the League of Nations should be based on a 'real peace of justice' so that a commission was able to travel to Paris within a month to present this resolution to the peace treaty negotiators. Ramsay MacDonald and Stuart-Bunning of the Postal Workers' Union were elected to the commission. MacDonald was an appropriate choice. Secretary of the Labour Party until 1912, he had attended International meetings from the 1896 conference when as a Fabian delegate, he witnessed the intense debate between socialists and anarchists.[5] He had opposed the declaration of war and thus temporarily sacrificed his leading position in the Labour Party. He believed the war should be pursued once begun and had demanded open diplomacy and democratic control of foreign policy. This stance had spelt the loss of MacDonald's parliamentary seat, so that he was somewhat in the political wilderness. He therefore had both the time and relevant experience to devote to the International.

To oversee British representation, an international joint sub-committee of the Labour Party executive and Trades Union parliamentary committee was formed. Representation at the International was agreed at twelve each for the Party and the unions, three for the Independent Labour Party, one each for the Fabians, the British Socialist Party and the National Socialist Party. The Trades Union Congress parliamentary committee became, temporarily, the International executive and equipped Ramsay MacDonald with a post-war role by engaging him as secretary, voting him, in his own words, 'the ridiculous salary of £600 per annum'. Gosling (later president of the Transport and General Workers' Union) became honorary secretary. However, British unions remained keen to recreate a specific trades union international body; the existence of the revolutionary Third International made the Henderson/MacDonald negotiations problematic and protracted. The TUC, therefore, called French and American delegates to a meeting in January 1919.[6] Thereafter, political and industrial international organisation took separate form, although the British continued for a while to manage their participation under the aegis of a joint committee.

14

International Federation of Trades Unions

Drawing on existing international contacts enjoyed since the 1903 Dublin agreement of national secretaries to share information, the trades unions were quick to re-establish networks. There was some British competition for international representation between the newly established Trades Union Congress and the General Federation of Trades Unions under William Appleton, who had managed pre-war contacts. The TUC won, claiming 4,532,085 affiliated members to Appleton's 844,210. Sam Gompers of the American Federation of Labour was much involved initially, but AFofL was out of step with the more radical European trades unionists and wary of possible negotiations with the communist unions of revolutionary Russia. Gompers considered that his efforts had been 'usurped' when Oudegeest, of the Netherlands, assumed responsibility for convening sessions, calling for an international parliament of trades unions.[7] The AFofL therefore stayed aloof when these sessions culminated in the institution of International Federation of Trades Unions headquarters at Amsterdam. Forty-four delegates represented 17countries at the 1919 meeting, claiming the support of 18,000,000 workers. By 1922 93 delegates from 19 European countries met with 21 international trade organisations. Edo Fimmen, of the International Transport Workers, claimed in *Labour Magazine* that:

> We go so far as to say that what had remained of working class unity is due, above all things, to those Trades Unions who comprise the International Federation of Trades Unions.[8]

IFTU, from its inception, organised beyond the borders of Europe. Canada, Argentina, Peru and the Union of South Africa were among the first members. The Dutch East Indies, Mexico, New Zealand, Palestine and South West Africa joined later. The American Federation of Labour, while it remained aloof, continued to send representatives to IFTU summer schools. Nonetheless, activity was centred in Europe. There were European competitors, the International Federation of Christian Unions based at Utrecht and the Syndicalist International based at Berlin. However, these were smaller and less effective that IFTU. There was also an attempt at forming a 'neutral' international for private employees and the self-employed.

That Fimmen should be asked to write on this subject in a British Labour periodical indicated a state of affairs with which the British were not entirely happy; without doubt influential, they did not predominate at IFTU. J.W. Brown was appointed British speaking secretary and Britain held four of the 22 council places. Oudegeest and Sassenbach held the other two secretarial positions. The Trades Union Congress lamented this tripartite arrangement, finding that none of the secretaries 'appeared to have final authority' while all were 'often away from the office'. The President was British; consecutively Appleton, presumably as a consolation prize; J.H. Thomas of Labour's leading 'big five' and then Albert Purcell, Furnishing Trades' Federation and Member of Parliament for Coventry. There were three European vice-presidents, of whom Jouhaux, the French union leader was particularly influential. In 1923 the TUC wanted 'to strengthen and safeguard British representation upon the Bureau and Management committee'. The bulk of affiliation fees came from Britain; Labour's International Secretary kept an account of salaries paid to IFTU officers and British trades unionists were signatories for IFTU cheques.[9]

The alternative designation of IFTU as 'the Amsterdam International' signalled rivalry to British leadership. Some of the International Trades Secretaryships affiliated to IFTU were in British hands: for instance, Tom Shaw (Textile trades) was secretary of the International Textile workers; Alec Gossip (Furnishing Trades' Federation) of the International Woodworkers; Frank Hodges (Miners' Federation) of the International Mineworkers. The largest and most powerful group, however, was Fimmen's own, also run from Amsterdam.[10] Ernest Bevin, of the Transport and General Workers Union was active in the reconstruction of ITWF but, despite his later prominence in British politics, his international influence at this stage should not be overestimated. Bevin helped to organise support for the 1920 Dutch dock strike but was impatient with the idealistic expressions of internationalism which came naturally to Fimmen. Bevin's motion to the 1920 ITWF Congress asked for issues strictly confined to trades union pay and conditions to be given more priority. Bevin was not a member of the British Labour Party and trades union Joint International Committee at this time. The failure of the 1921 Triple Alliance of British transport, mining and railway workers somewhat undermined pretensions to international leadership. While the TUC was right to claim:

> There is scarcely a Labour leader in the country who is not a secretary, president or member of a council of one of the organisations making up the International Trades Union Movement.[11]

the impression given of undisputed international leadership was erroneous. As the peace treaty negotiations continued without workers' representatives, disillusion made space for a paradoxical motivation for international participation; that of safeguarding British interests.

Part of IFTU's agenda was not controversial in Britain; boycotting dictatorship, preventing arms shipment for use against Soviet Russia, creating an international office to advise on the distribution of raw materials. However, the other aims adopted by IFTU in 1920 were more problematic: the cancellation of war debts and discussion of disarmament and a general strike against war. Before the war, the German influenced conservative majority block had succeeded in limiting trades union internationalism to statistics' gathering and information sharing. Now, the war was thought to have 'given a fresh impetus' and the results were disturbing.[12] Not in charge at Amsterdam, the TUC was unable to set the agenda for IFTU. This was to have important long term consequences and also had implications for the management of international contact. Running a joint party/union department presented difficulties when the trades union partner was bound to an international body outside its control.

War Debts

War debts and the related issues of reparations payments and war guilt raised various responses within the trades unions and Labour Party. Some, usually on the pacifist wing such as Lees Smith (a recruit from the Liberal Party) were of the opinion that demanding reparations was reprehensible, 'starving women and children in time of peace'. Trades unionists tended to agree with J. H. Thomas that: 'it is only fair that Germany should pay'. However, reparations payments caused currency destabilisation and enforced increase in German productivity meant competition. The formation of German trusts cartels was of continuing concern to the Labour Party and to the trades unions. Arthur Henderson wrote: 'shipbuilding has been crippled by the taking of German ships. Every ship we have received has meant a ship less built by British labour'.[13]

On these issues international discussion was helpful in smoothing over British difficulties. Delegates from France, Belgium and Germany at a meeting in April 1921 agreed that German materials and labour should pay for the restoration of devastated regions. Ramsay MacDonald's position was that compensation should be limited to an amount which would not cause hardship to German workers: 'sweating and burdensome reparations could not be separated'. MacDonald wrote of the German delegates at the April 1921 meeting:

> they had thought out details ... They produced maps of nationalities ... clearer than any I had seen ... They expected a heavy burden and they were willing to accept it ... their payments would have to be limited to a sum that could be paid.[14]

IFTU took the middle ground, deciding that reparations were legitimate, but that compulsory measures would be ineffectual and should be replaced by fraternal cooperation, impartial investigation and arbitration in case of dispute.

Strike for Peace

For the British, the more controversial issues were disarmament and the strike for peace. At its 1922 conference IFTU created the promised commission; this, in turn, proposed a committee to act with the national organisation in each country. The committee was voted Fr. 200,000.[15] Tensions within the British Labour Movement were revealed by this initiative. Some British unions were inspired to call for a World Congress on Disarmament, open to all unions, whether IFTU affiliated or not. The TUC, consolidating its power at home, insisted on 'representative internationalism':

the only official delegation from any nation which should be recognised should be that appointed by the National body forming part of the International Federation.[16]

The TUC refused to attend the World Congress, despite a plea from Ramsay MacDonald. The Congress went ahead and included contingents described by Karl Durr, of the Swiss Federation of Trades Unions, as 'societies of the pacifist bourgeoisie'. The resolution of the Congress was: 'to prevent the actual outbreak of such wars by proclaiming and carrying out a general international strike'.[17] Thereafter, this was IFTU policy; but it was not the policy of the British, who had declined attendance. This difference in policy outlook was to cloud relations throughout the inter-war period.

In line with its policy, IFTU planned international No More War demonstrations in 1924. In Britain, Labour Party and trades union leaders tried to regain control of the situation by arranging for demonstrations to be held under the auspices of local Labour Movement branches. The National Council for the Prevention of War, to which many of the peace societies were affiliated, preferred to create a national joint committee. There were further disagreements over the wording of the resolution to be proposed by local meetings. The National Council for the Prevention of War suggested:

> This mass meeting of Citizens sends fraternal greetings to the similar gatherings being held throughout the world ... it calls on our government to take the initiative ... in making a definite proposal for immediate disarmament.

The Labour leadership harked back to the idea of a League of Peoples, passing a resolution in which it called:

> upon its government to pursue a policy of international co-operation ... the convocation of an International Conference to reduce armaments.

The resulting demonstrations, held in August 1924, were well attended. Labour leaders, however, presumably found working with the peace societies difficult and it was decided the following year not to hold separate demonstrations, but to include No More War demonstrations in the May Day celebrations.[18] The Joint International Committee decided against attending the No More War congress in December 1924.

Anglo-Russian Committee

In view of its caution about working with other bodies and desire for representative, social democratic internationalism, the TUC's next moves need explanation. These moves included exploring collaboration with communist unions organised throughout the Soviet Red International of Labour Unions (RILU). Part of the reason for such initiatives was change in the membership of the TUC executive, which swung to the left in the early 1920s. Dissatisfaction with IFTU as then constituted also played its part.

The Russophile orientation of the Labour Movement as a whole in the inter-war years should also be noted as a contributory factor in the negotiations. The first, least controversial and arguably, most successful international act by the British Labour Movement had been its embargo on loading *The Jolly Roger* with weapons for use by the Allies in support of forces mounted against the new Soviet government. The Council of Action formed on this occasion had warned: 'the whole industrial power of the organised workers will be used to defeat this war' and the strength of the action matched the rhetoric.[19] Echoes of this expression of solidarity reverberated throughout the inter-war years so that Russophilism coexisted with Labour Party leaders' profound and warmly expressed differences with the Communist International and the Communist Party of Great Britain. Evidence in the early years included British representation in the delegation of international trades unionists organising relief in the 1922 Soviet famine.[20] A further delegation in 1924 included Albert Purcell, then IFTU president, Fred Bramley, TUC secretary, Swales (to the left of the TUC), Ben Tillett (TUC old guard), John Turner (TUC moderate). All were enthusiastic, especially Purcell. Their report was favourably analysed by Herbert Tracey of the TUC secretariat for *Labour Magazine*.[21]

At this time, the division of the international movement into communist and socialist wings was new. The Labour Movement at home had yet to ossify into its separate structures. Individual trades unionists, of course, might legitimately belong to any political party and some were communists; most, but not all unions were Labour Party affiliates. Some communists organised in the broad based National Workers' Committee Movement, which had grown out of wartime shop stewards' committees. This merged with the small British Bureau of RILU to form the National Minority Movement; the latter had 617 delegates representing 750,000 members at its inaugural conference in 1924. TUC negotiations with RILU should be seen in this context. Walter Citrine, who had succeeded Bramley, following the latter's illness and, later, death remembered that unity then seemed 'an ideal well worth striving for' and that:

> In my early days at the TUC I was so imbued with desire to see the success of the revolution in Russia that I was blind to the disruptive tactics of the Communist Party in Great Britain.[22]

IFTU itself was more cautious. A section of the French unions, the Finns, Latvians, Yugoslav and Bulgarian unions joined RILU. An IFTU commission in 1922, including Henderson, MacDonald, Gillies and Tom Shaw of the Textile Unions, investigated relationships between the two international bodies and recommended that RILU exchange its revolutionary doctrine for reformism as a step to joining IFTU. Two years later, a British left wing group of IFTU delegates, including Albert Purcell, inspired by his Russian trip, sought the inclusion of Soviet trades unions. IFTU was resolute in refusing admission in the face of letters from, amongst others, the Swiss National Centre (Purcell was 'chief witness in defence' of Moscow), Belgium ('the strongest protest must be made') and Germany ('the delegates should have spoken with discretion').[23] This criticism may have been effective in further diminishing British influence at IFTU, but had no impact on Anglo-Russian talks.

In June 1924 the 5th congress of the Communist International and the RILU conference discussed the formation of an Anglo-Russian committee as a method of achieving international unity. The National Minority Movement was ignored by both sides in subsequent negotiations. The discussions were typical of leadership internationalism; formal, taking place in committees, restricted to a few men and sensitive to ideas of status. Tomsky, the Soviet trades union leader (with four uninvited comrades) was made welcome at the 1924 Trades Union Congress. The following year, an Anglo-Russian trades union conference resulted in British agreement to press IFTU for unconditional talks with the Soviet unions and, on Bramley's suggestion, an Anglo-Russian joint advisory council was created. Other centres, for instance Finland, attempted to affiliate, but were refused on the grounds of the council's specific function.[24]

Gillies wrote to warn Citrine that German communists were using the Anglo-Russian talks to undermine social democratic trades unions.[25] However, the tide quickly began to turn. The TUC moved to the right, now including Ernest Bevin, who had achieved stature through his merger of the transport unions. There is no evidence that Bevin ever altered the opinion he later expressed: 'The philosophy of the Red International cannot mix with our form of democracy', although he never proscribed communists within the Transport and General Workers Union.[26] When Herbert Tracey analysed the 1926 All Russian Council of Trades Unions report his sympathy had noticeably diminished.[27]

In Moscow, the Anglo-Russian Council was hardly more welcome; the focus of a power struggle, it was denounced by the Trotsky/Kamenev/Zinoviev opposition as an alliance with the bourgeoisie which harmed the development of British communism, partly on the grounds of the exclusion of the National Minority Movement. Stalin's position was that talks should continue. In April and August 1926 there were acrimonious meetings of the Anglo-Russian Council at which the Soviet delegates attempted to discuss support for British miners.

Although the British negotiators continued to recommend inclusion of Soviet unions in IFTU, the TUC was content to merely forward, not endorse, their comments. At the following Congress, Brown represented IFTU and was invited to speak but the Soviet delegates, refused entry to Britain, were forced to make their comments by telegram. Citrine, in his annual report wrote that the TUC was:

> resentful at unwarranted intrusion in the shape of the 1,000 word telegram from Mr. Tomsky ... the General Council in its comments on this egregious minute made it unmistakably plain that the policy of the British trades union

20

movement is not to be laid down by the pedantic eccentricities either of the Russian Communist Party or of the All Russian Council of Trades Unions.[28]

At Bevin's suggestion, the TUC instructed its delegates to emphasise TUC autonomy. It appeared that the British were going to a great deal of trouble for little reward. IFTU did not even debate the next British proposal for meeting the Soviet unions, nor would IFTU affiliates give an opinion on their action should the British call a conference. Oudegeest, of IFTU's secretariat, insisted that the Soviet unions must write requesting affiliation.[29] Never conciliatory, the Communist International proclaimed the virtues of the united front from below, maintained its right to criticise British leaders and sought a single, revolutionary trades union International.

Although Tomsky had agreed to respect TUC rights,[30] he continued to mishandle negotiations. As Communist Party of Great Britain membership had fallen back, he chose the National Minority Movement, which now accounted for about 800,000 members as the focus of the united front campaign in Britain. He lost any chance of using this base to wield influence when, in a *Workers' Life* interview (8 May 1927) he lambasted the TUC leadership for failing to defend workers against the punitive 1927 Trades Disputes and Trades Unions Act. Citrine accused Tomsky of breaking the non-interference agreement by this action. A further meeting of the chair and secretaries of the British and Soviet trades unions (Citrine, Hicks, Tomsky, Dogadov), about possible threats of war against the Soviet Union, was acrimonious. In June 1927 the TUC International committee approved a statement of the breakdown of Anglo-Soviet relations. At Congress that year, documentation was distributed in support of a report recommending that the Anglo-Russian Council be disbanded. In Citrine's words, 'what we all considered to be a laudable purpose came to an end'.[31] For good measure, Citrine condemned the National Minority Movement.

TUC International Committee

During these negotiations and perhaps, partly impelled by the distinction between TUC and Labour Party attitudes to international communism, the TUC had withdrawn from the Joint International Committee and henceforward, managed its own international contacts. The TUC had simplified and strengthened its overall structure, following a process of merging smaller unions and the replacement of the parliamentary committee by a general council (1921); this was elected annually, unions being divided into trade groups which made nominations for council seats. While trades unions had their own section on the Labour Party national executive, affiliated trades unionists were not, necessarily, individual members of the Labour Party. The other, smaller sections on the Party executive were the constituency section, plus five women members and a representative of socialist, cooperative and professional organisations. The trades union voice in the Labour Movement leadership was maintained through the National Council of Labour on which unions, the Party executive and the Parliamentary Labour Party were represented.

A joint international department working within this structure was possible but, in fact, proved difficult to control and there was some danger of TUC policy being swamped. It seemed sensible therefore, that William Bolton, who had been appointed to the TUC as a financial officer, took the additional responsibility of secretaryship of the TUC International Committee. He worked very much under Citrine's supervision. His committee had to approve Bolton's journeys abroad, which were made in Citrine's company; moreover, the committee dealt with contacts between trades secretariats 'but not with what are usually called international affairs'. As Citrine deplored the fact that, apart from the textile workers, no trade secretariat was in British hands, Bolton's scope was limited.[32]

General Strike

As has been seen, one of the factors which undermined the Anglo-Russian Council was fear of Soviet interference in British trades unions. Immediate and sustained Soviet support was offered, not only for the 1926 nine day General Strike but also for the miners in their dispute which preceded and inspired the strike and was prolonged after the strike was called off by trade union leaders. It has been estimated that two thirds of the miners' funds came from the Soviet Union. An Anglo-Russian Council emergency meeting, proposed by the Soviet leaders 'for the sole object ... (of) rendering assistance to the miners' had been refused on the grounds that it would prejudice the chance of help from other countries.[33]

Help from social democrat sources, however, was no more welcome than that of the communists. Edo Fimmen claimed to have raised £27,000 in one hour. Bevin negotiated this amount as an interest-free loan, repayable in five years (and made early repayment in view of the Amsterdam dock strike). Altogether, the British raised a loan of £71,000 at five per cent interest. The problem was that IFTU regulations stipulated that support could be given only if several trades in one country were in trouble at the same time. Otherwise, the trade union involved should approach its own trade secretariat which would approach IFTU if necessary. The miners' cause, therefore, had to be presented *via* the International Miners' Federation, a step the British were reluctant to take partly because, if IFTU gave help, it assumed the direction of the action in the recipient country. The continuance of the miners' strike therefore placed British leaders in an invidious position. When the miners did ask for assistance IFTU proved extremely reasonable, merely circulating affiliates explaining the arrangements made and, in effect, leaving the direction of the dispute in British hands.[34]

The British response illuminated the difference between the trade union boss Bevin, powerful and identified with a particular body of workers, and the administrator Citrine, whose position rested on his ability to mediate between groups. Bevin wrote to Citrine that he would not accept IFTU instruction. Citrine could offer Bevin only limited sympathy, placing his note on the record; the TUC could not alter IFTU regulations. After angry correspondence, in which Bevin accused Fimmen of facetiousness, the latter tried to make peace by writing that the International Transport Workers' Federation had repudiated the relevant IFTU regulations. The Associated Society of Locomotive Engineers and Firemen cancelled its affiliation to the International Transport Workers' Federation, pleading poverty, although Fimmen offered to suspend, or raise a loan to cover affiliation fees. Perhaps in an effort to ensure that British interests were acknowledged, Bevin was elected to the general council of the International Transport Workers' Federation in 1927.[35]

British presidency

The result of these fears about British autonomy was a higher British profile at IFTU. First, the TUC began to attack IFTU administration; affiliation fees were withheld until IFTU sold its printing works and mortgaged its building.[36] Only the British, Germans, Danish, Swiss and Hungarians had paid substantial fees. The British were of the opinion that IFTU meetings should be restricted to delegates from fee-paying countries. Further, they insisted on one general secretary in place of three (having in mind Purcell) and headquarters in Paris, or Berlin. Underlying its wish for organisational, but not political unity, the TUC added 'to gain practical advantages of a Trade Union character, i.e. international wage and labour agreements' to IFTU objectives. Dissatisfied even with the success of these changes, the British considered whether unions affiliated to international secretariats should be contracted out of IFTU, but decided this was impossible.[37]

A British campaign to seize the IFTU secretaryship followed. J.W. Brown, by reporting an indiscreet letter written by Oudegeest in 1924, secured the latter's resignation. IFTU responded by nominating George Hicks (Building Trades Federation president) to the executive. The TUC thought this 'quite foreign to British practice' and Hicks refused nomination. The TUC then countered by declaring that no permanent president should be appointed until the question of British representation was settled. A compromise was reached, that the British would not nominate for the general secretaryship; that the president would be the British executive member; and one assistant secretary would be British. Citrine was nominated as British IFTU executive member and president.[38] George Hicks retained a seat on IFTU's general council, along with Arthur Hayday, MP, of the Garment Workers' Union. It was rather sudden promotion for Citrine, whose position as Bramley's replacement had been

23

temporary until the latter's death; presumably, both the TUC and IFTU thought him manageable. The result was that the man with the administrative background and skills represented British trades unions internationally, rather than one identified with work in a particular trade. This was a very different type of association that the networking between, for instance, Henderson, Vandervelde and Thomas, figures of the pre-war Second International. In turn, status abroad enhanced position at home, so that the way was open for Citrine to become a greater force in Labour movement politics. It should be remembered that the scope of the TUC International Department was limited and that unions had given a federated, rather than collective response to international affairs; Citrine's new position amended this. However, in this period immediately after the General Strike, the trades unions did not predominate in Labour's National Council, as the resumption of demands for the strike-for-peace showed.

Strike for Peace renewed

It was a function of the diversity of the British Labour Movement that while trades unions were aiming to ensure that British views were privileged, the next strike-for-peace call emanated from Britain. A resolution that members refuse to bear arms, produce arms, or give any assistance to war 'so called defensive or offensive', moved at the 1926 Labour Party conference by Fenner Brockway of the Independent Labour Party, resulted in a proposal for a joint committee of the political and industrial internationals to:

> prepare for a system of united international action in the event of war becoming imminent, including stoppage of work in the production of transport or war materials.[39]

This was, of course, in line with IFTU policy and the joint committee was duly created. Sassenbach, of IFTU's executive, summarised IFTU's position: that the strike for peace policy had been agreed at Congresses in 1922, 1924, 1927.[40] Jouhaux began to think in terms of a workers' peace pledge, involving a ban on manufacture or transport of arms; Citrine thought this would be 'decidedly inadvisable' and would have the effect of keeping America aloof from IFTU; as the trades unions were so badly organised in some countries, any embargo would be 'in danger of becoming a fiasco'. A note of Jouhaux's suggestion in 1929 was endorsed 'just a sentimental gesture' ... 'our GC is committed to call a special conference' (before declaring a general strike) ...'difficulties in defining munitions' and 'better to deal as a spontaneous action'.[41] The TUC International committee decided to tell IFTU that it supported the anti-war pledge in principle, but could not sign because to do so would be contrary to TUC policy. Action, therefore, was limited. Individuals attended international meetings; for instance, Bromley (ASLEF) and Ben Tillett represented the TUC at a peace meeting in Paris. No action was taken when, in

1931, IFTU discussed an embargo on war production along with economic planning, commercial credit, currency policies, production, transport and distribution.[42]

National Council of Labour

It was understandable, against this background, that the trades unions should seek to enhance their voice within the Labour Movement. The parliamentary debacle of 1931, with the fall of the Labour government and defection of leading parliamentarians, MacDonald, Snowden and J.H. Thomas, reduced Party representation on the National Council of Labour. The NCL was remodelled so that the TUC held seven seats, the Labour Party and Parliamentary Labour Party three each. Underlining the trades union contribution to policy, the NCL met monthly, the day before the Party executive. Henceforward the TUC-dominated NCL was active in international affairs and Citrine's role, as IFTU president, was enhanced. Furthermore, Ernest Bevin had become more powerful because, having persuaded the transport unions in 1928 to take out a mortgage on a mansion in Smith Square (Transport House) he was landlord to the TUC and the Labour Party. Citrine remembered that Bevin had sometimes been called 'Napoleon Bevin' even in Bramley's time as TUC secretary.[43] In determining Labour leadership response to the rise of fascism in the 1930s the TUC was of prime importance.

Nazism and Fascism

IFTU's broad 1931 agenda was a function of its discomfort with the strike-for-peace policy and its resultant need for alternative responses to fascism. Neither the International nor the British Labour Movement was ignorant of the reality of National Socialist and fascist terrorism; the Matteotti fund had been started in 1924, after the assassination of the Italian socialist leader and international meetings were attended by anonymous delegates from covert trades unions operating under the Italian fascist regime. William Gillies's *Germany* file abounded in accounts of Nazi cruelty. Finding an adequate Labour Movement response was an impossibility given the weakness of the left in much of East and Central Europe; the defeats suffered by organised Labour in Britain in the 1920s and 30s; the division of the International Movement into socialist and communist wings; the continuing aloofness of the Americans and the speed and efficacy with which reactionary forces came to power.

The National Socialist coup in Germany in 1933 rewrote IFTU's agenda. A general strike in Germany had been proposed, should the Nazis take power, although German unions had reported that their ability to initiate action was in doubt and that they feared bloodshed and civil war. In the event, IFTU decided on a money grant and agitation in the foreign press. Citrine had suggested that German delegates should visit IFTU affiliates to warn that a Nazi coup was possible and was somewhat scornful of his German comrades when his suggestion was rejected. In his memorandum to the TUC general council, *Dictatorship and the Trade Union Movement*, Citrine wrote that 'the International Movement was puzzled by the apparently passive attitude of the Trades Unions'. He was equally confused when, after the Nazi coup, German socialists did visit London, Paris, Copenhagen, Zurich and Vienna, but to plead for cessation of press criticism of the Nazis.[44] Gillies saved press statements from the German Social Democratic Party which appeared to advise appeasement. For instance, the trades unions welcomed the Nazi first of May festival.[45] Such conciliatory gestures were futile; the German trades union offices were commandeered on 2 May 1933, all parties except the Nazi party dissolved and the Cooperative Movement taken over. IFTU offices moved from Berlin to Paris and, opposed in elections to committees, German delegates withdrew from IFTU.[46] The size of the catastrophe appears to have caused Citrine to weigh his judgement. In his 1935 pamphlet *Dictatorship and the Trade Union Movement* he wrote:

> A good deal of criticism has been levelled at the Socialist and Trade Union Movement in Germany ... it should be borne in mind they were working under very difficult circumstances.[47]

In Austria, when resistance was mounted, IFTU's disabilities were even more fully revealed. At the October 1933 IFTU Vienna meeting, a general strike was planned. Czech and Swiss International Transport Workers affiliates promised to do their best to close frontiers to goods traffic, but reported that they could not bear the whole burden of the strike. The Miners' International thought an embargo impossible; the Metal Workers could not stop war production because of the weakness of unions in France, Belgium and Luxembourg.[48] British delegates promised diplomatic intervention. When the threatened attack on working class and socialist organisations took place (11 February 1934) the general strike failed. All TUC unions were invited to a special conference: £9,500 was raised by IFTU; later, a further £19,690.9s was sent.[49]

The Trades Union Congress (1933) called for a special conference to discuss strike action. The Labour Party Conference of that year having similarly resolved on action, trades union, party and cooperative executives met to consider their response. Union and party resolutions were held to run contrary to each other, while the former failed to specify which delegates should be invited (for instance, union executives or delegates elected in the normal manner). These quibbles enabled the leadership to defend the TUC position on the strike-for-peace; the unions were to retain the right to initiate industrial action, but the whole Movement should respond, even in the event of a one day protest strike: 'the responsibility of citizenship affected the industrial, the political and the cooperative section of the Movement'.[50] Legal advice on possible attachment of funds and deprivation of legal status was sought. This decision effectively enhanced the power of the TUC; authority over the industrial wing had been consolidated when the TUC won the right to be notified of and to approve strike action; that authority had now been extended to cover the Labour Party.

Given the changing balance of power between the industrial and political wings, the unity with which the Labour Party and trades union leadership addressed its task of representing working people was remarkable. It is noteworthy that union leaders chose not to separate their joint power base. Playing for once as a member of the team, Bevin effectively annulled the 1933 resolutions at Congress the following year, suggesting that; 'the responsibility for stopping war ought not to be placed on the Trade Union Movement alone'.[51] Bolton thereafter instructed Herbert Tracey to publish resolutions about a general strike only 'to the extent to which they are in line with British trade union policy'.[52]

Rearmament

It was a logical next step for Bevin to inform the 1934 Congress that the British government might have to 'give military forces in support' of League of Nations' action. Congress was further told that the League was a minimum obligation; membership 'did not diminish the responsibility of government for having a foreign policy'; 'there might be occasions when the Movement would assist any defensive action to preserve the nation and its democratic institutions'. The Labour Party conference that year was informed that:

> You may have to honour the covenant by taking part, even with capitalist states and even on behalf of a capitalist state that has been attacked in (financial sanctions) and in collective self-defence.[53]

It is important to note that this definite break with the guiding principle of disarmament, privileged within the Labour Movement since 1918, was taken as early as 1934. The outcome of the infamous Bevin/Lansbury debate at the 1935 Labour Party conference, was, in fact merely a restatement of the previous year's policy. George Lansbury was one of the mavericks; a Christian Socialist pacifist, he had become Party leader on Henderson's resignation, largely because the 1931 catastrophe had removed many of the National Council of Labour tested, tried and trusted parliamentarians. Lansbury rode out his differences with the NCL until he tried to overturn policy in an emotional speech at the end of a day's debate at the 1935 conference; seizing the chance of the few minutes left, Bevin, with more anger than style, was successful in winning support for the NCL position.[54] Lansbury resigned his leadership and Citrine had no trouble in winning Congress support for the NCL position.

United Front

In addition to setting in motion the policy change towards rearmament, the Nazi coup inspired attempts to unify the international Labour Movement. First attempts aimed at consolidating a united front of socialists and communists. This was not welcome to the trades union leadership, who had been denounced as 'lickspittles', selling out to the bourgeoisie, in the communist 'class against class' phase which followed the demise of the Anglo-Russian Council. They faced repeated communist challenges; it was the persistence, rather than the substance that was wearisome. Ernest Bevin was an example of someone repeatedly provoked by the communists. He had defeated the communist Fred Thompson in the ballot for Transport and General Workers' Union general secretary and successfully ignored a rival union which Thompson tried to establish, but was confronted in the 1920s by the Rank and File Movement of communist busmen. More generally, the leadership were irritated by the National Minority Movement which lingered until 1933 and then by the National Unemployed Workers' Movement, founded in 1921 by Wal Hannington and communist dominated.[55]

The Trades Union Congress debated the united front in 1933. Considerable conflicting opinion was presented in debate and the final resolution was ambiguous:

> ... to seek united front action against all forces which seek to usurp democracy in this country and to destroy the freedom of the people for the purpose of establishing some form of dictatorship.

However, Citrine showed how far he had moved from his initial revolutionary enthusiasm when he told Congress 'everytime they made a communist, they made a fascist'.[56] This argument gave the trades union leadership the necessary grounds for exerting discipline against communist collaborators. Trades Councils were among the first to feel the effect of stricter discipline. These had never developed into the TUC 'area counterpart ... divided into industrial groups' which Citrine had envisaged because of the blocking tactics of trades union secretaries, who, in Citrine's opinion feared competition and objected to shop steward involvement.[57] Model rules had been established in 1925, but the precise function of trades councils remained ambiguous and they had become a thorn in the TUC flesh, attempting on occasions to assume the right of independent action. Citrine re-exerted control when, in 1934, the Deptford and Greenwich Trades Council was disbanded and reconstituted on the grounds that its members had worked in communist front organisations.[58]

Greater powers of discipline were assumed at the 1935 Congress. Trades Councils were instructed not to cooperate with communist or united front organisations and were warned that they would lose recognition if they accepted delegates from these bodies. Trades unions, who were their own masters, were asked to draw up regulations to exclude such bodies or their members. This policy was approved by a mere 442,000 votes in a card vote after a fierce debate; the resultant discord was articulated by Will Lawther of the mineworkers who told congress: 'the miners are going to stand no interference in the democratic method of electing their officials'.[59]

Citrine used his otherwise pedestrian account of his 1935 visit to the Soviet Union to reinforce TUC policy. He had very much resented being tricked at an All Russian Council of Trades Unions meeting into an exchange of opinion with the head of RILU (Lovosky). German trades unions, meanwhile, although they appealed for help, expressed hostility to the united front by reporting to IFTU that German communists' priority was 'creating a Soviet Germany'.[60] Citrine, similarly, accused the Communist Party of Great Britain of weakening the faith of workers in trades unionism: 'have they not another purpose, namely to use our Movement for the advancement of their own plan of the dictatorship of the Proletariat?'[61] Yet, despite his hostility to the united front, Citrine's volume was curious in displaying the continuing romantic Russophilism of British Labour.

Spain

The Spanish popular front government, elected on 16 February 1936, faced fascist rebellion from its armed forces, assisted by Mussolini. It was in its reaction to this war that the British Labour Movement leadership confirmed both the change in policy direction towards rearmament and their resistance to collaboration with communists. By supporting non-intervention, the diplomatic response to the war negotiated by the European powers, the Labour Movement leadership effectively abandoned collective security. While it was easy for the leadership to win consensus support within the Movement for lowest-common-denominator resolutions of support for the Spanish government, their policy was challenged, not least by left wing socialists and trades unionists who went to fight in the International Brigade or sections of the Spanish forces.

The communists now proposed a popular front (encompassing workers' and broad left organisations). In giving approval to this, the Seventh Comintern Congress recognised moves that had already been made in practice.[62] In Spain, a programme of common action between the socialists and communists was drawn up and complete organisational unity was proposed by the communist party for military, economic, social and political programmes that were jointly supported.[63] Putting this programme into effect was complicated by separatist movements in the Basque country and in Catalonia, where there was a strong anarchist presence. This political situation, however, favoured popular front work. Those who went to fight might accidentally join socialists, communists, or anarchists as George Orwell did when he arrived in Catalonia. Although the number of combatants was small, they were supported at home by campaigns, fundraising and 'All In' conferences open to communist influence.

An Independent Labour Spain committee was set up within a month of the outbreak of the war, while the leadership's Spanish Campaign committee was not formed until 1937. William Gillies was secretary of the latter.[64] The trade union leadership was important in formulating policy on Spain. When the civil war began, several prominent Labour party politicians, including the Labour Party leader, Attlee, were abroad. At Transport House, Citrine and Bevin, together with Gillies, Middleton and deputy Party leader Greenwood were responsible for first reactions.[65] They were informed of the British government's position, supporting non-intervention. Thereafter, Citrine and Gillies controlled the flow of information, reacting with 'selective deafness' to international protests and accepting advice that the French popular front government had initiated the non-intervention policy in order to retain power and prevent European war. Non-intervention was also presented to the National Council of Labour as a device to allow a free trade in arms that would favour the Spanish government. Gillies gave the opinion that the Spanish government did not need arms.[66]

There were several reasons for the leadership position on Spain. One was caution that involvement with communists abroad would open the doors to communists at home. This was recognised by Middleton's American correspondent, Benetton, who wrote accordingly: 'You have sacrificed the workers of Spain to the expediency of your bureaucracy'.[67] The very vitality of support for Spain spelt a lack of control which caused the leadership discomfort; emigrés, reporters, those with a special cause to plead arrived unannounced at Transport House. Middleton wrote to IFTU and LSI secretaries that the National Council of Labour had felt 'considerable apprehension' about 'visits from unofficial delegations and individuals carrying unrepresentative credentials' and asked that such visitors be 'discouraged'.[68] In addition, some trades unions were sensitive about Roman Catholic members who might be presumed to support the clerical fascists. Ernest Bevin, for instance, took care to inform the Irish TGWU that medical supplies donated would be made available to both sides: 'The union has always stood by freedom of conscience'.[69] Middleton wrote that: 'Spain has not been made a special issue, frankly on account of the difficulties involved in its presentation'.[70]

In one major respect, however, the Spanish civil war was instrumental in promoting leadership policy; while rebels demanded action on Spain, consistency required that they supported domestic rearmament. Chapter three describes the debate within the Labour Party; arguments around these positions were resolved by the 1936 Labour Party conference emotive response to Senora de Palancia's speech calling for arms for the Spanish government.[71] The case for rearmament won, Citrine was consistent in endorsing a resolution at the October 1936 joint IFTU/LSI meeting (which he chaired) that the Spanish government should be helped to buy arms.[72] Bevin chaired the 1936/1937 TUC and, in the same period, jointly chaired the National Council of Labour with Dalton; at the end of their year in office, both the Labour Party conference and union Congress accepted the *International Policy and Defence* document prepared by Gillies which finally committed Labour to national rearmament, while asking the British government not to strike the first blow.

Sauve qui peut

While the Spanish situation helped firm up British Labour leadership international policy, it rendered decision making at IFTU and the Labour and Socialist International more difficult because it revealed these bodies' weaknesses. After a joint emergency meeting in September 1936, the Internationals issued a statement that: 'The International Labour Movement is not, and never can be, neutral in this struggle' but the problem of how to deliver support remained unresolved.[73] The piecemeal, reactive and understandably self interested policy of both the British Labour leadership and European socialist parties in the countdown to the Second World War was appropriately described by the Labour Party International Advisory Committee as *sauve qui peut* (every man for himself). [74]

In March 1937 the Internationals organised a conference in London of 200 delegates. Spanish delegates asked for an All-In conference, but had to settle for the exclusion of communists. They asked for arms and an international strike, but neither of these were forthcoming.[75] The refusal was not solely British, but Bevin, once again chosen to publicly articulate leadership opinion, spoke so vehemently that the rejection of the Spanish demands was made doubly offensive. *New Leader* (19 March 1937), the Independent Labour Party organ, admittedly biased against Bevin because of his resistance to united front collaboration with communists, reported Vandervelde's angry comment that Bevin's speech was 'possibly the funeral of the Second International'. There is some evidence that IFTU was more inclined to activity than the LSI. Dalton noted in his diary that Bevin and Citrine had told a private meeting held on 22 June 1937 at the House of Commons that the non-intervention policy had been breached. Their information seemed to have come from IFTU.[76] In July 1937 IFTU proposed a propaganda week for Spain; British leaders decided to call a weekend only because: 'in the circumstances existing in this country, such a project was not feasible'.[77]

There was a last attempt to reassert some confidence within IFTU. Suffering from a decline in membership because of the fascist advance, IFTU was forced to reduce affiliation fees, but, nevertheless, made a positive attempt at reform, trying to broaden its scope and to decide on resolute action.[78] The problems of expansion were illustrated when IFTU delegates to Moscow in the winter of 1937 exceeded their brief and recommended a united front. The TUC 'viewed (this) with very great concern', but, the following year, forwarded a TUC resolution recommending international unity to IFTU. In the event, IFTU decided it was bound by its previous decisions and rejected the British resolution by 46 votes to 37. Meanwhile, negotiations were in hand with the American Federation of Labor (AFofL) which would have considerably increased IFTU's geographic range. AFofL affiliated to IFTU in 1937. The Americans invited IFTU's general council to meet in America: 'as only by direct contact ... Americans could really understand and appreciate the difficulties which were facing their comrades in Europe'. Representatives of South American trades unions hoped to form links with IFTU, using the opportunity of the American meeting to establish closer contact. International trade secretariats hoped to win American affiliations. The main difficulty was the expense for the smaller national centres and trades secretariats; Sweden, Norway, the Textile, Factory and Landworker secretariats were keen to make the visit. It was decided that the executive, but not the general council, would go; however, the chance was lost when the meeting was postponed in April 1939 because of 'the grave international situation'. IFTU rules were amended to allow an American vice-president to be elected.[79]

At home, the TUC and the Labour Party organised work with refugees but otherwise concentrated on the need for rearmament. Citrine met the Prime Minister to put forward the TUC view that rearmament was an industrial matter. He was concerned with the engineering union view that dilution and changes in work patterns should be opposed.[80] Citrine recorded his own acceptance of the inevitability of war; he remembered that: 'I finished my underground air raid shelter on May 4 1938'.[81] The TUC that year instructed individual unions to deal directly with the government on the distribution of profits in the armament industry and the dilution of the workforce for increased production.[82] Herbert Tracey wrote to Gillies, reflecting trades union pessimism about the international situation:

> Far from rearming, there were moves at IFTU to revive the strike - for - peace. Even their (Nazis) downfall would not be much use, as long as there is no power able and resolved to organise the chaos which a breakdown of the Nazi system would leave behind.[83]

The strike-for-peace was still IFTU policy, as Jouhaux reminded delegates at the Oslo meeting of IFTU's general council in May 1938. Calling for obstruction of the transport of war material, abolition of the private manufacture of arms and a boycott of the aggressor, Jouhaux put forward the case that, when successful action had been taken against allied intervention in the Soviet Union, no-one had worried about the rights and wrongs: 'the League of Nations was powerless because the Great Powers which dominated it decided it should be so'; League of Nations policy was 'identical with the creation of production, transporting, sale and supervision of materials of war'. At first, Citrine accepted a draft of Jouhaux's speech, telegraphing to Schevenels that 'Trades unions must see to it war is no longer possible'. In Oslo, however, the British delegates said that 'Jouhaux has suggested nothing practical' and that 'so far as a boycott is practical it should be a consumers' boycott'. Citrine quoted (without much

32

justification) the success of boycotts arranged by his own Anti-Nazi Council (British and American members, non party-political) and cited the challenges made by the British unions to their government as evidence of good practice. He reiterated the British fear: 'We do not want our government to occupy our offices and tie up our funds in the banks'. He pointed out that it was not possible for German, Italian, Japanese, Spanish or Czech unions to operate a boycott: 'I will believe others can do it *when they can do it*' (his emphasis). IFTU set aside its president's realism and accepted Jouhaux's resolution.[84]

The distance between the TUC and IFTU positions were now considerable. The TUC clarified its position for the August 1938 IFTU meeting, forwarding the 1934 TUC/Labour Party resolutions which denied that responsibility for action lay solely with the industrial wing. Unfortunately, however, the TUC had never formally notified IFTU of its rejection of the strike-for-peace policy. A further IFTU memorandum listed all related decisions, including a 1936 call for industrial action in countries which refused arbitration. At the November 1938 IFTU meeting the Spanish unions asked for withdrawal of all invading men and war materials, the demand to be backed by an international general strike if necessary.[85] Citrine's realism was fully justified when no such strike was forthcoming.

It was Citrine who led the British Labour team in demanding rearmament in the series of meetings with the Prime Minister which punctuated Chamberlain's trips abroad in 1938 and 1939. Citrine's predominance was an indication of the power of the trades unions and he won an encomium from Hugh Dalton, who had become an influential Labour parliamentary speaker on international affairs:

> Citrine, although very reasonable and an excellent team man, is still inclined to be ... anti-Russia ... But he never lets his colleagues down publicly when facing the other side.[86]

Such negotiations were less well received abroad. IFTU condemned the Munich agreement whereby Chamberlain agreed to Hitler's annexation of the Sudetanland, planning simultaneous deputations to the French and British governments. Czech unions had thereby lost a third of their members and: 'they required all the help they could get if they were to do anything to remedy the great wrong done to Czechoslovakia'.[87] International Solidarity Fund aid was extended to Czechoslovakia, £2,000 being raised. For their part, the British guaranteed the upkeep of ten Czech refugees.[88]

Conclusion

By 1939 the TUC had consolidated its position of power within the Labour Movement at home, dominating the NCL, exerting power over trades councils, addressing individual trades unions from at least an equal footing, providing the leader for Labour deputations to the Prime Minister. The personal stature of

Citrine and of 'Napoleon' Bevin was immense. The British had been of central importance in recreating international organisations and participation in IFTU had helped considerably in strengthening the TUC domestically. Moreover, the British retained an influential position at IFTU while resistance to the strike - for - peace had underlined their continued national autonomy. Resisting united and popular front collaboration had been one of the means by which the TUC won legitimacy for its disciplinary powers. Citrine's IFTU presidency had raised his profile and made him a natural choice to inform trades union and Labour Party members of international affairs. National influence had been enhanced when the TUC led the demand for British rearmament. Of course, rearmament caused unemployment to fall (and with it, one of the Communist Party's power bases) and a larger workforce meant a growth in trades union membership, adding to trades union strength.

Abroad, international trades unionism was enfeebled, early optimism extinguished; trades unions had been either driven underground or hounded out of some countries. Trades unions had succeeded in forming their own organisation but had failed to influence the peace treaty or to win a League of Peoples. The division of the international Labour Movement into socialist and communist wings had not been overcome. Resistance to fascism had proved impossible, sanctions were not applied, the strike-for-peace had been tried in Austria without success. It had not been possible to prevent arms shipments to the Spanish rebels. Funds and membership were falling. Attempts to extend organisation beyond Europe remained ambitions rather than realities. Many of the original international leaders were no longer involved; Henderson and MacDonald had died. Citrine was a new type of leader, less flamboyant, more pragmatic. He led the TUC into the Second World War knowing that his air raid shelter was ready and preparations for managing dilution in hand. Speaking for an earlier generation which had formed international contacts before the First World War and had experienced the optimism of 1918, Katherine Bruce Glasier, veteran socialist, wrote: 'the dark winter of our International and socialist cause oppresses us all'.[89]

Notes

1. *Labour Party Conference Report* 1918, p. 7.
2. Henderson had opposed the Stockholm conference until his visit to the Kerensky government and Petrograd Soviet in 1917. Leventhal, F.M. (1989), *Arthur Henderson*, Manchester University Press p. 49 and pp. 64-73; right to represent labour, Wrigley, Chris (1990*), Arthur Henderson*, Wales, p. 128. AF of L, *Labour Party Conference Report* (1918), pp. 8-9. Meetings with Thomas and Vandervelde, *Labour and Socialist International Papers,* Labour Party archives, proposals of AF of L, September 1918, LSI/2/12/12, memorandum from the Parliamentary Committee of the TUC and National Executive of the Labour Party, 11

November 1918, LSI/3/95/1, Henderson to Frossard, 19 December 1918, LSI 3/140. For Vandervelde, see Polasky, Janet (1995), *The Democratic Socialism of Emile Vandervelde*, Berg, Oxford.

3.   *Labour and Socialist International Papers*, Henderson's internal memorandum considering competing claims to take the initiative, nd, LSI/3/135. *Labour Party Conference Report* 1919, p. 10-12.

4.   *Labour Party Conference Report* 1919, p. 10. *Labour and Socialist International Papers*, Henderson to Albert Thomas, 19 December 1918, LSI/3/101, cable from Gompers (Af of L) to Bowerman (TUC) nd, c 24 December 1919, LSI/3/158, note of British section of International Socialist Bureau meeting, 12 December 1918, LSI/3/150, Henderson to Vandervelde, 18 November 1918, LSI/212/18.

5.   *Labour Party Conference Report* 1919, pp. 12-15. MacDonald at International, see Kapp, Yvonne (1979), *Eleanor Marx: The Crowded Years, 1884-1898*, Virago, London p. 658.

6.   *Ramsay MacDonald Papers*, Public Record Office, Diary 10 November 1920, p. 140, PRO 30/69/1753/1. *Joint International Committee Minutes*, 10 November 1920. *TUC Papers*, Modern Records Centre, Warwick University, Memorandum submitted by the TUC for meeting 20 January 1919, MSS 292/910(1).

7.   Lorwin, Lewis L. (1929), *Labour and Internationalism,* New York, p. 186. AFofL ceased to pay IFTU fees in 1920 and renounced affiliation in 1921, Lorwin op. cit. pp. 255-70.   G.D.H. Cole noted that the Second International was in favour of recognising the Soviet government, while AF of L remained cautious, Cole, G.D.H. (1958), *Socialist Thought* , vol. iv part ii, MacMillan, London pp. 692-3.

8.   Fimmen, Edo (1922), 'The Industrial International', *Labour Magazine*, vol. i, no. 1, May, p. 34.

9.   *TUC International Committee Minutes*, 17 February 1924, 10 December 1923. *William Gillies correspondence*, Labour Party Archives, table of salaries of IFTU officers, January 1937, WG/IFTU.

10.   Reinalda, Bob (ed.) (1997), *The International Transport Federation (ITF) 1914-1945: the Edo Fimmen Era,* Stichting beheer 11SG, Amsterdam

11.   'Labour Abroad', (1923) *Labour Magazine*, vol. ii, no. 3, July. Lord Bullock, (1960), *The Life and Times of Ernest Bevin, vol. i, Trades Union Leader*, Heinemann, Oxford pp. 113-4, ITWF revival; p. 146, Dutch dock strike; p. 180, Bevin's 1920 ITWF motion.

12.   Conference Report, *Labour Magazine*, vol. i, no. 2, June 1922, pp. 88-89.

13.   Lees, Smith (1921), *Labour's International Handbook*, Labour Publishing Co., London p. 47. Thomas, J. H. (1920), *When Labour Rules*, Collins, p. 190. Henderson, Arthur (1923), *Labour and Foreign Affairs,* Labour Party, London, p. 7.   Henderson was opposed to reparations payments for pensions. Henderson, Arthur, op. cit., p. 4 'shipbuilding has been crippled by the taking over of Geman ships. Every ship we have received has meant a ship less built by British Labour'.

14.   MacDonald, Ramsay (1923), *Wanderings and Excursions*, London, pp. 196-7.

15.   Conference Report, (1922), *Labour Magazine*, vol. i, no. 2, June, pp. 88-9.

16. 'Labour Abroad' (1922), *Labour Magazine*, vol. ii, no. 3, July. *TUC Papers*, Modern Records Centre, International Memorandum, October 1922, MSS 292 906(1).

17. *TUC Papers*, Ramsay MacDonald to Bramley, 11 July 1922, Karl Durr to Bramley, 15 September 1922, MSS 292 906(1).

18. *Joint International Committee Minutes*, 20 March 1924, 21 May 1924, 14 December 1924, 17 June 1925. In 1925 Citrine refused to speak at a no. More War meeting: TUC Papers, Citrine to Northcott (Borough of Wandsworth Labour and Trade Council), 22 July 1925, MSS 292 906(1). In 1931 the Labour Party refused further cooperation with the National Council for the Prevention of War and the Central Disarmament Bureau.

19. *Council of Action: Report of a Special Conference on Labour and the Russo-Polish War*, 13 August 1920, London. 'Labour Abroad, (1922) *Labour Magazine*, vol. i, no. 1, May. (J. Grady, British Member of Parliament, who had formed part of the government delegation in 1917 and had negotiated the exchange of war prisoners, was the British delegate.) Tracey, Herbert (1925), 'The Real Soviet Russia', *Labour Magazine*, vol. iii, no. 11, March and continued vol. iii, no. 12, April.

20. For the origins of the National Minority Movement, see Martin, R. (1969) *Communism and the British Trades Unions, 1924-1931: A Study of the National Minority Movement*, Clarendon Press, Oxford, Chapter One.

21. Lord Citrine (1964), *Men and Work: The Autobiography of Lord Citrine*, London, p. 90, p. 253.

22. 'The International Federation of Trades Unions, Rome 1922', (1922), *Labour Magazine*, vol. i, no. 2, June 'Labour Abroad' (1923), *Labour Magazine*, vol. ii, no. 8, December 1923. See also A. Purcell (1924), 'A Worker's Parliament of Europe', *Labour Magazine*, vol. iii, no. 3, July. *TUC Papers*, Swiss letter 2 December 1924, Austrian 5 December 1924, Belgian 9 December 1924, Danish 13 February 1925, Hungarian 16 December 1924, Swedish 17 December 1924, Textile Workers 12 December 1924, Latvian 3 January 1925, Czechoslovak 4 January 1925, Roumanian 5 February 1925, MSS 292 910 3c(1). 'Labour Abroad' (1924, 1925*), Labour Magazine*, vol. iv, no. 7, November and vol. iv, no. 9, January. *TUC International Committee Minutes*, 11 September 1924, report of letter from IFTU rejecting advances of All Russian Council of Trades Unions.

23. For a full account see Calhoun, D. (1976), *The United Front: the TUC and the Russians 1923-1928*, Cambridge, *passim*.

24. *TUC Papers*, Lahika (Secretary of the Finnish Unions) to Hicks, 19 June 1924, MSS 292 910 3(1).

25. *TUC Papers*, Gillies's handwritten note, nd, to Citrine, MSS 292 31.6/2.

26. Bullock, A. (1960), op. cit. p. 559, citing verbatim transcript of 1935 conference speech. Communists in the TGWU were proscribed by Arthur Deakin in 1949.

27. Tracey, Herbert (1926), 'Trades Unionism in Russia', *Labour Magazine*, vol. iv, no. 11, March .

28. Calhoun, D.F. (1976), op. cit., p. 230. Full account of Trotsky's and Stalin's speeches, pp. 246-8, p. 272, pp. 301-7. Congress Report (1926), *Labour Magazine*, vol. v, no. 6, October.

29.   *TUC International Committee Minutes*, 23 November 1926, report of Anglo-Russian Council, 16 November 1926.

30.   *TUC International Committee Minutes*, 18 January 1927, 28 February 1927. That there may have been some support was indicated when German and Dutch 'neutral' unions attempted to form an independent bloc; see 'Labour Abroad', (1927) *Labour Magazine*, vol. v, no. 10, February .

31.   Lord Citrine (1964) , op. cit., p. 90. *TUC Papers*, Modern Records Centre, Tomsky to General Council, 25 June 1927. See Calhoun, D. F. (1976), op. cit., p. 362 for Lord Citrine's reminiscences of their meeting. *TUC International Committee Minutes*, 9 June 1927. TUC *Report*, 1927, pp. 324-31. Calhoun, D. F. (1976), op. cit., pp. 318-20, gives a full account of the Comintern debate.

32.   *TUC International Committe Minutes*, 20 January 1928. *TUC Papers*, Memorandum, TUC Research Department, 'Organisation of HQ Departments', 1926, MSS 292 28/1. Ibid, Citrine, *The TUC at Work (Pamphlet)*, MSS 292 28/1.

33.   *TUC International Committee Minutes*, 13 July 1926.

34.   Bullock, A. (1960), op. cit., p. 409. *TUC Papers*, IFTU Regulations, October 1926, MSS 292 910.2(1). IFTU Press Report no. 24, 1 July 1926, MSS 292 910.2(1).

35.   *TUC Papers*, Bevin to Citrine, 30 August 1927, MSS 292 910.2(1); Citrine to Bevin, 10 November 1927; Fimmen to Bevin, 1 September 1927, MSS 292 910.2(1); Fimmen to Citrine, 5 February 1928, MSS 292 912 (1). *TUC International Committee Minutes*, 20 August 1927 and 3 November 1927. The British had long memories; when in 1937 Fimmen was nominated for a Nobel Prize, the TUC refused to hold a London meeting in his support. *TUC Papers*, extracted TUC F & GP Minute, 23 October 1937, and George Snel, secretary of nominating committee to Citrine, 21 October 1937, MSS 906(1).

36.   *TUC International Committee Minutes*, 1 December 1926 and 18 January 1927 (latter includes auditor's report).

37.   *TUC International Committee Minutes*, 17 March 1927, 11 April 1927.

38.   *TUC International Committee Minutes*, 23 August 1927, Hicks Refusal; 12 December 1927, TUC declaration; 8 November 1927, IFTU acceptance of British right to nominate; 7 February 1928, compromise; 11 May 1928, Citrine's appointment.

39.   *Labour Party Conference Report* 1926, p. 256. *Joint International Committee Minutes*, 3 February 1927.

40.   *TUC Papers*, Sassenbach's memorandum for IFTU executive, 19-20 November 1928. There was, in fact, a minority vote at the 1928 Labour party Conference for direct action against war, which Brockway found inspiring. See Brockway, F. (1942*), Inside the Left,* Allen and Unwin, London, p. 169.

41.   *TUC Papers*, Citrine to Sassenbach , 27 August 1928, MSS 292 906.8(1), 19 August 1929, MSS 292 906.8(1).

42.   *TUC International Committee Minutes,* 26 August 1929. *TUC Papers*, Bromley's report to Citrine, 17 April 1931, MSS 292 906.72(1).

43.   Lord Citrine, (1964) , op. cit., p. 78, p. 80. Bevin first sat on the General Council in October 1925, the same week that Citrine became General Secretary.

44.   *Bevin Papers*, Churchill College, Cambridge, Report of IFTU meeting 16-18 February 1933, I 1/4/17 and I 1/4/18. Memorandum, Dictatorship and the Trade Union Movement, I 1/4/22. Ibid, I 1/4/23.

45.   *Germany: Correspondence, Reports and Memoranda*, Labour Party Archives, press statement, 7 March 1933, 10/GER/2/21, trades union note, 22 April 1933, 10/GER/2/26, SDP note, 12 April 1933, 10/GER/2/28. For full account of SDP attempts to find an accommodation with the Nazi party see Braunthal, J. (1967), *History of the International, 1914-1943,* vol. ii, London, p. 360 ff., for failure to prevent Nazi accession to power and the opinion that the German SDP was hindered by reluctance to use brute force, hoping the crisis would pass, and lacked confidence in its own ability to mount a successful resistance, and Cole, G.D.H. (1960), *A History of Socialist Thought: Socialism and Fascism, 1931-1939,* vol. v, Macmillan, p. 48 ff. Otto Wels withdrew his resignation on 18 May 1933, see Braunthal op. cit., p. 385.

46.   *Trades Union Congress Report,* 1933, pp. 169-170.

47.   TUC (1935), *Dictatorship and the Trade Union Movement*, TUC , London, p. 5.

48.   *TUC Papers*, Citrine's secretary to Wellock (ex MP), 10 October 1933, MSS 906.8(1).

49.   *Bevin Papers*, Report to the TUC GC of the IFTU meeting, Vienna, 6-7 October 1933, I.6, Statement of Fascism at Home and Abroad, 28 July 1934, I.6.

50.   *Bevin Papers*, Memorandum, nd., on points for discussion at review meeting of the three executives on the War and Peace report, Bevin, I 6.

51.   *Trades Union Congress Report,* 1934, p. 160.

52.   *TUC Papers*, Bolton to Tracey, Inter-Departmental Memorandum, 13 October 1934, MSS 292 906.8(1).

53.   *Trades Union Congress Report,* 1934, p. 156, pp. 158/9, *Labour Party Conference Report,* 1934, p.156.

54.   *Labour Party Conference Report,* 1935, pp. 177-8. Ceadel, M. (1980), *Pacifism in Great Britain 1914-1945: The Defining of a Faith,* Cambridge, pp. 46-9. Trades Union Congress *Report,* 1935, p. 67. See Naylor, J. F. (1969), *Labour's International Policy*, Weidenfeld and Nicolson, London., pp. 98-110 for a summary of contemporary opinion about the Lansbury/Bevin speech. It was again indicative of trades union power that Lansbury had previously been refused a platform at the Trades Union Congress. Herbert Morrison, not an admirer of Bevin, noted that Baldwin seized the occasion to call an election, 'carefully noting the divergence of opinion at the Labour Party Conference, the subsequent resignation and changes'. See Lord Morrison of Lambeth (1960), *Herbert Morrison: An Autobiography,* Odhams, London p. 162. Naylor op. cit., although generally in favour of Bevin, notes that Labour's 1935 election broadcasts were 'inept ... Lansbury's ommission emphasised the seriousness of Labour's internal difficulties and deprived the party of a powerful and effective speaker'.

55. TUC Conference *Report,* 1927, NMM rejected 3,746,000 to 148,000. See Citrine's attack on NMM, *Labour Magazine* (1927) vol. vi, no. 8, December. Martin's opinion is that 'class against class' was devastating to the NMM: 'The result (of confict over the new orientation) was a victory for international discipline and the "political" struggle over local flexibility and industrialism'. Martin, R. (1969), *Communism and the British Trades Unions, 1924-1933: A Study of the National Minority Movement,* Clarendon, Oxford, p. 102. Bullock, A. (1960), p. 372.

56. *Trades Union Congress Report,* 1933, p. 318, p. 325. Debate, p. 340.

57. Lord Citrine (1964), op. cit. p. 222.

58. *Trades Union Congress Report,* 1934, p. 232.

59. *Trades Union Congress Report,* 1935, pp. 110-112; of the trades councils who replied, 283 were in favour, 18 against (7 of whom later reversed their decision), 80 did not reply, 11 lost TUC recognition. Of the trades unions, 41 were in favour, 8 saw no reason for immediate action, 15 took no action, 10 were opposed, 14 had already taken action. *Trades Union Congress Report,* 1935, p. 262. For a full discussion, see Clinton, A. (1977), *The Trade Union Rank and File, Trades Councils in Britain 1900-1940,* Manchester University Press, pp. 150-56.

60. Lord Citrine (1964), op. cit., pp. 125-27.

61. Sir Walter Citrine (1936), *I Search for Truth in Russia,* London, pp. 285-87, cited p. 285.

62. For discussion of Comintern policy and its effect in Britain, see Fryth, Jim (1985), *Britain, Fascism and the Popular Front,* Lawrence and Wishart, London, pp. 14-19 and *passim* and Hobsbawn, E.J. (1986), 'The "Moscow Line" and International Communist Policy, 1933-1947' in Wrigley, C.J. *Welfare, Diplomacy and Politics: Essays in Honour of A.J.P. Taylor,* p. 171.

63. *Labour and Socialist International Papers,* LSI/16/6/81, programme of common action; LSI/16/6/38, International Information, 12 August 1937; LSI/16/6/43, International Information, 30 August 1937. Taylor, A. J. P. (1980), *Politics, Socialism and Historians,* Hamish Hamilton, London, p. 1919. Watkins, K.W. (1963), *Britain Divided: The Effect of the Spanish Civil War on British Political Opinion,* Nelson, London, chapter 5, *passim,* International Brigade, p. 168 ff., Communist manoeuvers, p. 175. Watkins illustrated the eclectic composition of the Brigade by citing the seven officers killed at Brunere; three Labour, three Communists, one Liberal. Michael Foot, reflecting the contemporary enthusiasm of the left wing in his biography of Aneurin Bevin, is of the opinion that because the importance of the Spanish Civil War is not properly recognised, socialist suspicions about 'the fibre and courage, if not the purpose, of the official Labour leadership' are not understood. See Foot, M. R. (1975), *Aneurin Bevan, 1897-1942,* vol. 1, Paladin, London, p. 220. See also Saville, John (1977), 'May Day 1937' in Asa Briggs and John Saville (eds), *Essays in Labour History* 1918-1939, Croom Helm, London, p. 241 for a left wing opinion of the vitality of 'the energies unloosed' (over Spain and fascism) which could 'at no point be credited to the Labour leaders'. Buchanan, Tom (1991), *The Spanish Civil War and the Labour Movement,* Cambridge, *passim,* and see p. 227.

64. *International Sub-Committee Minutes*, 27 October 1937. See Buchanan, Tom (1991), op. cit. chapter 6 for trades union rank and file initiatives in Spain.

65. Naylor, J. F., (1969), op. cit., p. 143.

66. Buchanan, Tom, (1991), op. cit., pp. 50-8. For leadership position see *Trades Union Congress Report,* 1936, p. 361. For the opinion that the non-intervention policy derived from British government opinion that the Spanish rebels were harmless to British interests, while the Spanish government was unreliable, see Moradiellos, Enrique, (1991), 'The Origins of non-Intervention in the Spanish Civil War', *European History Quarterly,* vol. 21, no. 3, July , pp. 339-64.

67. *James and Lucy Middleton Papers*, Benetton to Middleton, 18 March 1937, MID/59/22.

68. *Socialistische Arbeiter Internationale Papers*, International Institute of Social History, Amsterdam, Middleton to Adler, Faure, Jouhaux, Schevenels, 18 December 1936, SAI 27/63c 51 and 52.

69. Buchanan Tom (1988), 'The role of the Labour Movement in the origin and work of the Basque children's committee 1937-39', *European History Quarterly*, vol. 18, no. 2, April. See also *New Leader*, 2 October 1936, reprint from *Times*, 12 September 1936, Ernest Bevin's telegram to the Irish TGWU explaining a union donation for medical supplies available to either side: 'The union has always stood by freedom of conscience'.

70. *James and Lucy Middleton Papers*, Middleton to Baxter, 22 January 1937, MID 59/9.

71. *Labour Party Conference Report,* 1936, p. 214 ff.

72. For discussion see Watkins, K. W. (1963), op. cit. p. 166 ff.

73. *Labour Party Conference Report,* 1936, pp. 73-5; *Labour and Socialist International Papers,* Gillies's notes of LSI/IFTU meeting, 28 September 1936, LSI 21/7.

74. *International Advisory Committee Memorandum,* no. 479A, April 1937.

75. *Trades Union Congress Report,* 1937, p. 178.

76. *Dalton Papers*, British Library of Political and Economic Science, Diary, 23 June 1937, I 18.14.

77. *International Sub-Committee Minutes*, 15 October 1937.

78. *William Gillies Correspondence*, Financial Statement of IFTU 1938, WG/IFTU/3.

79. *TUC International Committee Minutes,* 19 October 1937, 26 October 1937, 21 December 1937, 20 November 1938, 24 January 1939, 25 April 1939 and 25 July 1939. *TUC International Committee Report,* 11 November 1938. *IFTU Records*, IISH, IFTU Conference Report, 5-8 July 1939, IFTU 60.

80. *Dalton Papers,* Diary, 11 April 1938, I 19.7. For AEU opposition to dilution, Citrine's initiative and subsequent negotiations between the unions and the Treasury, see Parker, R. A. C. (1981), 'British Rearmament 1936-9: Treasury, Trades Unions and Skilled Labour', *English Historical Review*, 96.

81. Lord Citrine (1964) , op. cit., p. 348.

82. *Trades Union Congress Report,* 1938, p. 443.

83. *William Gillies Correspondence*, Tracey to Gillies, July 1938, WG/LAB/79.

84.   *TUC Papers*, Jouhaux's Report for IFTU GC, 17-21 May 1938, MSS 292 906.8(1). Citrine's telegram to Schevenels, 3 May 1938, MSS 292 906.8(1). IFTU GC Report, 17-21 May 1938, MSS 292 906.8(1).

85.   *TUC Papers*, memoranda produced by Bolton, August and n.d. 1938, item produced by Bolton for Extra-ordinary IFTU GC, 9-10 November 1938, MSS 292/908.8(1), 9(1).

86.   *Dalton Papers*, Diary, 28 June 1939.

87.   *TUC International Committee Minutes*, 16 November 1938, summary of IFTU EC and Extraordinary GC, 9-10 November 1938, IFTU EC Report, 3-4 January 1939.

88.   *Labour and Socialist International Papers,* National Joint Council Circular, 3 October 1938, LSI 21/2/25, International Solidarity Fund Report, 1939, LSI 28/2/6.

89.   *James and Lucy Middleton Papers*, Katharine Bruce Glasier to Middleton, 21 August 1939, MID/62/51.

Table 1.1 British representation at the LSI

	1919 to 1923 (HQ in London)	1924 to 1925 (Labour Govt) (Move to Zurich)	1926 to June 1929	July 1929 to 1939 (Labour Govt)
PRESIDENT	Henderson	Cramp	Henderson	
BUREAU*	Henderson	Henderson (+ Gillies in advisory capacity)	Henderson (+ Gillies in advisory capacity)	July to Oct. 1929 Cramp from Oct. 1929 Gillies
EXECUTIVE COMMITTEE*	Henderson Thomas MacDonald (ILP)	1924 Cameron 1925 Henderson Cramp Allen (ILP)	Henderson Cramp Brockway (ILP)	Gillies plus Brockway (ILP) to 1932, Compton to 1935, Dallas from 1935
ADMINISTRATIVE COMMITTEE	Henderson Thomas MacDonald (British Secretary 1921) Allen Wallhead Webb Gosling (Hon. Sec. and Treasurer) Shaw (Joint Sec. 1923) (+ Gillies in advisory capacity)	1924 Cameron 1925 Henderson Cramp Allen Mrs Bell Brailsford C. R. Buxton Wallhead (Treasurer) Shaw (Joint Secretary) (+ Gillies in advisory capacity) (+ Morrison as deputy)	Henderson	

* Others attended Executive and Bureau meetings as substitutes or observers, the most frequent being Morrison and Jenkins. Mary Carlin, MacDonald, Kirkwood, Shaw and Williams were regular attendees until 1929, Dalton after 1935. As no congresses were held after 1931, there is no authoritative contemporary listing of executive members after that date.

Source: Labour and Socialist International Congress *Reports* (1925, 1929, 1931), secretary's report

Table 1.2   LSI conferences and congresses

Conferences

Lucerne, 1-9 August 1918 (Second International)

Paris, 21-25 August 1933 (LSI)

Congresses

Berne, 3-8 February 1919 (Second International)

Geneva, 31 July-4 August 1920 (Second International)

Hamburg, 21-25 May 1923 (LSI reconstituted)

Marseilles, 22-27 August 1925

Brussels, 5-11 August 1928

Vienna, 25 July-11 August 1931

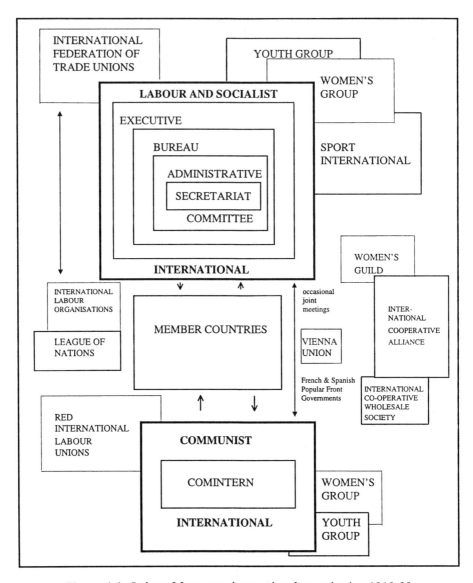

Figure 1.1 Labour Movement international organisation 1918-39

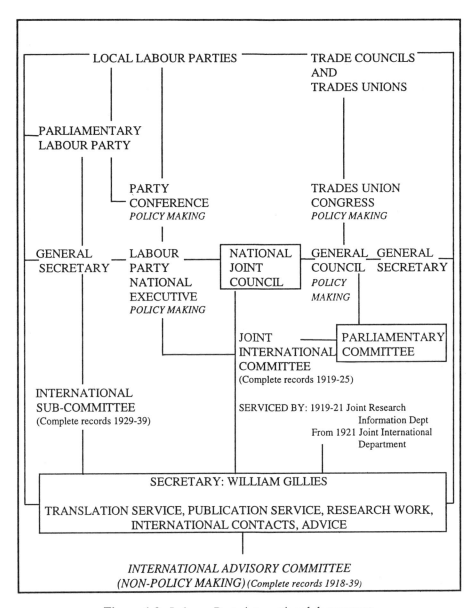

Figure 1.2 Labour Party international department

Paths of European Unity, 1918-33: The Labour Party and the Labour and Socialist International

The British continued zealously to pursue international activity following the creation of the International Federation of Trades Unions, channelling their efforts into the formation of a political grouping. The nature of the latter was hammered out in negotiation, but was underpinned by the memory and the surviving networks of the pre-war International. Then, ties of affection had consolidated relatively informal networks. Both Henderson and MacDonald could hark back to conference sessions balanced by peaceable conversation, pipe smoking on the hotel balcony, when socialism was an adventure not yet overshadowed by the scale of their administrative responsibilities and the 'dark winter' of total war was an inconceivable experience. This chapter describes the way in which the political International was rescued and contact managed, analysing the changing relationship of the Labour Party leadership to the Labour and Socialist International as the latter developed. The domestic impact of this international engagement is outlined.

Internationalism and the Labour Party programme

When Henderson and MacDonald engaged in international reorganisation, they were partly motivated by the need to unite the Labour Party and articulate its programme. The Labour Party had not split over the issue of participation in the war, but there had been different approaches, from Henderson's support of the war effort to MacDonald's opposition to the declaration of war. Some, particularly Independent Labour Party members, had refused conscription and avowed pacifism. Nevertheless, the Labour Party's political position at the end of the First World War had improved, the product of the strength acquired through workers' vital contribution to the war effort. This enhanced status built also on MacDonald's pre-war stewardship and Henderson's organisational ability. The latter found expression in the 1918 Labour Party constitution which provided a practical base as well as a philosophy, allowing for individual and affiliated membership based on constituency parties which were responsible to a national executive whose policy was settled at an annual conference. The Labour Movement remained heterogeneous; the constitution's triumph was to capitalise on this diversified membership, but there was need of a cause around which to unite. Reflecting Labour's war aims, the commitment to internationalism included in the constitution provided a point of purpose around which the Labour Party could cohere, eschatological, broad enough for widespread appeal. Indeed, recruits were attracted from the Liberal Party, their routes including the Union of Democratic Control and the No Conscription Fellowship. Its internationalism marked Labour's distinction from the older parties which had led the country to war. Recognising this, J.H. Thomas wrote: 'The politicians and the capitalists and the military fanatics have had their try and failed ... the world's hope lies in Labour'.[1] Similarly, Beatrice Webb commented:

> the one outstanding virtue of the Labour Party, a virtue which is its very own, not imposed upon it by intellectuals, is its high sense of international morality. Alone amongst British politicians, the leaders of the Labour Party do honestly believe in the brotherhood of man.[2]

Reform or Revolution

It was ironic that these hopes for the future were almost immediately checked by the recurrence of a problem which had beset the pre-war Second International, the difficulty of the choice between reform or revolution. Branting submitted a resolution to the 1919 Berne Conference in favour of parliamentary government which had the effect of institutionalising this conflict by excluding delegates from the Soviet Union.[3] A subsidiary problem was indicated when Adler (Austria) and Longuet (France), seeking unity between reformists and revolutionaries, refused to condemn the Soviet Union.[4] German, French, Spanish, Swiss and American revolutionary parties joined the Communist International, as did the British Socialist Party.

MacDonald and British leadership

As hopes of influencing the 1919 Peace Treaty and the character of the League of Nations slid away, and the trades unions formalised their own network, MacDonald came to the fore in recreating the political International. The tone of his book *Wanderings and Excursions*, which describes his contribution in detail, conveys MacDonald's enthusiasm and his 'international faith'. For example, he was much heartened by the reception he met with on his journey to Berne:

> the common people recognise their own ambassadors. Paris (official treaty) to them is little: Berne is everything. Our country, inspired by a vigorous democratic vision, can lead the continental democratic movement, be its rallying centre. And that is true whether one has in mind Foreign Offices or

the Socialist movement. For our foreign policy we shall create and use an international platform.[5]

However, progress continued to be difficult. Enjoying enforced freedom from parliamentary responsibilities, MacDonald found the International 'too parliamentary'. He lamented the lack of unity between representatives of socialist movements 'in such diverse state of political development ... and degrees of power'.[6] Attempting to encompass these difficulties and irritated at having his manifesto on the peace treaty disregarded, MacDonald confided to his diary that he was 'getting more and more struck with the work of Lenin as an administrator'.[7]

The British were the biggest group at the July 1920 conference of the International, followed by the German majority socialists. Only seventeen national sections were represented, five of these attending merely for information. Huysmans, pre-war International Secretary, feared: 'the condition of the International was a reflection of the condition of Europe ... a state of instability and despair'. Beatrice Webb recorded: 'a mixed impression of apparent futility and real usefulness' and that critics perceived: 'All that is senile in the Labour and Socialist Movement'. *In extremis*, other affiliates turned to Britain to rescue the International from despondency. Huysmans, a fraternal delegate to the 1920 Labour Party conference, urged that: 'the secretariat of the International must be based on a powerful party in a very powerful country'.[8] London was proposed as headquarters of a reformed administration; Huysmans would retain his secretaryship, assisted by MacDonald, with Henderson as president; these, with Branting, Louis de Brouckère, Otto Wels, Troelstra (Netherlands), J.H. Thomas and Tom Shaw formed the executive and British Labour provided the administrative committee.

For their part, the British were hesitant. Affiliation to the Third International was decisively rejected at the 1920 conference (2,940,000 against affiliation, 225,000 for) but an Independent Labour Party resolution in favour of secession from the Second International was rejected in a less impressive manner (816,000 for secession, 1,010,000 against).[9] The Joint International committee of Party and trades union leaders was cautious: 'we doubt the wisdom of making London the permanent centre of the International' and the latter's records were therefore kept at Brussels.[10] MacDonald, accepting the secretaryship, was less than optimistic and faced censure from the Independent Labour Party (on whose national executive he sat). Offered a fee, he refused, in order not to be tied. Although ILP censure was rescinded, the ILP refused to join in reconstruction efforts and its relationship with the International was always problematic.[11]

International Department and William Gillies

The Labour Party had two related muddles to resolve: how to manage contact with, and the remit of, the International body. These arose from the loose, federal nature of both domestic and international pre-war bodies and their need to adjust to new responsibilities and expectations. The Labour Party leadership could be commended for expending considerable effort in its tidying operation, especially in view of the difficulties of international organisation so eloquently expressed by the files of this period.[12] For instance, applications for affiliation had to be dealt with, typewriters bought, stationery organised, passports arranged, hotels booked for international conferences, delegates provided with admission cards, against a background of endless argument about place and time of meeting, telegrams flying to and fro, translation services' estimates, arrangements for printing, press releases. Miss Coe was appointed by the International to help with this mass of administration and William Gillies was appointed to head an International Department, which, as has been seen, initially served both the trades unions and Labour Party.[13]

Gillies's joint appointment presented difficulties when the Labour Party and Trades Union Congress had each their own leadership and bureaucracies, while relations between the Party and TUC were subject to a continuous process of negotiation and the two groups might differ in policy. The Labour Party was well aware both of its need for union fees and of the possibility of policy differences. MacDonald wrote: 'Something must be done to coordinate the political and industrial interests, or we shall always be open to disastrous waves of popular impulse and mood', while Philip Snowden wrote that Henderson's 'favourite saying ... (was) that we must take the trade union movement with us'. It was Henderson who had taken practical steps towards coordination, instigating first, a Trade Union Coordinating Committee (1919) and second, the more formal National Council of Labour (1920).[14]

Gillies's scope for influence in his new job arose from the check-and-balance nature of Party and TUC relations:

> On the industrial questions the Department shall be at the service of the General Council and its General Secretary; and on the political questions it shall be at the service of the Labour Party and its General Secretary.[15]

Moreover, Gillies's direct supervisors were occupied with day-to-day administration of their respective empires. Mary Hamilton, Henderson's first biographer, noted the latter's ability to delegate, an attribute to which the enormity of the tasks Henderson regularly undertook bore testimony; she described Gillies as 'the expert head of the Party's International department'.[16]

Gillies joined the Labour Party research staff in 1912 and had risen to the secretaryship of the Information Bureau. He had been exempted from wartime service because of his position on the Labour Party staff. Duly appointed to his new post in January 1922 (Arthur Greenwood replaced him at the Information Bureau), Gillies received a salary of £525 per annum. His personality was not retiring. Denis Healey (who succeeded Gillies as International Secretary after the Second World War) remembered him as a 'cantankerous Scot who distrusted foreigners and hated all Germans'; the latter part of this opinion was

Party folk-lore, although there is no evidence of xenophobia in this early period.[17] A contemporary opinion, distastefully phrased by Beatrice Webb, acknowledged both Gillies's obstinacy and his expertise: 'there is that little dwarf Gillies - an honest, oversensitive and obstinate minded but well informed little Glaswegian Fabian'.[18] Gillies was fiercely proud of his department; Christine Howie, an ex-governess, proficient in French, German and Italian (she could also speak Spanish) was appointed chief assistant in 1922 and worked for Gillies until her retirement. Gillies's well documented and extensive files indicate that he was meticulous, dry and had a temper.[19]

The International Advisory Committee

Gillies was also a member of the International Advisory Committee, a non-elected forum of unpaid, volunteer experts in foreign affairs, whose secretary was Leonard Woolf. Membership was open to the Parliamentary Labour Party but members were not, necessarily, Party members or trades unionists. This body reported initially to the Joint Research Department and, from 1924, to the Joint International Department. It met infrequently, often in the House of Commons. Sidney Webb, H.N. Brailsford and G.D.H. Cole, the latter two to the left of the Party, were among the Labour intellectuals at the first meeting, although the time they gave thereafter was limited. More to the centre of the Party, Susan Lawrence, Philip Noel Baker and Noel and Charles Roden Buxton were regular members. The latter two (brothers) had been Liberal Members of Parliament, attracted by Labour's pacifist outlook. With Philip Noel Baker they sought to use League of Nations machinery to further Labour foreign policy goals. This policy was also pursued by Arthur Henderson and later, Hugh Dalton, under whom Philip Noel Baker was to work in the Foreign Office (1929-31). The committee has, therefore, been seen as a centre of League of Nations support within the Labour Party and indicative of Liberal influence.[20] Although the committee considered widely ranging subjects and its homogeneity should not be overestimated, this generalisation is substantially true. Former Liberals on the committee should not, however, be seen as the sole source of League of Nations support, as discussion of the Labour Party's war aims has indicated. As Gillies was a constant committee attender, the evidence would suggest that he also looked to the League of Nations to realise Labour's goals. The committee's success in promoting the League of Nations was doubtful; Ramsay Macdonald was cautious about the efficacy of the League, as was his 1924 under secretary Arthur Ponsonby (also a Liberal recruit). From its inception, even its foremost supporters wanted the League's revision.

The Advisory Committee continued to give advice on foreign affairs in the inter-war period, but was not concerned with managing international socialist contact. It should be remembered that lengthy memoranda produced at monthly intervals by academics were of limited use within the Labour Party and only one source of advice, others being the unions and International organisations. Gillies's department collated all the advice. Committee members appeared to realise their limitations. Throughout 1921 Ernest Bevin declined invitations to speak at its meetings and in July 1921 the committee decided to limit the number of its recommendations because it was 'losing influence'.[21]

The quest for international unity

While these preparation for management of international contact were being made, negotiations abroad centred around the attempt to unite the International Movement. Together with those who had doubted the wisdom of Branting's resolution on reformism (the Austrian, French and Norwegian parties), the Independent Labour Party founded in Vienna on 15 January 1922, the Union of Socialist Parties for International Action. This body became known as the Vienna Union or disparagingly, by the Third International, as the two-and-a-half-International (which aimed to provide a bridge between reformists and revolutionaries). Friedrich Adler was the leading figure in the Vienna Union; his credentials were twofold. First, his father Victor had been prominent in the Second International and second, he had assassinated the Austrian Prime Minister and was released from life imprisonment in the general amnesty of 1918. MacDonald's task was to clear the ground of the subsidiary difficulty of the Vienna Union in order to achieve an 'all inclusive' International by negotiation with the communists. Renaudel (French Socialist Party) wrote to MacDonald:

> Il n'est pas encore clair si Vienna voudra devenir un centre d'attraction pour une nouvelle Internationale, la 4, ou bien si l'organisation ainsi preparée se contentera d'être un centre ... pour une véritable unité Internationale (sic).[22]

> (It is not clear whether Vienna would like to become a centre of attraction for a new International, the 4th, or if the organisation will be content to become a centre for a truly united International.)

Such perceptions of ambiguity of motive were the weakness of those who tried to find a middle ground between revolution and reform.

Adler, trying to explain his motives in a characteristically lengthy letter (Philip Snowden called it a Papal Encyclical.[23]) wrote:

> I am not by any means, one of those who condemns everything connected with the Second International, for ... the whole of the world's proletariat was represented in it.[24]

Nevertheless, in Adler's opinion this body had 'become the select group of those unrepentant sinners' who would not condemn the war; its wartime anarchy had allowed Lenin to rush into revolution; *'there is no International today'* (Adler's emphasis); 'there is only an international association of parties'.[24] The subsequent course of Labour Party relationships with the International is illuminated by this exposition of Adler's principled position; he wanted to create an International whose decisions would be binding on members and which looked to eventual inclusion of the Soviets.

MacDonald noted that the International was: 'in a bad way and (the) difficulty is to organise office and staff. Moscow is weakening and Vienna not much consequence ... Must try to put my back into this'. He was somewhat helped by Snowden who intended starving the Vienna Union of funds ('I am determined not to allow ILP money to be spent on the Vienna affair'). Adler made the running, however, in seeking to unite the Internationals, calling six conferences in 1921/22, with IFTU and the executive of the Second International. Debate was fierce. MacDonald was in despair at a particularly unhappy session in October 1921, Vienna Union affiliates insisted on being treated collectively while addressing Second International affiliates separately, Britain insisted on Scandinavian attendance; these matters were left to London headquarters to decide and MacDonald made difficulties over meeting Adler.[25]

Adler's initiatives, MacDonald's attention and, most importantly, the adoption of the New Economic programme and consequent political change in the Soviet Union resulted in a meeting (held, after much difficulty with venue and date at Cologne, May 1922) of all groups identified with the class struggle: the executives of the Second and Third Internationals and the Vienna Union. A committee of nine was set up to prepare an International Congress of Workers. Rights of defence, exercised by the Second International were agreed for Soviet political prisoners and a joint examination of the case of Georgia (whose socialist government had been overthrown by the USSR) was promised. Preliminary and joint declarations were drawn up but the Vienna Union and the Third International listed further points of disagreement. The committee of nine had soon to report failure. Nothing was done about Georgia; Vandervelde, defending the political prisoners, was harassed and had to resign in the prisoners' own interests.[26]

Abandoning all attempts at uniting the Internationals, Second International parties called a conference in London (June 1922); because of the difficulties of failing European exchange rates, many delegates could not afford the fare; the Vienna Union groups stayed apart. British representatives included MacDonald, Henderson, Clynes and Thomas of Labour's 'Big Five' and Tom Shaw.[27] It was decided to carry on trying to unite with the Vienna Union and a number of joint demonstrations were arranged and carried through, particularly between the British, Belgian and French delegates. After further difficulties, in July 1922 the trades unions helped by convening a meeting of the executives of the Second International and Vienna Union in the Hague; in December of that year these bodies formed a committee of action to convene an International Socialist conference.[28] MacDonald's involvement ended with his 1922 re-election to Parliament, but had been important in reconstructing the International.[29] It was, perhaps, a legacy of their differences in the war that he and Henderson had made separate contributions, rather than uniting in a team effort.

Finally, at Hamburg, in May 1923 a general conference was convened and chaired by Adler; ethical and doctrinal points were avoided, allowing merger with the Vienna Union. William Gillies wrote a postcard to James Middleton: 'Unity is achieved!'. Tom Shaw believed the September 1922 merger of the German socialists to be the decisive factor allowing unity; the Labour Party executive cited 'the growing intimacy of the French and British parties' as the major contribution. The conference discussed action on the peace treaty; international action against reaction; an eight hour day and international social reform; organisation of workers internationally. A constitution was agreed, of which the four main parts were; first, to engage in class struggle to empower workers' organisations and build a socialist commonwealth; second, to unify the activities of affiliates; third, that resolutions of the International were binding; fourth, that the International was necessary in peace and war and would be the biggest authority in conflict between nations. Although not substantially different from the 1900 Second International regulations, the terms of the new constitution reflected Vienna Union ideals rather than those held by MacDonald. Britain had opposed binding resolutions while Branting's 1919 resolution in favour of reformism had been effectively annulled. Administrative arrangements agreed were that congresses should be held (delegates from each party based on its size of membership), conferences (thrice the party's executive representation); the executive was to consist of four representatives from each party (smaller parties being grouped together). As these were unwieldy bodies for decision making, a bureau was elected of 11 members of the executive. The country that hosted the International's office nominated a small administrative committee to work with the secretariat (Secretary, president, treasurer).

The reconstituted Second International was, henceforth, more usually known as the Labour and Socialist International (LSI). Adler and Tom Shaw agreed to be joint secretaries for six months. With Henderson and J.H. Thomas, MacDonald had a place on the executive. The TUC withdrew from running the now redundant British International secretaryship. That the latter's work had been only partly achieved was indicated when the 1924 Labour Party conference unanimously resolved to continue working for a fully united International.[31] The Labour Party, nonetheless, retained a position of considerable authority because it housed the LSI secretariat and therefore, formed the LSI administration committee.

London headquarters

The LSI's London base was first, Victoria Street and then Southampton Street. MacDonald, Henderson, Thomas and Shaw were joined on the administration committee by Gosling (Transport Workers), Sidney Webb (Fabian Society), Lees, Clifford Allen and Wallhead (Independent Labour Party). Gillies was coopted to the committee, attending every one of the 18 meetings from June 1923 to June 1925, an unequalled record.[32] British authority was, however diluted when Labour became the party of government following the December 1923 election; LSI rules dictated that no government minister could serve on the executive and Henderson, MacDonald and J.H. Thomas accordingly lost their places. There had been attempts during the election to damage the Labour Party through its membership of the LSI, which was dubbed 'a supernatural monster'; *Labour Magazine* was used to refute the charges and to assert that LSI decisions were not binding on member parties. As LSI resolutions were both collective and binding this illustrated important differences in perspective. The report also indicated that, should it become an electoral liability, the LSI's attractions would diminish.[33]

The position of the secretariat in London was not always comfortable; the legacy of MacDonald's and Adler's difficulties remained to be overcome. Adler does not seem to have taken the occasion to endear himself to British Labour; for example, he failed on several occasions to accept invitations to Bristol, a centre of Labour activity.[34] London was inconvenient for Adler, whose home with his wife Kathia remained in Austria. He did not fit easily into London Labour life, perhaps expecting an intellectual rigour more characteristic of European parties. For instance, Adler failed to understand why the *Daily Herald* editor (Hamilton Fyffe) printed merely extracts of LSI resolutions and Fyffe's explanations were brusque ('In an eight page paper that is all the resolutions were worth from a newspaper point of view').[35] Adler's dealings with MacDonald, and with Hamilton Fyffe indicated that Adler shared both Gillies's obstinacy and his sensitivity; these traits of character did not bode well for their future collaboration. However, Labour Party influence was clear; together with the German Social Democratic Party, it had the maximum 40 votes at LSI congresses; France had 26, Austria 23 votes and all other countries less than half Britain's representation.[36]

The Move to Zurich

It was, perhaps, an indication of Adler's discomfort in London that in 1925 he offered his resignation. The reasons given were family responsibilities and what Adler referred to as his 'dream of securing leisure for theoretical and critical study'; Adler described himself as a Marxist who wanted to campaign against 'so called communists'. To the *Daily Herald* he wrote; 'From the Marxian point of view I believe the reconstruction of the International to be the supreme task' and that 'it was not easy to relinquish the secretaryship'.[37] Austrian politics, however, were of absorbing interest, for instance pioneering experiments of city socialism in Vienna and the expression of Austromarxist theory led by Otto Bauer. Tom Shaw, who had been given leave of absence from his joint secretaryship, decided to resign his LSI position in order to devote himself to the International Textile Workers. The Labour government having fallen in 1924, Henderson retained the LSI presidency and his position at the bureau and was re-elected to the LSI executive. He was successful in persuading Adler to stay on condition that its offices moved to Switzerland: Henderson recorded his 'immense satisfaction' ... '(Adler) would continue the work, and in the event of our going to Switzerland, he would place his services at our disposal'.[38] The administrative committee was reformed, Grimion of Switzerland reinforcing Adler, Henderson and Van Roosbroeck (treasurer).

Settling on the continent seemed to give the LSI secretary a feeling of permanency; Adler made a huge effort to organise the archives, which had been split in the war.[39] By the time the offices next moved (1931) there were eight full time and two part time employees. Adler had not become more conciliatory; the move had been occasioned by:

> a dispute with the bank which owned the building in Stockenstrasse where the secretariat had rented accommodation since 1925, in connection with the hoisting of a red flag on the occasion of the May day celebration.[40]

A contemporary commentator was of the opinion that there were now three centres of leadership within the LSI; the British, who had been extremely influential from 1923-25; the Austromarxist centre, whose influence rested on Adler's secretaryship and Bauer's prestige; and the right wing, represented by Otto Wels (Germany) and de Brouckère (Belgium).[41]

Gillies's promotion

Switzerland was a long way for busy politicians to travel. Gillies, however, was free to attend; he became the most regular and often the only British delegate. His international position was reflected in an accretion of power at home. This caused problems with Citrine who, newly appointed TUC secretary, wished to establish trades union rights *vis à vis* the Labour Party. Citrine asked for 'closer collaboration', paradoxically because unions catered for members 'irrespective of their politics and must retain their right to an independent political position'.[42] This, of course, was at the time of the Anglo-Russian Council experiment and the TUC international political outlook therefore differed from that of the Labour Party, which had given up trying to cooperate with international communism.

Citrine began to attack Gillies, complaining of the latter's lack of supervision. Appalled that Gillies attended international meetings without obtaining permission to absent himself, Citrine rang to object, only to find that Gillies was in Paris. Gillies insisted on his rights:

> I shall, of course, be delighted to comply with the wish, now expressed for the first time, that when I am instructed to leave the country by the Labour Party, I should acquaint the secretary of the General Council of the fact.

Further, he claimed that the TUC did not use him properly:

> For although the Labour Party has made the Department responsible for all the administrative work arising out of the Party's foreign policy and relations with foreign parties and the Labour and Socialist International, the General Council has not called upon the Department to do the corresponding work on the Trade Union side.[43]

The International Department and committee remained joint ventures for one more year until the unions backed out, ostensibly as part of a cost-cutting exercise. Citrine reported that 'the trade union service has been in no way commensurate with financial liability'; 'Mr. Bramley has never known of any disciplinary condition ... nor has it been possible to exert any proper supervision'. Once rid of Gillies, Citrine was able to write: 'the relationship between the two offices is very much better ... no hostilities exist'.[44]

Gillies was now substantially free from trades union control, despite occasional joint meetings of the Labour Party and TUC International Committees, until the fall of the 1931 Labour government altered the balance of Labour Party/TUC power. Then, Citrine again asked that trade union policy be given more weight; however, by then, differences in international policy had largely dissipated. Gillies was, apparently, quick to see that trades union influence would grow because he developed a good relationship with Ernest Bevin, who told the TUC congress: 'There is a little chap you do not know very well; I refer to William Gillies, who is an asset to the Labour Party and Movement'.[45] Gillies was punctilious about joining in the social life of Transport House and was a member of its club (president Bevin, vice-presidents Henderson, Middleton and Citrine), whose objects were: 'to provide fellowship among the officers and administrative staff of Labour organisations in Transport House', which it did through music, drama and social functions.[46]

Gillies originated much of his own work, suggesting letters to socialists abroad, providing drafts for comment or following up policy decisions by suggesting relevant Party circulars. His proposals were usually for comments by leading socialists on current affairs; for instance, from Vandervelde on Belgian politics, from Adler on working class unity. He contributed to publications, frequently *Labour Magazine* and its successor *Labour,* edited by Herbert Tracey.[47] His reports were eclectic, covering trades unionism, the progress of the LSI and detailed accounts of European politics. From 1934 to 1939 Gillies himself produced *International Service*, a brief account of LSI affairs for domestic production. Gillies's rôle was illuminated by its contrast to that of Bolton, TUC International Committee secretary who had very little room to manoeuver; Gillies's position was analogous rather to that of Citrine at the TUC, exerting influence within the constraints of formal policy decision; in Citrine's words: 'I could work through and with the staff to influence policy and I knew that, as time went on, I could do much to initiate it'.[48]

With parliamentarians, MacDonald in particular, Gillies's relationship was ambiguous. He represented the conjunction of two international worlds in which the parliamentary leadership operated, that of the Labour Movement and that of foreign secretaries, ambassadors, governments and civil servants. The leadership aimed, understandably, at good relations with and information from the Labour world, but freedom of action in the foreign office world. Collision of the two was, occasionally, embarrassing. For instance, Gillies was involved in the 1925 Barmat scandal which embarrassed German socialists and, through them, MacDonald. However, MacDonald continued to use Gillies for information and was untroubled by the only occasion extant when Gillies was caught out by the press. A French reporter posing as a trades unionist had managed to get an interview with Gillies on reparations. Gillies arranged through Blum for an apology from the editor and wrote to MacDonald: 'It is the first time in 15 years that I have been caught like this. I am very angry about it, and am sorry if it brings trouble to you'. MacDonald merely thanked him for his letter of explanation; there was no hint that, quite apart from publication, Gillies had exceeded his duties by discussing reparations with the (supposed) trades unionist; exchanging information in order to extend his formidable knowledge of the international scene seems to have been accepted as part of his duties.[49] Gillies translated for MacDonald when the latter was Leader of the Opposition and annotated the translation with comment.[50]

Gillies became a generally respected figure in international affairs. He joined the committee of the Royal Institute at Chatham House, lending books from the Labour Party library, suggesting speakers, taking the opportunity to present Labour opinion. His expertise was of use, for instance, when he gave a memorandum about the economic and financial situation in Italy, or outlined the procedure for the committee stage of a Bill for the ratification of a treaty with a foreign power. Although Sheila MacDonald (Ramsay's daughter) worked at Chatham House and asked for Gillies help with suggestions for guest lists, Gillies tried in vain to interest MacDonald in the Royal Institute, writing that: 'The institute is now a very valuable non-party organisation' and pointing out that other former prime ministers (Balfour, Lloyd George) were presidents.[51]

In short, Gillies enjoyed a central position in the Labour Movement, presenting ideas to the leadership directly through Departmental advice and indirectly through the Labour Press, the Advisory Committee and the social life of Transport House. He also had contact with the whole range of the Labour Party membership; for instance, he prepared annotated bibliographies (*Aids for Study in International Relations*) for local Labour Parties and acted as travel agent, inviting European socialists and arranging trips abroad. Instances of the diverse people seeking his advice were Sidney Silverman, when a parliamentary candidate, asking for introductions to socialists in Oslo; York Labour Party League of Youth asking for European contacts; Ellen Wilkinson, making an extensive trip to Germany, receiving addresses and a rap on the knuckles for not paying enough attention to protocol (she intended taking a flag and greetings from British Labour women but had failed to ask the appropriate Labour Party women's committee for its support).[52] Gillies was content with a background rôle at home; he never claimed to be a politician and never stood for parliamentary office; but he was the Labour Party expert in his field, his knowledge of European socialism outmatched only by that of Henderson and MacDonald.

Gillies at the LSI

Abroad, Gillies came more to the forefront because the Labour Party's second spell in government (1929-31) obliged Henderson, who took the Foreign Secretaryship, to renounce his LSI presidency. Vandervelde took over as president, with de Brouckère in the chair. Henderson was thanked in the LSI *Report* for his 'devotion'; 'under your presidency the LSI was reconstructed and became strong and active'. Gillies replaced Henderson on the executive and in 1930 was elected to the Bureau, the major decision making forum.[53] One of his actions was to arrange for a fraternal delegate from the LSI to visit the Labour Party conference; he argued that the Party never reciprocated, although European parties often requested a British delegate to their conferences; he won his point and the process thereafter became automatic.[54]

Before 1933, and in contrast to IFTU debates on the strike-for-peace, LSI relationships were managed relatively smoothly, Gillies and Adler maintaining regular contact. An instance was the potentially controversial issue of reparations and their effect on employment, in particular the damage to mining, shipbuilding and engineering jobs in creditor countries; this was raised by Pat Dollan of the ILP at the 1925 LSI Congress, but dissipated in sub-committees.[55] Henderson, as Foreign Secretary, attempted to satisfy French demands for guarantees of mutual assistance in case of German aggression and to find a way of resolving the reparations issue, although he had scant assistance from Ramsay MacDonald (premier) or Philip Snowden (Chancellor).[56] A French plan for European federal union was not supported by Henderson; raised at the League of Nations in 1929, this was investigated by Philip Noel Baker (Henderson's junior assistant). Vandervelde shared British scepticism, writing that 'the private presence of opposing class interests' in Europe ensured the failure of European federalism and that the International 'relying above all upon itself, will work in the most effective manner to open up the paths of European unity'.[57]

At this time, the LSI tried to broaden its appeal by attracting delegates from outside Europe. Non-European Labour movements tended to be small and therefore poor, so it was decided to take best advantage of meetings of the League of Nations (to which their governments paid Labour delegates' expenses) and the British Commonwealth Labour Conference. Vandervelde made trips to Argentina and the Far East. Finland and Japan affiliated to IFTU in 1931, following a visit to Japan the previous year.[58]

Gillies showed his ability at international negotiation in 1931 when he was called on to co-chair the LSI conference session on disarmament. In view of TUC disquiet at the strike-for-peace policy and leadership insistence on holding the reins at home and directing the peace campaign, his was not an easy task. He achieved a creditable compromise between British and international interests, the Labour Party supporting a pious LSI majority resolution in favour of a joint campaign with the unions on disarmament. Subsequently, the Party International sub-committee decided to support a policy of the largest possible measure of international disarmament by mutual agreement.[59] This was in line with Henderson's decision (1931) to accept the presidency of the League of Nations Disarmament Conference. Dalton reinforced the commitment to collective security in a resolution at the 1931 Labour Party conference which demanded drastic disarmament by national agreement in the numbers and equipment of all armed forces. The British contribution to the international disarmament campaign was, however, modest; perforated postcards were prepared for affiliates to send to the Prime Minister indicating support.[60] Cooperative societies, unions not affiliated to the TUC and the Labour press were asked to publicise the campaign. When Adler tried to take the campaign further by arranging a conference (Zurich, May 1932) on the methods by which workers would carry on the struggle for power, the way to working class unity and the position of the workers on the outbreak of war, the Labour Party International sub committee recommended the Labour Movement should not commit itself: it had 'no objection in principle' but would need early notice of the precise terms of the motion for full discussion: 'if there were irreconcilable differences of opinion, we should probably wish to avoid a premature conference'.[61]

Relationships with the Communist Party

It was during Gillies's time of greatest influence at the LSI that the issue of collaboration with international communism arose. His position abroad meant that Gillies was able also to input his opinion to decisions on united front work at home.

The Labour Party response to communism was more consistent than that of the trades unions. The championship of reformism and the establishment of a mass membership political party capable of office were two sides of the same policy. For these ends, the Labour Party needed to mould the diverse Movement into a homogenous and loyal following. While the Independent Labour Party, which accepted the Labour Party's objectives, was an acceptable affiliate, the Communist Party of Great Britain (CPGB), which rejected these goals, clearly was not. Clause three of the Labour Party constitution stated that members should: 'abstain strictly from identifying themselves with, or promoting the interests of, any other political party'. For its part, the Communist International was hostile to reformism, while employing the rhetoric of 'united front from below' among the Labour Movement mass membership. *Labour International Year Book* recorded in 1923 that the first two years of the Third International's existence: 'were devoted to the primary work of drawing the sharp, theoretical lines of demarcation between the revolutionary and the reformist elements of the proletariat'.[62] Some of the difficulties of this phase were expressed by MacDonald:

> We wanted to know whether the 'united front' was only a phrase for tactics or an idea for action ... in England it is being declared, in order to satisfy the Communist Party here, that the Moscow leaders have devised the catchword in order to expose and entangle us and to accuse us face to face.

At the International, MacDonald wrote, 'we had reports of meetings broken up, Trades Union Conferences attacked, unions split, rival candidates'.[63] The CPGB, nevertheless, repeatedly applied for affiliation to the Labour Party. This was held by the latter's negotiators to be inconsistent with the CPGB affiliation to the Communist International. Labour Party affiliates could not serve two masters. There was little difficulty in winning Labour Party conference support for rejecting each CPGB application, although the majority in favour of excluding individual communists was relatively small (1924); conference reports showed that many found working with the communists a dispiriting experience; they were unused to the discipline expected and grew bored at the insistence on procedural points.[64]

A firm line with the CPGB, however, did not protect the Labour Party from attack on its associations with communism. Ironically, although the Labour Party was wary of the Communist International because it acted in accordance with Soviet foreign policy, the Labour Party's Russophilism rendered it open to Soviet diplomatic approaches. The 1924 Labour government discussed Soviet trade, possibly to its detriment at the polls and the 1929-31 Labour government continued the negotiations. Failure to handle criticism over the Campbell case was the immediate cause of the 1924 government's fall. Campbell, editor of the communist *Worker's Weekly,* had advocated in its pages solidarity of the armed forces with industrial action in peace or war; his prosecution for sedition was withdrawn, an action inadequately defended in the House of Commons. The production during the subsequent election of a letter (now thought to have been forged) from Zinoviev, president of the Third International, which set out plans to revolutionise the British proletariat added to the charges of communist connections and contributed to the government's defeat. Soviet foreign policy, British communist activity and Third International plans seemed, with justice, to be intertwined. If it countenanced the former, the Labour Party opened itself to charges of collaborating with the latter. The second effect of the Zinoviev letter was to deepen the hostility which the denunciation of Labour's leaders by the Third International obviously aroused.

Much of the Communist approach was not direct but clandestine. The Communist Party operated cells within other parties, the system of '*noyautage*', or under cover of apparently innocent 'front' operations with impeccable aims. Labour learnt by experience how to respond. An early example, which first directed Gillies to the need for vigilance, was that of Russian Famine Relief; this body's petition was circulated by the Second International in 1921 and money was collected worldwide. IFTU reported however that the Communist Party was using the organisation to attack them. Invited to a meeting to further its work, both the Second International and IFTU declined attendance and the TUC set up its own relief fund. In 1924 the organisation re-emerged as Workers' International Relief; the TUC International committee met representatives, who gave assurances that their work would not overlap that of other relief organisations; however, information was received from the German SDP via the LSI that: 'the WIR is nothing other than one of the many forms of communist cell building' and that its inspiration was Willi Münzenberg, known as 'the patron saint of fellow travellers', later described by Gillies as 'the true inventor of the sympathising mass organisations'. The TUC International committee, then pursuing its links with Soviet unions, took no action. Not content with this passive reception, WIR attacked, demanding an enquiry into how the LSI information was obtained and agreed that all relief work in Britain would be 'entirely disassociated from political propaganda'; if and when these conditions were complied with, the Labour Party and TUC promised support. In April 1925 WIR claims that the conditions had been met were rejected. Outmanoeuvred, WIR was not particularly successful in Britain.[65] It should be noted that at this time both Gillies in Britain and Adler at the LSI were equally wary about communist methods and motivation. Indeed, Gillies was, to an extent, instructed by Adler in the need for caution. Adler advised all affiliates that International Workers' Relief was a Communist organisation 'which, under the cloak of the united front, would work politically for the communists'. He warned Gillies also about international Class War Prisoners' Aid, also known as International Red Aid. In February 1928, Adler refused an invitation for the LSI to be affiliated to the International of Proletorian Freethinkers because an invitation had also been sent to the Third International.[66]

The Communist Solar System

From 1928, the Communist Party adopted a 'Class Against Class' openly hostile attitude to reformist organisations.[67] Front organisations came under greater suspicion. Because of his international connections, Gillies played a major rôle in deciding who, and which groups, should be doubted. When the 1917 Club had been formed to 'Hail the Russian Revolution', Gillies had been a founder member. However, his work in the International Department fostered a prejudice against the Third International and the CPGB which became obsessive. The investigative work Gillies undertook reflected the bias against the communism of Labour Party and trades union leaders such as Ernest Bevin, who had to deal with the busmen's committee. How far Bevin, and others, inspired Gillies's research is uncertain; the records suggest that this was very much carried forward on Gillies's own initiative. He scanned letters and pamphlets arriving in the International Department and marked the names of known communists; subsequent letters would then be studied to see if *any* of the names on the original letter heading reappeared; if so, this second organisation was also suspect. Working in this way, Gillies built up a whole collection of Third International ancillary organisations; seven large boxes containing seventy-eight files. The collection resulted in a pamphlet, *The Communist Solar System* (1933). The authorship of the pamphlet is open to doubt; Morrison's biographers claim his authorship; others suggest that Gillies, with the help of colleagues at Transport House was the author.[68] Its production seems to spring naturally from Gillies's files; it may be judged a team effort to which Gillies substantially contributed.

No doubt Gillies's suspicions of communist infiltration were at times justified; at others, they were inappropriate: the Marx Memorial library, for instance, was hardly a communist cell. Münzenberg, Gillies's arch villain, had his own problems with the Third International.[69] Making a judgement was not easy, as the case of the Labour Research Department shows. This was, as its name suggests, a fact finding and reporting service; there were communists on its executive which was elected at an annual conference. LRD officers asked why they came under suspicion; there appeared to be a *prima facie* case, *Inprecorr* (the Third International press service) having reported:

> The Labour Research Department collects statistics, conducts investigations into wages, movements etc. This Department is not a Party concern, but is under control of the Party.[70]

Inprecorr printed a correction and the LRD survived (until the war years, when it was proscribed for a year and then reinstated) because it had strong trades union and District Labour Party support. The naivety of the ordinary Labour Party member should not be overestimated; s/he was able to withstand communist persuasion while making use of the indisputably helpful facts and figures.

The Independent Labour Party

Its diversity was the major difficulty in policing the Labour Party.[71] Affiliated socialist societies were likely to act on their own initiative. The 1918 constitution, imbued with the chiliasm of the war years, had committed the Party to the common ownership of the means of production but the Party's identity and programme could more accurately be expressed as the representation of working people and their organisations; with this, the trades unions could agree. While the socialist societies had insufficient representation to offer an effective counterpoise to the influence of the parliamentarians at leadership level or of the unions in the constituencies, their persistence indicated that they retained an attraction for the rank and file.

The most important of the socialist societies was the Independent Labour Party. That its international perspective differed from that of the Labour Party had been made clear by its 1920 condemnation of MacDonald's British International secretaryship; its membership of the Vienna Union; Dollan's attempt to debate reparations and unemployment at the 1925 LSI conference; Brockway's 1926 resuscitation of strike-for-peace. In 1926 the ILP proposed that the LSI approach the Third International with a view to holding an exploratory conference. Nine arguments were put forward in support of this move, the chief being the need for solidarity against capitalist reaction and others that the Soviet Union had proved it was capable of change by initiating the new Economic Programme. The case of the Georgian prisoners could also be reopened. This proposal was rejected by 247 votes to three at the LSI, the majority reiterating that while unity was desirable, it was impossible. An offshoot of the Vienna Union, the International Bureau of Revolutionary Socialist Parties continued to meet spasmodically.[72] The ILP was to the left of the Austromarxist centre group at the LSI and even further removed from the British influenced group (including the German, Belgian and Czech social democrats), although these groupings were loose. At the 1928 LSI congress Dollan, serving on the commission on the 'World Political Situation and the International Labour Movement', abstained from endorsing a resolution containing a condemnatory reference to the Soviet Union, stating on behalf of the ILP that:

> We do not accept the view ... that the Russian workers stand for war as a means of social revolution ... We also fail to take the view ... that the Russian Government and its tactics are responsible for the oppressive measures in other countries.[73]

The ILP delegates were persuaded to accept the resolution in full congress. The ILP was hampered from articulating a separate viewpoint by being admitted only by grace and favour of the Labour Party to the commissions (workshops), the main discussion bodies of LSI congresses. Each national delegation was entitled to two representatives on the commissions; until 1928 the Labour Party and ILP had shared these places. Then, the Labour Party claimed both places. The difference was submitted to the LSI bureau; albeit advising that the goal was 'unity of the socialist movement in each country', Adler left the decision on inclusion of ILP delegates to the British Labour Party.[74]

In August 1930 the ILP joined with others in founding the International Labour Community, a group whose aims included international unity. Brockway wrote that: 'it was the growing Nazi challenge ... which compelled reconsideration'. The International Labour Community decided not to set up a formal committee which would risk being disciplined by the LSI, but to issue a manifesto. John Paton, ILP secretary, wrote to Adler in 1931 of the need for unity and asked also for closer unity with IFTU. Some IFTU members were, of course, communists.[75] That year, the ILP called a meeting at the 1931 LSI congress, which attracted support for the International Labour Community from the German left social democrats (who later became the German Socialist Workers' Party), the Swiss Socialist Party, the Polish Bund and the Independent Socialist Party of Poland. This grouping moved a minority amendment at the congress session which Gillies chaired, condemning cooperation with capitalist parties and coalition governments. As the Labour Party was then a minority government, reliant on Liberal Party support, this was a direct challenge. The minority amendment was not included in the final resolution (Julius Deutsch, Austria, having found that 'a resolution should not be a crossword puzzle'), which the International Labour Community parties voted against.[76]

From an international perspective, the British Labour Movement seemed divided. At home, the distance between the Labour Party and the ILP increased when, following the election of the 1929 Labour government, the ILP committed the unforgivable sin of moving an amendment to the government programme presented in the King's speech. The ILP took the campaign for a living wage as a central thesis, declaring it stood for: 'the speedy solution of poverty and decisive transition to socialism while the Labour Party stood for a gradualist policy of piecemeal reform' . Fenner Brockway looked back on this period in which he was one of the chief negotiators of ILP relationships with the Labour and Communist Parties as one when: 'the ILP began its immense struggle towards a revolutionary socialist position'.[77]

The 1931 general election was a fraught one for the Labour Party, bereft of MacDonald, Snowden and Thomas following the collapse of the Labour government. Refusing to move to the right with these defectors to the National government ensured the Labour Party's political survival. It was hardly surprising that thirteen ILP candidates were refused endorsement by the Labour Party because they insisted on retaining the right to criticism, refusing to pledge themselves to obey Parliamentary Labour Party standing orders. Lansbury, according to Brockway, 'rejected altogether the federal conception of the Labour Party which the ILP urged' while Henderson questioned whether the ILP had 'real faith' in parliamentarianism.[78] The ILP was, in fact, divided on the virtues of the parliamentary road and remitted decision about continuing its Labour Party affiliation to its conference. C.K. Cullen and Jack Gaster (London members of the ILP) had formed a Revolutionary Policy Committee that campaigned for disaffiliation and association with the Third International.[79] Meanwhile the International Community group, meeting in Berlin, discussed the forlorn hope of 'ways and means of speeding up or capturing leadership of their respective parties'.[80] Reports were scathing: 'it may be the beginning of another attempt to bridge the gulf between the Second and Third Internationals ... a futile move'.[81]

A communist activist in Glasgow, Harry McShane, who had been a pacifist and an anarchist, has left a vivid account of fluctuating boundaries at local level.

The bitter election battle of 1930, when John McGovern, ILP Member of Parliament and local ILP chair, was challenged by the communist Saklatvala was followed by cooperation in the Free Speech campaign the following year. One of the troubles of the ILP, in McShane's opinion: 'was that they were a bunch of hero worshippers who couldn't distinguish the real left wing from the false'.[82] The communists fought equally fierce battles in local elections against Pat Dollan, who was leader of the Labour group at Glasgow corporation.

Caught between hostile revolutionaries and obdurate reformists, the ILP tried negotiating with the latter; reports of failure caused a special conference to vote in favour of disaffiliation. Those who wanted to retain Labour Party membership (including many local councillors) were given an honourable exit.[83] McGovern, who had been expelled from the Parliamentary Labour Party for his refusal to accept standing orders was instrumental in seeking disaffiliation and moved further towards the left, appearing on a National Unemployed Workers march in 1933 and being arrested with McShane, again campaigning for free speech.[84] The *Yorkshire Post* neatly summarised the ILP problem: 'not left enough for the Communist Party but not right enough for the official movement'.[85] The Labour Party was not freed from criticism from within, because the Socialist League was formed (1932) from ILP-ers who wished to stay within the Labour Party and the members of a small research group, the Socialist Society for Inquiry and Propaganda.

Disaffiliation domestically, obviously put an end to ILP hopes of generosity at the International. Gillies complained when Adler reported the disaffiliation in the LSI newsletter.[86] Excluded from effective LSI participation, the ILP assisted the International Community parties in the creation of the International Bureau for Revolutionary Socialist Unity, known as the London Bureau. Fourteen organisations from eleven parties joined the London Bureau, which was always fragile and divided. The ILP had resisted creation of a Fourth, Trotskyist International 'by a thesis into a vacuum' but its actions led to that effect.[87]

United Front

The creation of the London Bureau raised the question of international unity; as early as December 1932 Adler wondered: 'whether the time had come to make an approach to the Communists'. Vandervelde's biographer Janet Polasky is of the opinion that the LSI president moved to the left after the failure of the Belgian coalition government and socialist losses in the 1929 election and, in default of support at home, thereafter worked closely with Adler to invigorate the LSI.[88] Gillies made haste to inform the TUC International committee of Adler's change of heart and his fears that Blum and Bauer were moving in the same direction. He underlined the fact that the communists were still attacking the trades unions, the Third International having decided at its 1932 congress:

'to expose on the basis of actual and well known facts all the sophisms and manoeuvres of the bourgeoisie (sic) pacifists and especially of the social democratic parties'.[89]

Gillies had to move on two fronts because, while the LSI was considering central negotiations with the communists, the latter were responding nationally. Under pressure of events in Germany the LSI bureau decided on 18 February 1933 to try for 'a fighting unity of Social Democrats and Communists'. The Third International replied: 'every vote for the Social Democratic Party is a vote for Hitler'. The LSI persisted, asking affiliates to abstain from national talks. The Third International's biggest tactical error may have been to refuse these executive level talks: 'the United Front can only be forged in relentless struggle for the defeat of the Second International'.[90] Henri Barbusse, of the Syndicalist International (*Comité Mondiale de Lutte contre La Guerre Impériale*), wrote to Adler, Vandervelde and Bauer in support of the United Front. Vandervelde was not sure if Barbusse's help would be useful, but told Adler that preliminary talks would be acceptable. In April 1933 Vandervelde was of the opinion that he could have carried the Belgian social democratic party with him on this issue; a month afterwards, Belgian opposition to the united front had hardened. In March 1933 the Labour Party International sub committee instructed Gillies and the British representatives at the LSI that 'an unconditional cessation of hostilities was the only condition acceptable' although 'they should not oppose conversation between the two Internationals'. Gillies interpreted his instructions as a broad mandate to resist communism but his difficulty lay in the willingness of some LSI affiliates to engage in national negotiations which were beyond his control.[91]

The International sub committee meeting had also to consider appeals for unity from the CPGB and the ILP. At first, it was decided to await for advice from the Labour and Socialist International; just a few days later the National Executive decided, without awaiting LSI consideration, not to cooperate. It may have seemed an opportune time for the communist approach; Lansbury was the party leader, notoriously tolerant to the communists. He had met Lenin in 1920 and, according to his biographer, 'the effects of his Russian visit never wore off'.[92] The ILP was persistent: Fenner Brockway in May 1933 invited Ellen Wilkinson and G.D.H. Cole, among ILP and CPGB leaders, to a meeting: 'to see whether a policy can be worked out which will hasten the coming together of all sections of the working class in a common struggle'. Tracey, intercepting the note, forwarded it to Citrine marked 'Intrigue!'.[93] The lengthy ILP search for unity was genuine: ILP-ers attempted to work with the communist rank and file, but refused to accept Soviet 'tutelage'. Brockway remembered that the ILP 'slipped into a united front with the Communist Party'.[94]

Support for united front activity within the Labour Party was indicated when conference challenged the 1933 NEC report of groups deemed to be communist inspired, whose adherents were therefore ineligible for membership. Collick (ASLEF) spoke out against 'heresy hunting' while Ellen Wilkinson criticised

The Communist Solar System as propaganda for communist efficiency and said: 'The time has come for the big organisation in the Labour Movement to take the first step and heal the breach'. Herbert Morrison, the most effective and consistent NEC speaker against the united front, put the NEC case successfully, stating that 'cooperation with the Communist Party was an impossible thing'. It was Gillies's research work which provided the substance for the charges.[95]

Conclusion

Refusing to cooperate with the relatively small CPGB at home may have been justified as the Labour Party sought to strengthen its own organisation, challenged by the fall of the 1931 Labour government. The split between Communists and Social Democrats was, however, a major weakness in international organisation and the value of the search for a middle ground was underestimated by contemporaries, as it has been by historians.[96] Creating the LSI had been a difficult task and, as the ILP experience showed, the organisation was vulnerable to schism and to the effect of domestic quarrels.

Nevertheless, the existence of the LSI represented a considerable achievement. Before 1933, LSI files give evidence of a vibrant organisation with an expanding central office, firming up European contacts and attempting, if failing, to extend its remit. The Labour Party had contributed largely to its formation, of which Henderson and MacDonald could be justifiably proud. Labour Party engagement in the LSI had been moulded by its fluctuating fortunes at home. Success at the polls meant deputising quotidian contact to William Gillies, who engineered for himself a unique position, shrugging off trades union control, feeling free to advise MacDonald, presenting Labour opinion to Chatham House, managing a network of contacts throughout the Party. His position as International Secretary was steadily enhanced as his rôle grew, so that he became Britain's representative at the LSI Bureau. The development of Gillies's rôle at home was matched by that of Adler abroad, so that British initial prominence in international organisation diminished. The Labour Party remained, however, an influential affiliate and its part in the recreation of the LSI was not forgotten. This was crucial to the conduct of unity negotiations with the Third International. It was the rise of fascism which inspired the unity talks and called into question the efficacy of the LSI. The response to fascism is dealt with in the following chapter.

Notes

1.   Thomas, J.H. (1920), *When Labour Rules*, Collins, London p. 115.
2.   MacKenzie, Norman and Jean (eds) (1983), *The Diary of Beatrice Webb, vol 3, 1905-1925*, Virago, London, entry for 12 December 1918, p. 326.

3. Although Branting was relatively successful in achieving consensus, MacDonald found his chairmanship 'a great misfortune' in view of his other responsibilities. *Ramsay MacDonald Papers*, Public Records Office, *Diary*, 3 May 1919, p. 124, PRO/30/69/1753/1.

4. *Labour and Socialist International Papers*, resolution of French and Serb parties, September 1918, LSI/2/13/12.

5. MacDonald, Ramsay (1925), *Wanderings and Excursions*, London, cited, p. 193-94.

6. MacDonald, Ramsay (1925), op. cit., pp. 196, 212, 228 (later there was tension between the Labour Movement and foreign office worlds on this score).

7. *Ramsay MacDonald Papers, Diary*, 3 May 1919, p. 124, 24 May 1919, p. 137, PRO/30/69 1753/1.

8. MacKenzie, Norman and Jean (eds), (1984), op. cit., p. 363. Huysmans, *Labour Party Conference Report,* 1920, p. 118.

9. *Labour Party Conference Report*, 1920, p. 184.

10. Joint International Committee of the Labour Party and *Trades Union Congress Minutes*, 10 November 1920; *Labour Party Conference Report,* 1921, p. 314.

11. *Ramsay MacDonald Papers, Diary*, 10 November 1920, p. 140, PRO/30/69/1753/1; *Diary*, 16 December 1920, p. 143, PRO/30/69/1753/1. *Labour and Socialist International (LSI) in London,* International Institute of Social History, Amsterdam, MacDonald to Gosling, 20 June 1922, LSI IISH 102.

12. The papers for the *LSI in London* are held at the International Institute of Social History, Amsterdam, while those for its period in Zurich are held at the Labour Party Archives, Manchester.

13. *Trades Union Congress Papers*, Modern Records Centre, Warwick University, memorandum of Trades Union Coordinating Committee, n.d., MSS 292/28/1. *Joint International Committee Minutes*, 17 November 1921. *Ramsay MacDonald Papers*, *Diary*, 17 November 1921, PRO 30/69 1753/1.

14. *Ramsay MacDonald Papers*, *Diary*, 15 October 1920, p. 139, PRO 1753/1. Philip Viscount Snowden (1934), *An Autobiography, vol. 2, 1919-1934*, London, p. 941. Leventhal, F. M. (1989), *Arthur Henderson*, Manchester University Press, Chapter 4, 'Uncle Arthur' *passim* and p. 104 summarised Henderson's administration. See also McKibbin, Ross (1974), *The Evolution of the British Labour Party, 1900-1924*, Oxford, p. 208 and pp. 210-14.

15. *Trades Union Congress Papers*, Memorandum from Sidney Webb in the capacity of chair of joint Labour Party/TUC finance and information committee meeting, 20 May 1923. *Joint International Committee Minutes*, 3 January 1922.

16. Hamilton, Mary Agnes (1938), *Arthur Henderson, A Biography*, Heinemann, Oxford p. 225 and cited, p. 184.

17. Healey, Denis (1990), *The Time of my Life*, Penguin, London p. 57.

18. MacKenzie, Norman and Jean (eds), (1984), op. cit., p. 303. Konni Zilliacus was later MP for Gateshead. He was appointed to the Information Section of the League of Nations secretariat in 1919 and became

Henderson's private secretary when the latter was president of the World Disarmament Conference when he wished to accuse a colleague of a fault, he wrote: 'He is more obdurate and less amenable to reason than anyone I know, not excluding Willie Gillies's, *Noel Baker Papers*, Churchill College, Cambridge, Zilliacus to Noel Baker, 13 December 1934.

19. There is an unconfirmed story that Gillies proposed marriage to Miss Howie after his own retirement. Information given to Stephen Bird, Labour Party library by Miss Howie's aunt, 1986. *William Gillies Correspondence*, for example memorandum from Gillies to library staff, 29 June 1934, WG/LIB: 'In view of my discovery that you have been receiving *Lavora fascista* and throwing it out, kindly note in future no Italian documents are to be thrown out without my knowledge or consent'.

20. Winkler, H. J. (1956), 'The Emergence of a Labour Foreign Policy in Great Britain', *Journal of Modern History*, xxviii, 3, pp. 247-58.

21. International Advisory Committee of the Labour Party *Minutes*, Labour Party Archives, Labour History Museum, Manchester, 23 February 1921, 9 March 1921, 6 April 1921, 6 July 1921. McKibbin, R. (1974), op. cit., pp. 220-221. Even Winkler, who championed the importance of the International Advisory Committee, accepted that its rôle was modest by the 1930s. Winkler, op. cit., p. 248. MacKenzie, Norman and Jean MacKenzie (eds) (1984), op. cit., p.382. There were, of course, fundamental political issues which caused the split.

22. *Ramsay MacDonald Papers*, Renaudel to MacDonald, 24 January 1921, PRO 30/69 1165/57.

23. *Ramsay MacDonald Papers,* Snowden to MacDonald, 1 August 1921, PRO 30/69 1165/56.

24. *Ramsay MacDonald Papers,* Adler to MacDonald, 10 February 1921, PRO 30/69 1165/1.

25. *Ramsay MacDonald Papers*, Public Record Office, *Diary*, 18-19 March 1921, PRO 30/69 1753/1; Snowden to MacDonald, 1 August 1921, PRO 70/69 1165/54; *Diary*, 20 October 1921, PRO 30/69 1753/1. *Socialistische Arbeiter-Internationale Papers*, Amsterdam, Henderson to MacDonald, 5 January 1922, SA1 85/1; Adler to MacDonald, 19 January 1922; MacDonald to Adler, 29 April 1922, SA1 88/30.

26. Vandervelde's Report, *Labour Magazine*, vol. i, no. 4, August 1922, p. 178. *LSI in London*, trial and notes, LSI IISH 83-98. Polasky, J. (1995), *The Democratic Socialism of Emile Vandervelde,* Berg, Oxford p. 151 ff.

27. Report *Labour Magazine* (1922), vol. i, no. 2, June, p. 90. Tom Shaw, an anti-militarist, became Secretary of State for War in 1929 and was described by G.D.H. Cole as a good linguist. Cole, G.D.H. (1958), *Socialist Thought,* vol. iv, part ii, MacMillan, London p. 684.

28. *Sozialistische Arbeiter-Internationale Papers,* MacDonald to Adler, 3 May 1922, date of meeting inconvenient; Adler to MacDonald, 23 May 1922, notice of meeting date, SA1 88/65; MacDonald to Renaudel, accusing Adler of delay, 27 November 1923, SA1 89/15.

29. *Ramsay MacDonald Papers*, Wels to Henderson, 6 December 1928, PRO 30/69 1173/47.

30. Labour Party Photograph Library, Gillies to Middleton, 1923. Shaw, Tom (1923), 'The Rebirth of the International', *Labour Magazine*, vol. ii, no. 1,

May. *Labour Party Conference Report* 1923, p. 4. *Labour and Socialist International Papers*, Labour Party Archives, Memorandum written by Adler, 1939, recording 1923 decision, LSI 22/4/29. In particular, Vienna Union resolutions were binding on affiliates. See Dowse, R. G. (1966), *Left in the Centre: The Independent Labour Party, 1893-1940*, Longmans, p. 56.

31.   *Labour Party Conference Report* 1924, p. 156.

32.   Members of the administrative committee were Shaw, Gosling, Lees, MacDonald, Thomas, Webb, Henderson, Clifford Allen, Wallhead. *Labour Party Conference Report* 1923, p 6. *Labour and Socialist International Congress Report* 1925, p. 82.

33.   *Labour and Socialist International Congress Report*, 1925, p. 65. 'The International: Facts and Fallacies' (1924) *Labour Magazine*, vol. ii, no. 9, January, p.409.

34.   *Sozialistische Arbeiter-Internationale Papers*, Walter Ayles (Labour candidate) to Adler, 7 September 1923, 26 September 1923, 19 November 1923, SA1 1770.

35.   *Sozialistische Arbeiter-Internationale Papers*, Hamilton Fyffe to Adler, 27 February 1924, SA1 1786/7.

36.   *Labour and Socialist International Congress Report*, 1931, p. 781.

37.   *Daily Herald*, 6 January 1925. *Labour and Socialist International Congress Report* 1925, p. 209.

38.   *Labour and Socialist International Congress Report*, 1925, p. 198.

39.   See bibliographical note.

40.   *Labour and Socialist International Congress Report*, 1931, p. ii 33.

41.   Lorwin, Lewis L. (1929), *Labour and Internationalism*, New York, p. 437.

42.   Lord Citrine (1964), *Men and Work: The Autobiography of Lord Citrine*, London, p. 79.

43.   *TUC Papers*, Citrine to Gillies, 11 May 1925, MSS 292 30/8, Gillies to Citrine, 27 April 1925, 12 May 1925, MSS 292 30/8.

44.   *TUC Papers*, unsigned memorandum, n.d., headed 'Staffing of Joint Departments 1925-1926': 'The Joint International Department is being discontinued'; (?by Citrine), n.d., (?1925), MSS 292 28/1; Citrine to Robert Williams, n.d., MSS 292 752 (1). *TUC International Committee Minutes*, 1 November 1928.

45.   Pimlott, B. (1977), *Labour and the Left in the 1930s*, Cambridge University Press, p. 19. Trades Union Congress *Report*, 1936, p. 367.

46.   *William Gillies Correspondence*, Transport House Fellowship annual meeting agenda, 1932, WG/TH/ii.

47.   *William Gillies Correspondence*, Memorandum from Gillies to Miss Davey about Vandervelde, 10 August 1932, WG/LAB/1, Gillies to Adler, 7 April 1933, WG/LAB/3, memoranda from Gillies to Tracey, n.d., 3 January 1934 WG/LAB.

48.   Lord Citrine (1964), op. cit., p. 27.

49.   Barmat was an industrialist who had given hospitality to International delegates before 1914. He had mediated in the stevedore strike which froze German food supplies, lent money to the communists and negotiated with the 1924 Labour government a successful change in postal clearing house procedures. Gillies had been introduced through the German SDP and promised help from the Labour Postmaster General, Vernon Hartshorn. The

following year Barmat's Communist connections were used to smear the SDP. *Ramsay MacDonald Papers*, Breitscheid to Gillies, 30 July 1924, Gillies to Rostini, 7 August 1924 and 8 August 1924, *Telegraph*, 5 February 1925, Wels to MacDonald, 22 February 1925, Gillies to MacDonald, 19 February 1925, Hartshorn to MacDonald, 5 March 1925, PRO 30/69, 3. Reparations, *Ramsay MacDonald Papers*, Gillies's telegram to MacDonald, 25 May 1929 and letter to MacDonald, 25 May 1929, PRO 30/69/1174/445 443-444; Gillies to Blum, 27 May 1929, PRO 30/69 1174/450.

50. *Ramsay MacDonald Papers,* examples, Gillies to MacDonald, 15 December 1926, translation of French Parliamentary Labour Party constitution, PRO 30/69 1171/1/463; Rose Rosenberg to Gillies, request for translation of letter from Kronstadt, 3 March 1928, 1173/437; Gillies to MacDonald, 18 December 1928, on an article in the French press about past talks between MacDonald and Herriott, Gillies wrote:'the whole article is really propaganda in favour of the foreign policy of the Left Bloc in the Chamber of Deputies, which, in my opinion, has been reconstituted in anticipation of a Labour victory this summer', PRO 30/69 1173/428.

51. *Ramsay MacDonald Papers*, Gillies to MacDonald, 22 February 1927, MacDonald to Gillies, 23 February 1927, PRO 30/69 1172/535/6. *William Gillies Correspondence*, Information Committee to Gillies and reply, 22 April 1932, Information Committee to Gillies and reply, April 1935, Sheila MacDonald to Gillies, 7 November 1933, WG/20.

52. *William Gillies Correspondence*, Sidney Silverman to Gillies, 22 July 1935; York Labour Party League of Youth to Gillies, 16 March 1935, WG/VIS. *International Department Correspondence*, Labour Party Library, Wilkinson to Gillies, 12 July 1932, Gillies to Wilkinson, 13 July 1932, Gillies's telegram to SDP. Ellen Wilkinson had lost her parliamentary seat in 1931.

53. *Labour and Socialist International Congress Report* 1931, p. 119; Ibid, Secretary's report, 1925, 1928, 1931.

54. *William Gillies Correspondence*, Gillies to Henderson n.d., (1932), WG/FRAT DEL.

55. *Labour and Socialist International Congress Report* 1925, pp. 247, 285.

56. For a full account, see Carlton, D. (1970), *MacDonald versus Henderson: The Foreign Policy of the Second Labour Government*, MacMillan, London chapters two and three.

57. *Noel Baker Papers*, Churchill College, Cambridge, Memorandum 'Advantages and Difficulties', 3 June 1930, 4/222, LSI *International Information*, vol. vii, no. 27, 31 May 1930, 4/222. For a full analysis of the Briand plan see Boyce, R. W. D. (1980), 'Britain's first "No" to Europe: Britain and the Briand plan, 1929-30', *European Studies Review*, 10, pp. 17-49.

58. *Labour and Socialist International Congress Report,* 1931, pp.107-9 and *TUC International Committee Minutes*, 6 January 1931.

59. *Labour and Socialist International Congress Report,* 1931, p. vii, 43-65, resolution text p. xl-x8. International Sub-Committee *Minutes*, 20 April 1931.

60. *Labour Party Conference Report,* 1931, p. 184. TUC International Committee *Minutes*, 21 July 1931.

61. *International Sub-Committee Minutes*, 26 April 1932 and 10 November 1932.

62. Dutt, Palme (ed.), (1923), *Labour International Year Book*, Labour Publishing Co., London p. 67.

63. *LSI in London,* MacDonald's manuscript notes, pre-meeting of Second International, 20 May 1922, LSI IISH 7. MacDonald, Ramsay (1925), *Wanderings and Excursions*, London, p. 221.

64. See Royden Harrison (1974), Society for the Study of Labour History *Bulletin*, No. 29, Autumn, pp. 16-34 for transcript of meeting to decide affiliation. Members of the Labour Heritage Women's Research Committee, previously CPGB members, have expressed continued surprise at the relative informality of Labour Party procedures. For instance, Annie Leff (interview 1987) would have been expected by the CPGB to visit the same day interest in membership was expressed.

65. *LSI in London,* LSI appeal, August 1921, IFTU Bulletin 18, correspondence Münzenberg / MacDonald / Fimmen / Shaw, 1921-22, LSI IISH 99. *TUC International Committee Minutes*, 11 February 1924, 10 April 1924, 17 July 1924. *TUC Papers*, Modern Records Centre, Memorandum on Workers' International Relief with confidential information from Dr Adolf Braun, of the discovery of WIR notes on the Berlin underground railway, note from Gillies and Minutes of WIR meeting, 14 June 1923, MSS 910.2(1). *Joint International Committee Minutes*, 4 December 1924, 21 January 1925, 20 April 1925, 21 May 1925. Helen Crawford (WIR) had been prominent in the Independent Labour Party faction which proposed affiliation to the Communist International and on defeat of the proposal left the ILP to join the Communist Party, Dowse, R. E. (1966), *Left in the Centre: The Independent Labour Party, 1893-1940*, Longmans, London, pp. 56-8. Carew Hunt, R.W. (1960), 'Willi Münzenberg', in Footman, D. (ed.) *International Communism*, Chatto and Windus, London p.73. Koestler called Münzenberg: 'the grey eminence and invisible organiser of the anti-fascist world crusade', Koestler, Arthur (1954) *Invisible Writing*, London, pp. 189-21. Theo Pinkus, who worked with Münzenberg in Paris denied that Workers' International Relief was anything more than a relief organisation and was of the opinion that Münzenberg was a great, if idiosyncratic, individual. Interview at IALHI Conference, Helsinki, 1990. See also Pinkus, Theo (1990) *Willi Münzenberg, Eine documentation zur Münzenberg - Tagung*, Studienbibliothek, Zurich.

66. *Sozialistische Arbeiter-Internationale Papers,* Adler to all affiliates, 6 May 1924, SAI 3050. This file is also titled 'Gillies and Münzenberg'. International Red Aid Adler to Gillies, 21 July 1925, SAI 3050. International of Prôletarian Freethinkers, notes for LSI Executive 28 February 1928, SAI 3052.

67. Howkins, Alun (1980), 'Class against Class: the Political Culture of the CPGB 1930-1935' in Frank Gloversmith (ed.), *Class, Culture and Social Change*, Harvester, Sussex p. 243 is of the opinion this policy must be perceived against the industrial and political failures of the Labour Movement in the 1920s and the fall of the 1931 Labour government.

68. *Ancillary Organisations of the Communist International 1926-1940* (Labour Party Headquarters Archives). Donoghue, Bernard and Jones,

G.W. (1973), *Herbert Morrison: Portrait of a Politician*, Weidenfeld and Nicolson, p. 227; Williams, Andrew J. (1989), *Labour and Russia: The Attitude of the Labour Party to the USSR, 1924-1934*, Manchester University Press, p. 230.

69.   Carew Hunt, R. W. (1960), op. cit. Münzenberg was called to Moscow for investigation in 1936. Carew Hunt is of the opinion that as Stalin consolidated his power, Münzenberg's independence could not be tolerated.

70.   *James and Lucy Middleton Papers: The Ruskin Collection*, Middleton to Labour Research Department, 17 October 1933, MID/30/35.

71.   Seyd, Patrick, 'Factionalism within the Labour Party; the Socialist League 1932-1937' in Briggs, Asa and Saville, John (eds) (1977), *Essays in Labour History, 1918-1939*, Croom Helm, analysis of factionalism as a function of the Labour Party ideology.

72.   Archives of the ILP, series 2, part 1, Bodleian Library, Oxford (microfiche), ILP NAC *Minutes*, 24-25 June 1926, note of invitation from BRSP to ILP.

73.   *Sozialistische Arbeiter-Internationale Papers,* ILP proposal, n.d. (1926), SAI 3035). *Labour and Socialist International Congress Report,* 1928, p. vi. 165, p. vi, 166.

74.   Brockway, Fenner (1942), *Inside the Left*, Allen & Unwin, London p. 169. *Labour and Socialist International Papers*, Labour Party Archives, ILP to Henderson, 14 March 1929, LSI 16/1/2; Henderson to Adler, 16 March 1929, LSI/16/1/3; Adler to Henderson, 16 March 1929, LSI/16/1/3.

75.   Wim Bott (1982), review of Willy Bushak, 'Das Londoner Buro', *International Review of Social History*, 2. Brockway, Fenner (1942), op. cit., p. 237, p. 277. *Sozialistische Jugend Internationale Papers*, Paton to Adler, 21 October 1930, 10 February 1931, SJI 741/1.

76.   *Labour and Socialist International Congress Report,* 1931, p. vi, 59-61, Deutsch's comment, p. vii, 43, final resolution, p. vii, 62-63.

77.   *Archives of the ILP*, series 2, part 1, Bodleian Library, Oxford (microfiche), head office letter signed 'Brockway', November 1931, 67/1. Deteriorating relationship of the ILP and Labour Party, see Dowse, R. E. (1966), op. cit., Chapter Twelve. Brockway, Fenner (1942), op. cit., p. 238, p. 239.

78.   Brockway, Fenner (1942), op. cit. p.239

79.   Ibid, p. 280, pp. 325-6. The Revolutionary Policy Committee joined the CPGB in 1935 on the issue of sanctions against Italy over Abyssinia.

80.   Archives of the ILP, Bodleian Library, Oxford, series 2, part 1, card 68: British report of meeting; card 24, NAC *Minutes*, 31 March 1932 shows decision to convene ILC meeting taken during negotiations with the Labour Party on domestic differences.

81.   *Labour and Socialist International Papers, Yorkshire Post* report, 6 May 1932, LSI/21/1.

82.   McShane, Harry (1978), *No Mean Fighter*, Pluto Press, London   p. 174. Ibid., p. 170.

83.   *Archives of the ILP*, series 2, part 1, (microfiche), Bodleian Library, Oxford, card 24, ILP NAC *Minutes*, 30 March 1932 on negotiations and ILP NAC *Report*, 30 April 1932. *William Gillies Correspondence*, Labour Party Archives, note from Henderson, n.d., constituencies to receive into membership those who wished to join, WG/ILP/3. Pat Dollan was one of

those who stayed in membership; he later formed the Scottish Socialist Party.

84. McShane, Harry (1978), op. cit., p. 199.

85. *Labour and Socialist International Papers, Yorkshire Post* report, 6 May 1932, LSI 21/1.

86. Gillies remained on friendly terms with Fenner Brockway; they addressed each other 'Dear Willie/ My Dear Fenner'. *William Gillies Correspondence*, letter from Gillies to Henderson, August 1932, letter from Fenner Brockway to Gillies, 17 December 1934; letter from Gillies to Fenner Brockway, 17 December 1934, WG/ILP.

87. Wim Bot, (1989), op. cit. *Archives of the ILP*, Bodleian Library, Oxford, series 2, part 1, p. 344, card 71, Report of Meeting 26-27 January 1934. After many changes the group chose the title International Revolutionary Marxist Centre. Brockway, Fenner (1942), op. cit., p. 263.

88. Polasky, Janet (1995), op. cit., chapter nine.

89. *TUC Papers*, Note of International Labour Position by Gillies to TUC International Committee, 13 December 1932, MSS 292 901.2. Some light is cast on the beginning of the deterioration in Gillies's and Adler's relationship by Andrew Williams's account of Gillies's disquiet at Beatrice and Sidney Webb's favourable report on their visit to the Soviet Union and Gillies's inability to win support from Adler over this. Williams, Andrew J. (1989), *Labour and Russia: The attitude of the Labour Party to the USSR, 1924-1934,* Manchester University Press, pp. 185-86.

90. Braunthal, J. (1967), *History of the International, vol. 2, 1914-1943,* London, LSI Bureau decision pp. 391-92, communist reply p. 392, Comintern reply to LSI Executive Committee, p. 471.

91. *Sozialistische Arbeiter-Internationale Papers,* Barbusse/Comité to Adler *et al.,* 20 March 1933, 4 April 1933, 10 April 1933, Vandervelde to Adler, 3 April 1933, 2 May 1933. *International Sub-Committee Minutes,* 16 March 1933.

92. *International Sub-Committee Minutes,* 13 March 1993. Postgate, R. (1951), *The Life of George Lansbury,* London, p. 207 and p. 236 ff. for Lansbury's support of communists arrested during the general strike and advocation of communist admission to the Labour Party.

93. *TUC Papers*, Modern Records Centre, Fenner Brockway to Dear Comrade, 9 May 1933; Herbert Tracey, memorandum to Citrine, 23 May 1933, MSS 292 752(1).

94. Brockway, F. (1942), op. cit., p. 249-501.

95. *Labour Party Conference Report,* 1933, Wilkinson's speech p. 224; Morrison's speech, p. 221; see also Donoghue, Bernard and Jones, G. W. (1993), *Herbert Morrison: Portrait of a Politician,* Weidenfeld and Nicolson, London pp. 223-27.

96. Eley, Geoff (1992), 'Reviewing the Socialist Tradition' in Lemke, Christiane and Marks, Gary (eds), *The Crisis of Socialism in Europe,* Duke University Press, London, p. 29.

Table 2.1 Münzenberg's 'front' organisations

b. 14 August 1889

August 1914	Secretary General of *Sozialistische Jugendverland*
November 1919-April 1921	President of reformed SJ , now k/a Communist Youth International
September 1921	International Workers' Aid (relief for USSR famine) aka MRP (Russian initials), aka Münzenberg Trust, aka Workers' International Relief
February 1922-35	League Against Imperialism
March 1929	Anti-Fascist Bureau
1930s	Paris publishing house; WIR financing of Soviet films
August 1932	Committee of Action of AFB
June 1933	World Committee Against War and Fascism
1933	Committee for the Relief of Victims of German Fascism
1933	Committee of Enquiry into origins of Reichstag fire
July 1936	Committee for War Relief for Republican Spain/Committee for Enquiry into Foreign Intervention in the Spanish Civil War
1939	Expelled from the Communist Party
1940	Murdered near Lyons

Source: Carew Hunt, R. N. (1960), 'Willi Münzenberg' in D. Footman (ed.), *International Communism*, Chatto & Windus, London; Koestler, A. (1954), *Invisible Writing*, London, pp. 198-212; Pinkus, T. (1990), *Willi Münzenberg: Einer Documentation zur Münzenberg Tagung*, Studienbibliothek, Zurich

The Fascist Challenge, 1933-39: The Labour Party and the Labour and Socialist International

Hitler's accession to power in 1933 was a devastating blow to international organisation. The effect of Nazi success was compounded by the loss of the strong German Labour Movement. The prime purpose of the Labour and Socialist International became its resistance to fascism. Finding an international, consensus position was problematic. The strategy of combating fascism by working with communists had failed and was not acceptable to the British Labour Party leadership. This chapter records other attempts to find a solution, internationally and domestically. At home, there was intense debate within the Labour Movement on leadership international strategies, and support of the leadership position was used as a criterion for discipline.

Anti-fascism

Although the LSI was well aware of the need for an urgent response to the situation in Germany, its records convey curiously little sense, at this stage, of the enormity of the potential collapse of international socialism. The LSI bureau met in May 1933, with IFTU, to discuss sanctions. There was 'a deep seated difference of opinion on the wisdom of a boycott', some fearing this would consolidate Hitler's power against a hostile world.[1] A commission of enquiry was set up to investigate the conditions of political prisoners and Gillies began to collect his reports of ill treatment and torture.[2] In August, the LSI criticised the German SDP's paralysis of will, calling for a general strike and united front collaboration within Germany. These last two points were opposed by the British.[3] Fraternal delegates (Smith and Crompton) to the Austrian SDP congress in October 1933 reiterated that the Labour Party would call on the British government to exert its influence against fascism.[4]

Although the 1933 Labour Party conference rejected united front activity, it did accept a series of composite resolutions in favour of international workers' collaboration against fascism. It was at this conference (1933) that the strike-for-peace call was renewed. The Socialist League had inspired these resolutions and worked for mass support, calling for consultation with the LSI, the cooperative and trades union movements: 'The working class of any country has no quarrel with the working class of any other country'. Collick seconded: 'we believe, as socialists, that capitalist imperialism is the cause of war'.[5] As a composite resolution could not be amended by the platform, the NEC avoided confrontation by indicating its acceptance.

It was Henderson's articulation of the International Faith which drew the conference together. Henderson recalled the 1918 ideals: inimical to class, racial or national injustice, he reaffirmed support for collective security, drawing inspiration from the LSI: 'we must make a living reality of the international solidarity of the workers'; a socialist world community would organise economic and social justice and freedom: 'if we abandon our international faith, we shall be powerless to save the world from another war'. Labour must organise for peace, 'subordinating national sovereignty to world institutions and obligations'; with its International Labour Office, the instrument to hand was the League of Nations. Britain could take the lead at Geneva in an efflorescence of the activities of the League, which covered the whole field of public life. Socialist internationalism, as depicted by Henderson, was gradual; the existing institutions had to be moulded into its pattern to provide collective security. 'Never shall we surrender our International faith - that faith is the very soul of socialism'. Henderson's broad and visionary proposal was acclaimed by all sides; although the Socialist League had termed the League of Nations 'a thieves kitchen', Stafford Cripps, one of the League's most prominent members, took the rostrum to ask for reproduction of the speech in pamphlet form.[6]

Although this hegemony was welcome, Labour leaders remained determined to sail their own ship. An instance was the response to Cripps's suggestion of a peace campaign, '"Labour Party Committee" or something ... an alternative form of activity to the Anti-War committee etc.' to be opened at the Albert Hall by Arthur Henderson. This, of course, was exactly the sort of body the Labour Party wished to avoid. Henderson replied:

> The International Committee has to keep a watchful eye on such movements as have occasioned the creation of such outside committees ... it naturally follows that the International Department will also keep a viligant eye on the movement in order that we can do the work ourselves.[7]

In 1934 the ILP rejected 'sympathetic affiliation' to the Third International and, too late, decided members should pay the trades union political levy and retain individual Labour Party membership.[8] Fenner Brockway and James Maxton met Labour Party leaders but there could be little chance of mending fences when such vague 'somethings' of Stafford Cripps were seen as a threat. The Labour Party stated that it had recognised and taken action on the menace of fascism, would defend democracy and freedom and 'work for the achievement of socialism by the democratic exercise of the will of the people'. Furthermore, the CPGB was reminded of its fundamental difference, that it was non-parliamentary and denounced reformists, its attitude to the Labour Party being one of 'misrepresentation, denunciation and disruption'. This time the Labour Party conference not only accepted the rejection of a united front but also approved disciplinary powers for the National Executive against members who took united action with the Communist Party or 'organisations subsidiary or ancillary thereto'. Exception was made in the case of Spain; however, this initiative was negated when *Pravda* denounced the conference as traitorous to the working class because an emergency resolution had not been taken, which shrivelled the olive branch.[9]

Communazis

In 1933 Gillies was still able to be generous; about an appeal fund for German prisoners he wrote: 'After all, the Communists also have stomachs'.[10] At this stage, the Labour Party International sub committee decided to invite German emigrés to meetings.[11] There was, however an important emendation to Gillies's philosophy which had the effect of bringing socialist emigrés into the category of suspect politicians. The reason seems to have been their supposed tolerance of communism. Gillies had coined the term 'communazis; in his opinon, communists led to Hitler's accession to power, therefore communists were tantamount to fascists; so were communist sympathisers. Otto Wels rather played into Gillies's hands, by resigning from the LSI because of the latter's denunciation of the Nazi regime; the German SDP set up headquarters in Prague. Gillies's caution led him to object to an emigré speaker at Chatham House, whom he alleged to be a Nazi; he persuaded *Labour* and the *Daily Herald* to broaden the base of their German commentary.[12] Gillies's battle against Lord Marley, Labour's chief whip in the House of Lords, may serve to indicate both his growing suspicions and the extent of his influence. Marley was associated with the Relief Committee for the Victims of German Fascism, which Gillies suspected to be a Münzenberg/front organisation allied to his old enemy, Workers' International Relief. Marley defended himself against Gillies's detailed prosecution at the International sub committee and lost. Morrison condemned Marley at the 1934 conference, when the latter tried to save the Relief Committee from proscription. Marley retained his position as chief whip, but the Relief Committee was proscribed.[13]

The LSI and the United Front

His suspicions of 'communazis' caused Gillies to wage battle against emigré (largely German and Austrian) representatives at the LSI; in May 1934 he successfully sought International sub committee backing to cut emigré votes in the bureau 'when the opportunity presented itself'. Nazi successes meant the Austromarxist power base at the LSI disappeared, leaving Adler in an exposed position. The German Social Democrat Party, of course, similarly lost influence.[14.] As a cororally, the British representative(s) - usually Gillies alone - increased in influence.

Adler may have drawn conclusions about the need to collaborate internationally. Moves towards a united front in France had put the issue back on the LSI agenda and the Third International asked for a joint meeting, inspired by 'the great revolution that has begun in Spain' and change in Soviet foreign policy (Stalin's mooted alliance with Hitler having failed). The French experience had convinced the communists that 'we have been making mountains out of difficulties'. Vandervelde and Adler met French communists Thorez and Cachin for exploratory talks. Both sides' mandate was restrictive; Thorez and Cachin could talk only on Spain, Vandervelde and Adler were permitted only to listen and report, but the participants were cautiously optimistic. Vandervelde's and Adler's difficulty lay in the differing opinions they had to represent. Adler told Thorez and Cachin that because the Labour Party was 'a pretty powerful force' while the Communist Party of Great Britain was 'far from being as strong as it is in France', it would be impossible to persuade the Labour Party to work with an organisation it considered 'negligible'. LSI affiliates had, therefore, been instructed to work independently to assist Spain; 'systematic and lengthy preparations' would be needed before joint action became possible. Frankly conducted, this unique meeting was probably as close as the two Internationals ever came. A verbatim report, rather than a joint communiqué was distributed. Much care was taken to produce a mutually agreed report.[15]

Vandervelde and Adler were not able to convince the LSI to change its position, although great efforts were made. Britain, Sweden, Finland and the Netherlands remained opposed to the united front. Vandervelde and Adler argued that the LSI executive, having made its 1933 approach to the Third International, should remain consistent. They pointed to united front pacts already in place, for instance in Spain, and noted that the LSI could not prevent affiliates from collaboration, writing: 'One may believe, and must hope ... that people on both sides are beginning to realise the necessity of rallying all the forces of the workers against fascism'. Nenni of Italy was in favour and Clarence Senior of the United States was reported to have said 'leave no stone unturned to get a united front'. Adler tried to get the communists to discuss principles and organisation. However, Gillies, with Albarda of the Netherlands proposed to the LSI executive: 'we are ... obliged to conclude that under present conditions there is no possibility of concluding a general pact for unity of action which, moreover, you (Adler) have not proposed'. The executive would not prohibit Vandervelde and Adler from engaging in talks 'for information only'. This was a fairly desperate attempt to maintain an appearance of LSI unity, but in reality the LSI had become deeply divided into pro- and anti-united front wings.[16]

The Third International made a further round of discussions possible when it committed itself to a popular front in 1935. France and Spain had continued in united front activity and their social democratic parties were never condemned by the LSI for their participation; their 'united action' was, indeed, reported a success. It was not repeated; in Belgium, under Vandervelde's guidance, there were attempts at unity. In Iceland and Czechoslovakia negotiations broke down. In Norway, Denmark and the Netherlands there were attempts to achieve community of action. In Austria, the Revolutionary Socialists decided against the united front; in Poland, the Socialist Party conference decided against unity. The Third International repeatedly tried to arrange the executive level talks it had refused in 1933. With de Brouckère (who had taken over from Vandervelde) Adler continued to meet Thorez and Cachin from time to time, for discussion and an exchange of information.[17] The LSI office moved to Brussels in 1935, a safer distance from the fascists; this brought Adler into closer contact with those Belgian socialists, who favoured united front action.

Following Labour Party gains at the 1935 general election, Hugh Dalton joined Gillies as British LSI representative. Gillies had heavyweight political support at the LSI for the first time since 1929. Although Dalton was not elected to the executive, Dalton and Gillies won the support of the 'Scandinavian' countries (Netherlands, Sweden, Denmark, Czechoslovakia - the 'real parties' according to Dalton) in resisting united or popular front collaboration. Dalton wrote that there was 'a silly waste of time' over the united front. To British disgust, there was an LSI majority in favour of cooperation; Dalton stated that the British would not accept the decision and threatened to reconsider British relationships to the LSI; the point of this threat was that Dalton, in Gillies's words was 'taking the British navy in my pocket' and they won the day.[18] Gillies wrote:

> There will be no merger of the Second and Third Internationals ... a hard core ... of the living democratic parties ... had no relationship with domestic communist parties.[19]

Nevertheless, the LSI did plan a joint meeting with IFTU following Mussolini's attack on Ethiopia, which was also to discuss meetings with the Third International. Adler produced a preliminary memorandum for the LSI executive and sadly concluded that any communist contribution to a joint body: 'would be under the control of the Communist Party, just as before'. The Swiss, Italian, Spanish and Austrian parties and the Polish Bund wanted talks to go ahead. Bauer cautioned that this could cause the LSI to break up and that, although contact with Moscow was important, so was contact with London. Gillies and Dallas again refused to reopen discussion on collaboration. By now, they had plenty of justification. Stalin's attack on the Bolshevik old guard, including the public trials of Bukharin, Kamenev and Zinoviev, people well known to international socialists, meant that any chance of united front work receded. Albarda (Netherlands) for instance, wrote that communist hands 'were dripping with the blood of their comrades ...the very last thing to win over the opponents of the united front'. However, Vandervelde and Adler again met with Thorez and Cachin in Blum's private room, to discuss the situation in Ethiopia. News of this leaked out and caused further discussion in the LSI.[20]

Labour's new men

Domestically, the change in Labour Party policy to rearmament mirrored changes in Labour Party personnel. Party influence at the National Council of Labour was increased by gains at the 1935 general election. Dalton and Morrison were elected; Dalton's *Practical Socialism for Britain* (1935) argued the case for an armed international police force and his views contributed to leadership policy thereafter. Morrison, as indicated, was important in articulating resistance to the united front; his was the healing speech reuniting the delegates after the Lansbury/Bevin debacle at the 1935 conference, when Lansbury's defence of pacifism was derided. Attlee, a new aquaintance for European socialists, replaced Lansbury as leader. Both Attlee and Dalton had fought in the first world war; it was, perhaps, easier for them to break with the policy of war resistance that had characterised international socialism. Attlee was, apparently, more congenial to the Labour Party staff, who had difficulty accommodating Lansbury's pacifist and religious attitudes. Henderson was succeeded by Middleton as party secretary; the latter never stood for political office and had not represented Britain at the LSI. The old personal networks were thus largely extinct.[21]

Moreover, Middleton's international philosophy was different to Henderson's; discussion with socialists abroad would serve 'genuine nationalism', the inclusion of working people in a fully democratic state. Dalton found Middleton awkward in international affairs: 'talking to diplomats in front of office boys is difficult', he wrote, after a meeting with the Polish ambassador at which Middleton had been present.[22] Middleton's succession had been a compromise choice and he recognised the need to restore harmony among the leading figures. He wrote to Lansbury: 'I feel really anxious to do what is possible to reconcile the difficulties that are activating some of leading men and sections in the Movement'; he would attempt more 'rubbing of shoulders between Cripps, Morrison, Bevin and Citrine'.[23] While there were personality clashes and old scores to settle, a large part of the differences between these men was due to divergent international perspectives and attitudes to the united front.

Peace or confrontation

It was, of course, necessary to export the rearmament policy to the LSI. In the opinion of the German Socialists, the LSI was hampered by harbouring three conflicting aims; to refuse all negotiation and prepare for war; to negotiate and confront Hitler with collective resistance; to seek peace at all costs. The latter two had failed, as the LSI bureau more or less admitted in May 1935, stating: 'Only by their own efforts can the German people reconquer their freedom'. German socialists had reported to the meeting: 'German people can never win their freedom from the points of foreign bayonets'[24] but now demanded foreign criticism of Hitler's régime in order to facilitate domestic rebellion. Reaction to Hitler's 1936 occupation of the German demilitarised zone illuminated the problem; the LSI secretariat and enlarged bureau met with IFTU, the TUC general council, Gillies and Bolton. The sense of the full impact of the rise of fascism was now apparent in the LSI files. However, the joint meeting was still unable to address the question of whether and how to operate sanctions. The joint manifesto produced was little more than a reiteration of opposition to fascism and the desire for peace through collective security. Despondent, the LSI summarised its position in 1936; apart from events in Spain, the Austrian SDP had been eliminated in 1934; the Bulgarian regime 'hesitated between fascism and the peoples front' and elections had been postponed; in Czechoslovakia the Nazis were exploiting economic distress to win over German subjects; Danzig, thanks to the weakness of the League of Nations, suffered 'unbridled Nazi terror'; Estonia had a reactionary government which included fascists; 'domestic policy in Germany is dominated by food rationing and the executioner's axe'; the Netherlands, although peaceful, feared Nazi attack; in Italy there was Mussolini; Latvia had a peasant fascist dictatorship; in Poland 'rule rests on bayonets'; Roumania was conservative and, it was feared, would ally with Hitler; Stalin's terror in Soviet Russia had intensified; Switzerland was fearful, bounded by fascists; in Yugoslavia, the dictatorship had cancelled elections.[25]

Twelve months of Spain

The Spanish civil war was the watershed for the LSI. War with fascism had begun; unlike that of 1914, the situation LSI member parties faced was not whether to give support to national governments against foreign enemies, but how to support a Popular Front government against domestic rebellion. It was the more frustrating that reaction to the Spanish civil war illustrated policy differences both at the LSI and at home. Vandervelde, who resigned from the Belgian government on the issue, moved further to the left.[26] The LSI allowed individual centres to decide policy, a sure sign that a consensus could not be reached. At home, Cripps's differences with other leading figures were exacerbated by his opposition to the Labour Party's cautious reaction. Morrison was also opposed to the policy of non-intervention, although he did not press his differences on this issue.[27] Middleton, despite Dalton's scepticism, was on friendly terms with Maisky, the Soviet ambassador in London, whom he invited to attend International sub committee meetings; Maisky suppported formal non-intervention while covertly sending arms to the Spanish government.[28] A consciously hostile racism was displayed when the Labour Movement deplored the Spanish rebel generals' use of Black troops, often referred to as 'Moors'. Ernest Bevin spoke of:

the organisation of the Moors to be brought across from Africa to kill the Spanish people - and we resent that as much as we resented the putting of black troops into the Rhineland.[29]

As the Labour leadership used the issue of Spain to consolidate the move to rearmament, Gillies was asked by Dalton to prepare statistics on armament expenditure; he questioned whether rearmament 'is not essential merely on the grounds of prudence'.[30]

Leadership attitudes to united front work remaining unchanged: the CPGB 1936 application to affiliate to the Labour Party was refused. Gillies used a May Day London District Communist Party circular to illustrate the cell building technique to local Labour parties, describing such campaigns as 'directed against working class organisations which voice the democratic aspirations of their countries'.[31] The National Council of Labour presented *The British Labour Movement and Communism: An Exposure of Communist Manoeuvres* to the 1936 Labour Party and trades union conferences, reinforcing Gillies's efforts and denouncing popular and united fronts. Trying to reconcile war resistance and action on Spain, united front activity and party loyalty, this conference was particularly unhappy: 'Everybody grumbling', wrote Dalton. There was a futile attempt by the left wing to reassert Henderson's 1933 policy: 'I hope the Labour Party will have some other policy to offer (Spain) than their sympathy accompanied by bandages and cigarettes', said Sir Charles Trevelyan of the Socialist League, arguing for League of Nations intervention. As Party critics complained rather of the application than the substance of the leadership policy on Spain their numbers are difficult to estimate; the 1936 conference, for instance, voted 11,836,000 to 519,000 in favour of leadership policy.[32]

Chair of the Labour Party from the 1936 to the 1937 conferences, Dalton concentrated on consolidating the leadership position on rearmament and on building party loyalty in order to resist communism more efficiently. He satisfied constituencies with amendments to the voting arrangements. Taking Bevin's advice, he planned meetings of picked loyalists with 'a few of the professional non-cooperators' such as Cripps; Bevin was to 'frankly face Cripps up to the question "Do you want us to win or not"?'. Dalton advised Maisky to: 'liquidate the Communist Party in this country and let the members join the Labour Party as individuals' in order to 'improve relations between your country and the Labour Movement'.[33]

In view of his later championing of the cause of Czechoslovakia, Dalton's aloofness from the Spanish cause needs explanation. He did not believe Spanish aid appealed to the electorate. In July 1937 he told Kingsley Martin (editor of the *New Statesman*):

This year, after twelve months of Spain, many of my colleagues take the view ' Arms for Spain, but no arms for Britain' is not a slogan on which to win the country.[34]

On the issue of Spain, Dalton was out of step with some of the other leaders. In

June 1937 he told Maisky that: 'the attitude of our Party now was that ... the non-intervention agreement had completely broken down'.[35] With Dallas and Jenkins, Gillies attended an LSI bureau meeting that month which instructed all affiliates to meet their obligations to Spain, a position endorsed by the National Council of Labour in July 1937. Gillies spent some energy trying to persuade a reluctant Dalton to listen to Spanish troubles: he accompanied Dalton to an abortive LSI/IFTU meeting in September 1937, Dalton noting privately: 'six Spanish present, glaring at each other. A Spanish bullfight is anticipated when they get going'. De Brouckère, indeed, reported argument among Spanish government supporters, that food and arms were in short supply and Catalonia in disarray. Dalton was much assisted in avoiding committment to intervention by Blum's equal eagerness to avoid the issue. Lunching at Blum's house with Gillies, Dalton wrote that Blum had made it clear: 'we should not now, as a year ago, embarras him by denouncing the non-intervention agreement'. Dalton reported that Gillies, nonetheless, told Blum: '"Britain and France will guarantee the right of Russia to send arms to Spain"'. Dalton concluded: 'our talk leaves me -partly too, as a result of Gillies!- quite tired and very miserable'.[36]

Dalton's otherwise triumphant 1937 conference was marred by continuing divisions over Spain. The *New Statesman* did not report the conference at any length; Kingsley Martin, just back from Spain, had become an enthusiastic convert to the Republic's cause. He wrote to Dalton:

> The muddle, comes, I think, from a certain difference in what seems important to us at the moment. I came back from Spain very deeply moved- and ought not a great many of us have been to Spain earlier?

Dalton replied:

> As to Spain, I found last year that many people were focussing on that rather than strengthening the Labour Party.[37]

and that private discussions with Blum prevented him from saying more.

Positions taken on Spain were not simply 'left' (in favour of popular front activity) or 'right' (for party loyalty), nor militarist versus pacifist. An indication of the complexities was the International Advisory Committee's May 1937 decision, having considered a number of memoranda on the situation, 'to take no further action at present'. The committee met a further 15 times until April 1938 but was unable to construct an agreed policy; it therefore reduced its numbers and limited its meeting time. John Price, Lucy Middleton, Douglas Jay and R. H. Crossman joined the Committee which perhaps reflected Lucy Middleton's pacifist position in emphasising the desire for peace.[38] As Dalton told Kingsley Martin, there were parliamentarians and trades unionists in both camps: 'the people who try to divide us into "intellectuals" or Trades Unionists are always getting things in a muddle'.[39] That said, it was the Socialist League which articulated with most vehemence the case for a united front by setting up the Unity Campaign with the ILP and the Communist Party. Unity Campaign organisations were themselves at odds over their manifesto: the CPGB, obedient to Third International popular front policy, was rather to the right of the Socialist League and ILP at this time. Support for the ILP had been, in part, due to traditional affection which did not apply to the Socialist League, whose members were still paying Labour Party subscriptions and open to disciplinary action. Therefore, according to Brockway at Harry Pollitt's suggestion, the Socialist League dissolved itself rather than face wholesale proscription.[40]

The weakness of the LSI was fully revealed by its inability to offer an effective response to the Spanish government's predicament. As fascism triumphed over LSI affiliates, Britain approached, by default, the predominant position held before 1925. The strength of the British made LSI joint meetings with the communists impossible. De Brouckère was so enraged and despondent that he resigned. Adler also offered his resignation in the face of what he termed a 'grotesque' situation: in some places the united front was in operation, while in others such as Britain, Scandinavia and the Netherlands, LSI affiliates would not even talk to communists. However, if communist members of IFTU arrived for joint meetings, they were, of course, included in discussions. Van Roosbroeck, LSI treasure also resigned on this issue. All three LSI officers were re-elected at the subsequent executive but still had no consensus policy to operate. Adler recognised this in 1937, when the communists again asked for joint meetings; he replied that this was impossible, and asked Dimitrov to understand his position.[41]

Sensational tales

Gillies's work with refugees now took an increasing amount of time. This work was far from easy: the British government had suspended rights of asylum, so that a special case had to be made for each potential immigrant. Gillies helped Spanish refugees by negotiating fees for articles in *Labour Magazine* and arranged for republication, commanding a further fee, in the *Daily Herald*. The International Solidarity Fund spent over £16,000 in 1937 helping Spanish workers and Basque children. His contact with refugees possibly increased Gillies's hostility to German people. Dalton later commented that Gillies 'always brings sensational tales from refugees'. Gillies warned Labour travellers not to accept hospitality in Nazi or fascist countries, lest their hosts suffer and asked Members of Parliament, prospective parliamentary candidates, International sub committee and Advisory Comittee members to inform him of visits abroad so that he could arrange for information to be gathered.[42]

Attlee made a last attempt to reassert Henderson's policy of collective security. He wrote to James Middleton that Chamberlain's policy had failed. Franco was obdurate, assisted by Mussolini, who had made an anti-British broadcast: Roosevelt, however, was making strong speeches in favour of the allies; Hungary had made a pact with the Little Entente (a pro-democratic collection of states); there was much anti-German feeling in Poland. The time was, therefore, favourable for rallying the democracies: 'We all over-estimate the strength and solidarity of the fascist powers'. In Attlee's opinion, the National Council of Labour should give a strong lead, aiming for a British and French initiative. Attlee was strengthened in this viewpoint by the continuing friendliness of Maisky, who in 1938 made Middleton a present of Tolstoi's *Peter the Great* and continued to help trace people who had been arrested.[43] While rejecting united front collaboration, the Labour Party supported a miltary alliance with the Soviet Union. A substantial effort to persuade the Soviet Union to engage in collective security ensued. Dalton was in almost continuous contact with Maisky until the outbreak of war, pressing for Soviet involvement at diplomatic and military levels. This position was generally endorsed within the Labour Party which, as Dalton told the Polish ambassador, was 'Russophile but not communist'.[44]

In 1938 the Parliamentary Labour Party finally opted for national self interest, voting for the government's armed service estimates (a position opposed by Morrison).[45] Formal Labour Party policy making was delayed bcause there was no conference in 1938; the traditional meeting time had changed to Whitsun, leaving an eighteen month gap from the October 1937 conference. Many party members deplored this lack of opportunity for debate. Supporters of the Spanish government held their own National Emergency Conference on Spain (April 1938), which expressed the need for material and political support for complete national independence in The Republic. 1,205 organisations sent 1,806 delegates, and ten Members of Parliament attended. The aim was a working conference, sharing ideas and considering methods of support. Sir Charles Trevelyan called for a popular front: 'the end of his speech was drowned in cheers'.[46]

The alternative position was put by Julius Deutsch (then acting as ambassador for the Spanish government) at a luncheon with Attlee and others; that the LSI and IFTU should press the Spanish government to begin negotiating peace; 'a gloomy, desperate business', wrote Dalton, Deutsch's only supporter. He denounced the majority: 'what pathetic drivel and self-delusion this is. It nearly made me sick'.[47] Given that the Labour Party leadership would agree to neither united front work, nor intervention in Spain, his irritation is understandable. The International sub committee, indeed warned: 'the defence of Prague and of Paris lies in Catalonia now' but did not heed its own lesson. An indication of the worsening situation was the incorporation of the International Brigade into the Spanish Regular Army (1938) and the abolition of the Brigade's separate base at Albacete: clear evidence of a diminution in international assistance. The Labour Party's aim thereafter was confined to minimising reprisals and caring for refugees. The implications of defeat were the end to hopes of both collective security and united front activity. A conference called by the Labour Spain committee and 18 Divisional Labour Parties in Autumn 1938, chaired by H.N. Brailsford, expressed its homage to the people of Czechoslovakia as well as requiring recognition of the International Brigade, help for their dependants and aid for Spain. For the single purpose of Spain it called for collaboration with other opposition parties, a parliamentary popular front. This was a last throw which received no recognition from the leadership. In January 1939 the leadership refused to cooperate with a Labour Spain poster campaign on arms for Spain.[48]

Decline of the LSI

In contrast to his attitude to Spain, Dalton, with Gillies, championed Czechoslovakia at LSI bureau meetings, delaying for the arrival of Czech delegates. However, Bauer's motion that there be 'no concessions by Czechoslovakia to Nazi Germany' was rejected.[49] Informed of British Labour's lobbying of the Prime Minister, the LSI wrote to the *Times*

> since Hitler came to power it has been clear that stage by stage allied diplomacy has been compelled to concede to the dictator the rectification (of the peace treaties) steadily refused to democracies.

and asked for real self-determination and democracy in Czechoslovakia, mourning the people 'in exile, in concentration camps, in prison or in their graves'.[50] Both the Sudetan German and Czech social democratic parties were lost to the LSI. The effect of the LSI's announcement was nullified when the remaining Scandinavian affiliates announced their neutrality. Presumably in a fraught moment, Dalton suggested Papua as a good sanctuary.[51]

At the LSI, Gillies became the prime mover in translating Britain's rejection of the popular front and its determination to rearm into an aggressive and obstructive stance, whereby the Labour Party revealed the reassertion of its nationalism. Gillies's personal relationship with Adler deteriorated, perhaps because Adler was Austrian and Gillies had been attempting to cut the emigré parties' vote; Gillies's suspicions of German socialists may also have cast a shadow. Issues of personal dispute were mirrored by philosophical differences; Adler was returning to his beliefs of 1921-22, when he had perceived the Vienna Union as an international workers' council, representing all tendencies of socialist thought. During the 1930s, as Adler modified his position towards the united front, engaging in occasional discussion with representatives of the Third International, Gillies saw the distance between himself and Adler grow. Expressing his own comittment to reformist socialism and electoral choice, Gillies wrote to Adler: 'we do not regard Democracy as a means but we consider it a fundamental part of our socialism ... we do not use the terms bourgeois democracy and social democracy'. At the April 1938 LSI executive Gillies 'inaugurated a vigorous debate on the neutrality of many Continental Socialist parties'.[52] Rejection of the united front had made collective European resistance problematic; smaller European states felt too threatened to choose rearmament as a policy option. Adler spent the next two years trying to achieve a consensus LSI position, in line with its statutes. These, of course, declared that LSI affiliates were bound to collective decisions on international questions and further, that during war, the LSI was 'an indispensable instrument' and 'in the case of conflicts between nations the LSI will be recognised by affiliated parties as being their supreme authority'.[53] Adler first tried to inaugurate discussion by asking for theses on Gillies's statements; Gillies was irritated and eventually sent the current National Council of Labour a statement condemning fascist aggression.[54]

The British position was a difficult one; the continuing refusal to be bound by collective LSI decisions was in conflict with the desire to win support for the Labour party's policy of armed resistance. Gillies wrote:

> we did not discover during the crisis of last autumn (1938) that the International was capable of making pronouncements on the basis of a common policy for all parties. We also discovered that the leadership was not only taken by the British Labour Movement, it was left in their hands.[55]

In effect, the British sought to control a reformed LSI that would be a loose confederation of affiliates. The International sub-committee illustrated its contradictory strands of opinion by calling for the reduction of affiliation fees and asking for economies in organisation while suggesting the administrative centre be moved to London. It reiterated its opinion that the LSI was a purely consultative body.[56]

Peace Alliance and Lib/Lab pacts

The Labour Party's resistance to the CPGB was in no way diminished by its failure to win LSI support for rearmament. Cripps was opposed when, in 1938 he extended his united front campaign to include Liberals, setting up the popular front Peace Alliance the following year. The Liberal, Communist and Cooperative parties joined but the Peace Alliance was denounced by the Party national executive. This did not prevent simultaneous exploration of Liberal/Labour parliamentary links, in which Dalton was involved but which Middleton opposed. Looking back at these moves, Attlee considered that although he was 'prepared to make overtures', he had no mandate for talks and 'neither the Labour Party nor any considerable body of Conservatives was prepared to take action'.[57] Cripps insisted on issuing a direct appeal to the rank and file in support of the Peace Alliance; although some of the national executive wanted Cripps's immediate expulsion, he was given leave to appeal to annual conference. Dalton's suggestion of a special conference on this issue was not accepted, in his view because: 'there is ... a danger of appearance of division between the Trades Unions and the District Labour Parties'. In the face of such possible division, the leadership remained curiously complacent, Dalton likening the Peace Alliance campaigners to: 'a lot of old hens scratching in the dirt heap'. In the event, despite substantial backing from the constituencies, Cripps's appeal to the 1939 conference failed; Dalton noted: 'when we come to the Popular Front ... opposition (to its denunciation) has crumbled'.[58]

Internationalisation of domestic quarrels

Adler committed the heinous crime of allowing Cripps to publish in the LSI newsletter a statement about his exclusion from the Labour Party. Gillies wrote: 'we are really not very much interested in the internationalisation of domestic quarrels'.[59] He then made life impossible for Adler, for instance, by denying notice of a joint meeting of the LSI bureau and IFTU executive to be held in Transport House in April 1939 and therefore refusing to make the necessary arrangements, although several European delegates had overcome grave difficulties in order to attend.[60]

Gillies's position was strengthened when de Brouckère resigned from the LSI presidency (being 70 years old) and was succeeded by Albarda of the Netherlands. Albarda was part of the British/Scandinavian wing and British politicians wasted no time ensuring his support. Gillies and others met Albarda in Dalton's flat, where Albarda stated the Netherlands' need for collective security. According to Dalton, de Man (Belgium) was:

> very emphatic that the 2nd International must be cleaned up, its scale of action greatly reduced and, if possible, Adler got rid of and the staff, which now consists of Austrian Jews, diversified.

De Man also wanted refugee parties eliminated. This was, of course, the British position, although Gillies did not display anti-semitism. Dalton, indeed, acknowledged that 'none of my colleagues much liked de Man'.[61]

Gillies took the opportunity to strengthen links with the reformists by inviting Albarda to the Whitsun 1939 Labour Party conference. Albarda was grandly welcomed and reciprocated by talking of the British as the oldest and the greatest Labour Movement. His speech set out the reformist position:

> It would ... be contrary to my conception of the duty of the Labour and Socialist International if I were to recommnd to you a certain course of action, or were to force on you a solution of the problems which you must solve yourselves. The LSI cannot and may not be a power imposing directions and decisions on the various national parties.[62]

Adler made a last attempt to reassert the collective nature of the LSI. He reported that the British were a stumbling block to unity; that due to their obstruction for ten years there had been no conference of the International, for eight no congress; that the British representative (Gillies) had declared the Labour Party no longer accepted clauses one to four of the LSI constitution (those directing that collective action should be maintained and the LSI continue to function in case of war). How the LSI should operate if war broke out was a question which urgently needed to be addressed. Gillies said the Labour Party: 'would refuse to take a position on problems which war could pose for the policy of the working class'. Adler, however, leaned more to revolutionary defeatism, using war to overthrow the existing capitalist regimes: 'rouse the popular masses and bring about the fall of capitalist dominance'. Adler concluded that while the Scandinavian bloc suggested the LSI limit itself to the activities of an information bureau, it was not capable even of that limited rôle without immediate attention being paid to these various problems.[63]

Until war was declared, Adler tried to force the LSI to address the question of its rôle and the need for unity. In 1925 it had seemed Adler's moral duty not to resign his post; in 1937 he had resigned and been re-elected; in 1939 he offered not only his own resignation but that of the whole International. He believed his position to be part of the political questions 'which have always constituted a real problem of conscience for me concerning my office in the LSI'. Fascism, he thought, had driven apart the LSI; panic had meant the isolation of the small states which sought neutrality, while the bourgeoise democracies supported defence and hoped for concessions to peace. Adler reported to his executive that:

> every fresh sign of the progressive deterioration of the LSI adds now to the pangs of disillusion and bitterness, to the disheartening experiences which the attitude to the International for years past has again and again inflicted.[64]

The Labour Party, in Adler's opinion, in changing its attitude to rearmament had put Britain first and 'desires to free itself from the obligation of participation in the LSI' so that:

> the LSI is falling to pieces from the antithesis between the policy, exclusively adapted to the national interests of the great Reformist parties and the principles of international action. The liquidation of the LSI is most eagerly pursued by that Party which today amongst all parties of the LSI has the most active foreign policy and the most decisive attitude towards fascist aggression: the British Labour Party.

The Labour Party now wanted to exclude from the LSI altogether the 'illegal' parties in the countries overrun by fascism. Adler accused it of imperialism:

> it wages the struggle against Fascism not for the sake of the working class ... but on the basis of the general interests of the nation or the Empire ... this is a pure revival of the patriotism of 1914.[65]

The LSI split into two camps. The French asked Adler to stay on. The Hungarian Party, which reported it was 'compelled to fight desperately for its very life' was reluctant to take action against the bigger parties, but begged Adler to continue because of his knowledge of Central and Eastern Europe and appealed to the British Labour Party to 'make it possible that Adler remains'. Luxemburg, Russia and Poland backed Adler. Gillies announced himself surprised at the debate. Adler had said he would resign if someone else would take over his duties, Gillies had suggested an adjournment, during which a candidate (unnamed) had been found and Britain: 'therefore accepts your resignation'.[66]

The Scandinavian bloc did not accept that the LSI could make binding decisions: 'the previous collapse, as well as the present crisis, has something to do with the far too simple idea we had of internationalism'. Gillies believed that the LSI should not be dominated by the emigré parties which had no contact 'with the living Labour Movement'; 'the difficulty consists in finding the proper form reconciling international with national interests'; what was necessary and what the International should have addressed was a 'possible and concrete peace programme and a constructive plan for a new Europe'.[67]

Albarda took his presidency seriously, working for reconciliation. The administrative committee was enlarged to include the disaffected British, French and Scandinavian delegates. The Labour Party hoped Albarda would take over the secretaryship of the LSI and did pay part of its fees, although it did not resist the opportunity to remind Adler:

> the International could only be consultative, not authoritative, as explained by the President, Albarda, in the address he made to the Annual conference at Southport.[68]

Albarda tried to mollify Adler who was, in fact, unanimously re-elected secretary; Albarda wrote that Adler had been over sensitive about criticism from 'the British representative'; that there had always been agreement not to adopt resolutions which some parties found it difficult to fulfill, that the 1907 resolution against participation in war was not binding and that; 'since 1933 we live in a totally different world'.[69] These efforts failed when Albarda entered the Dutch government and had to resign his LSI presidency. The International Solidarity fund continued to assist refugees, British Labour maintaining 43 people whom the government allowed to stay, but not to work, in Britain. There were said to be very few social democrats or trades unionists left in Germany: 'they ... were the original inhabitants of the concentration camps'.[70] When war was declared, the LSI was still divided; Adler finally resigned, on British insistence, as the Nazis advanced through Europe and the LSI's members were scattered.

Having fought so hard to preserve its independence of action, the Labour Party was consistent in deciding, in late August 1939, not to join the government. Finally, proudly, Labour reasserted its nationalism when Greenwood almost took the declaration of war into his own hands, rising to reply for Labour to Chamberlain's speech in the House of Commons on 2 September 1939. Chamberlain had failed to indicate a time limit for German withdrawal from Poland: 'Arthur Greenwood had a magnificent opportunity', wrote Dalton, 'He rose to follow the PM and was greeted with cries ... "Speak for England" ... "Speak for the working classes" ... "Speak for Britain" '.[71] The immediate effect on the Labour Party of the imminent war was chaos: 'It is impossible to say what the Party will be doing and where we shall be functioning at the beginning of next week', wrote Middleton.[72]

In the face of war, Adler retained a guarded optimism, perhaps the best epitaph for the LSI, writing:

> Those sceptics who never took internationalism seriously will now consider themselves in the right. Those for whom International Socialism was an integral part of their life will be a little discouraged by the present defeats as they were by the defeat of 1914. Just as during the world war, and after its termination, the will to construct the International arose, so will historic events - even after serious drawbacks - bring about the final triumph of the International of the fighting proletariat.[73]

Conclusion

Despite Adler's optimism and his unremitting efforts, the LSI had failed to meet the fascist challenge. Unity talks with the Communists had broken down and it had not been possible to agree sanctions. Adler, the Marxist and original leader of the Vienna Union parties, sought a middle ground between Social Democracy and Communism. He was assisted by Vandervelde, whose move to the left was confirmed by the Spanish Civil War. This was also the watershed for the LSI, fully revealing the latter's weakness. The LSI had been powerless to prevent the annihilation of the German and Austrian parties by their respective governments; in 1936 it was unable to help the Spanish Popular Front government against fascist rebellion.

As the search for a response to fascism had caused closer contact between LSI and IFTU, so it resulted in greater collaboration between the Labour Party and trades union leadership. Trades unions were at the height of their influence at the National Joint Council following the fall of the 1931 Labour government; Lansbury's resignation had shown that it was not wise to ignore trades union opinion; but, thereafter, there was little difference in the international outlook of the Party and trades unions leadership. Gillies, who had reached the zenith of his powers at the LSI with the rejection of the united front and the reduction in the emigré vote, and at home with the proscription of united front groups, saw his rôle diminish as Party leaders again resumed control of contact with the International. Attlee, as Party leader, and Middleton, as secretary, were less engaged than their respective predecessors MacDonald and Henderson and lacked the intimate, personal links; Dalton, one of Henderson's protegés, filled the breach.

Although disputes about international strategies within the Party were sometimes bitter - 'everyone grumbling' - alternatives, the united and popular fronts, proposed respectively by the Socialist League and Peace Alliance, failed to win majority support. Henderson's 1933 expression of the International Faith remained the bottom line which all could agree. Henderson had spoken of the possibility of the need to rearm. At first in support of the League of Nations, and then for domestic defence, rearmament became accepted policy. It was again the Spanish cause which confirmed this policy. The commitment to rearmament, however, changed the British profile at the LSI; at least for the small parties who sought neutrality, Britain was no longer the hero of the LSI's renaissance, but the villain of its demise.

It is difficult, nevertheless, to see what other options were open to the British. The left had condemned non-intervention in Spain; the strike-for-peace had failed; the LSI had proved unable to agree a response, and was weakened by the unremitting series of fascist victories. When Arthur Greenwood spoke 'For England', Labour found new expression of its international faith by joining the military adventures of a national government. In so doing, it made space for emigré LSI leaders to gather in London and to maintain Adler's vision.

Notes

1. Braunthal, Julius (1967), *History of the International, vol. 2, 1914-1943,* London, p. 392. *International Sub-Committee Minutes*, 29 May 1933.
2. *Germany: Correspondence, reports and memoranda*, Labour Party Archives, Manchester, Communications on the Conditions of Political Prisoners, 17 May 1933, ID/GER/32.
3. Braunthal, Julius (1967), op. cit., pp. 399-401.
4. W. R. Smith, Nation of Boot and Shoe Operatives, was Chairman of the National Executive 1933-34; Joseph Compton, National Union of Vehicle Builders.
5. *Labour Party Conference Report,* 1933, p. 188.
6. *Labour Party Conference Report,* 1933, p. 188ff. Reproduced as *Labour Outlaws War.*
7. *International Sub-Committee Minutes*, 11 October 1933.
8. Brockway, F. (1942), *Inside the Left,* Allen & Unwin, London, p. 243, 248. *Archives of the ILP*, series two, part 1, card 25, note 2.1. Report to National Administrative Committee, 11 November 1934. Of 335 branches, 137 replied to a question about cooperation with communists; 18 branches had no communist local; 42 cooperated; 77 did not; 63 answered in favour of more limited cooperation; 30 wanted to cease all cooperation. Ibid, p. 243.
9. *Labour Party Conference Report,* 1934, pp. 138-42, p. 232.
10. *William Gillies Correspondence*, Labour Party Archives, Manchester, Gillies to Schiff, 17 July 1933, WG/LAB/6.
11. *International Sub-Committee Minutes*, 17 May 1933.
12. *William Gillies Correspondence*, Gillies to Chatham House, 7 November 1933, WG/RI/3-9; Gillies to Tracey, 16 August 1934, WG/LAB/28; Gillies to Catlin, 27 May 1938, WG/LAB/84. *International Sub-Committee Minutes*, 9.5.34, 26.11.34.
13. *International Sub-Committee Circular*, June 1933, *Minutes* 13 July 1933, *Note*, 3 November 1933, *Minutes* 10 November 1933, 7 December 1933,

Gillies's *Statement*, n.d., *Minutes*, 7 December 1933, *Report* of Marley's statement, 14 December 1933, letter from Lathan to Marley, 22 November 1934, 26 November 1934. *William Gillies Correspondence*, draft note of Gillies/Marley meeting, 7 December 1933, WG/ISC/9. *International Sub-Committee Minutes, Labour Party Conference Report* 1934, pp. 138-42. Morrison's biographers credit him alone with the attack on Marley, a statement not borne out by the records. Donoghue, Bernard and Jones, G. W. (1973), *Herbert Morrison: Portrait of a Politician,* Weidenfeld & Nicolson, p. 227. Marley wrote a forward to the WIR account of the Reichstag fire (*Brown Book of the Hitler Terror*), Koestler, Arthur (1954) *Invisible Writing*, London, pp. 198-212.

14.   *International Sub-Committee Minutes*, 9 May 1934, 26 November 1934.

15.   For Stalin's foreign policy, see Braunthal, Julius (1967), op. cit., pp. 469-71. For full account of meeting see *Labour and Socialism International Papers*, Labour Party Archives, LSI/16/2, verbatim report of negotiations, *Documents and Discussions*, vol. xi, no. 15, 24 November 1934. *Sozialistische Arbeiter-Internationale Papers,* Amsterdam, Adler to Citoyens Cachin and Thorez, transcript sent for amendment, 24 October 1934, SAI 3041; stereographic record, SAI 3040.

16.   *Sozialistische Arbeiter-Internationale Papers*, papers for LSI Executive, 13 November 1934, SAI 3042.

17.   *Labour and Socialist International Papers, International Information*, 1 December 1934, 30 May 1936, 5 July 1937, 30 July 1937, 11 October 1937, 22 November 1937, 9 March 1939. *Documents and Discussions*, vol. xiii, no. 8, August 1936, vol. i, xiv, no. 13, 22 September 1937, vol. xiii, no. 9, September 1938, LSI/16. Braunthal, J. (1967), op. cit., pp. 480-82.

18.   Braunthal mentions Dalton as an executive member, but Dallas and Gillies appear to have been executive representatives, Dalton a frequent attender. Dalton was a delegate to the 1928 Labour and Socialist International Congress. *Labour and Socialist International Papers*, report of Joint Conference LSI/IFTU, 11-12 October 1935, LSI/16/5/7. *Dalton Papers*, British History of Political and Economic Science, *Diary*, 10 October 1935, I 16.13.

19.   *Labour and Socialist International Papers*, Gillies to R.L. Ball, 31 January 1935, LSI/16/5/4.

20.   *William Gillies Correspondence*, report of LSI Bureau, 2 October 1936, Gillies to Albarda, October 1936, WG/COM. Braunthal, J. (1967), op. cit., p. 486, citing *Het Volk* (17 June 1935). *Sozialistische Arbeiter-Internationale Papers*, LSI Executive meeting, 12 October 1935, SAI 3043; Vandervelde's and Adler's talks, SAI 3044.

21.   For a full account of the leadership contest see Donoghue, Bernard and Jones, G. W. (1973), op. cit., pp. 234-43. Dalton had written in his preface to *Towards the Peace of Nations* (1928), p. ix, 'I am of that generation which during the Great War was massacred in droves upon the battlefields'. Postgate, R. (1951) *The Life of George Lansbury*, London, p. 293.

22.   *Dalton Papers, Diary*, 24 September 1938, I 19/59, *Diary*, Summary, I. 10, p. 3.

23.   *Dalton Papers, Diary*, Summary, I. 10, p. 4. Donoghue, Bernard and Jones, G. W. (1973), op. cit., p. 234, records contemporary opinion that

Henderson wished his son to assist Middleton and eventually succeed to the secretaryship. *James and Lucy Middleton Papers*, Ruskin College, Oxford, Middleton to Ponsonby, 25 January 1935, MID/47/10; Lansbury to Middleton and reply, December 1934, MID/46/65.

24.   *Noel Baker Papers*, Churchill College, Cambridge, report of LSI bureau, 5-7 May 1935 and Labour Party International Department *Memorandum*, 8 May 1935, 2/30. *International Sub-Committee Minutes*, 16 May 1935, citing German SDP memorandum to LSI bureau, 6 May 1935.

25.   *Labour and Socialist International Papers*, Labour Party Archives. This is a verbatim report of the meeting in note form, sometimes in pencil, much of it in shorthand, often illegible. *William Gillies Correspondence*, 'Report on Various Countries by the Secretariat of the Labour and Socialist International from 1 January 1936 to 31 December 1936', WG/19/9.

26.   Polasky, Janet (1995), *The Democratic Socialism of Emile Vandervelde,* Berg, Oxford, p. 242 ff.

27.   Donoghue, Bernard and Jones, G. W. (1973), op.cit., p. 258.

28.   *International Sub-Committee Minutes,* 11 October 1933, record of standing invitation to Maisky.

29.   *Trades Union Congress Report,* 1936, p.308

30.   *International Sub-committee Note* (signed WG), 1 September 1936.

31.   *William Gillies Correspondence*, Communist Party of Great Britain, London District *Circular*, 10 February 1936, Memorandum from Gillies to constituency Labour Parties, 2 June 1936, WG/COM.

32.   *Dalton Papers*, note, n.d., (1936), II 3.1.31. *Labour Conference Report* 1936, p.181, p. 214ff.

33.   *Dalton Papers*, *Minute*, 11 November 1936, II 3.1.4. *Diary*, 24 June 1937, 18.17.

34.   *Dalton Papers*, *Diary*, 26 July 1937, I 8.2.33, 11 April 1938, I 19.7.

35.   *Dalton Papers*, *Diary*, 23 June 1937, I 18.14.

36.   *Dalton Papers*, *Diary*, 13 September 1937, I 18.14, 14 September 1937, I 18.24.

37.   *Dalton Papers*, Martin to Dalton, 26 October 1937, Ii 5.3.10. Dalton to Martin, 28 October 1937, II 5.3.12. Martin made his first reference to Spain in *The New Statesman*, 18 July 1936, and was much less enthusiastic before his visit; see Hyams, Edward (1963), *The New Statesman: the History of the First Fifty Years, 1913-1963*, Longmans, London p. 193ff.

38.   *International Advisory Committee, Memoranda* no.480, May 1937, no. 484A November 1937 *Agenda* 26 May 1937, *Minutes* 26 May 1937, 17 November 1937.

39.   *Dalton Papers*, Dalton to Kingsley Martin, 6 July 1937, IIA 5.2.33.

40.   For discussion of Unity Campaign manifesto, see Dewar, H. (1976), *Communist Policies in Great Britain*, Pluto, London p. 113ff. Brockway, Fenner (1942) op. cit., p. 269.

41.   *Sozialistische Arbeiter-Internationale Papers*, de Brouckère to Adler, 19 June 1937, Adler to De Brouckère, 21 June 1937, Dimitrov to de Brouckère, 12 June 1937, 16 June 1937, SAI 3046. *Labour and Socialist International Papers, Documents and Discussions*, vol. xiv, No. 16, 28 November 1937, 27 December 1937, LSI 16/6/60 and LSI 16/6/85.

42.   Interview with Irene Wagner, 1986; academic skills not sufficing to gain

entry to Britain, Irene Wagner worked as an au pair in the Jay household. Labour Heritage Women's Committee *Bulletin 2: In Face of War* (1987). *William Gillies Correspondence*, Gillies to Tracey, n.d., Gillies to Middleton, 4 August 1935, Gillies to Oliviera, 11 December 1936, WG/LAB/50,51,72. *Labour and Socialist International Papers*, International Solidarity Fund Account, 1937, LSI/21/2/37. *William Gillies Correspondence*, Schiff to Gillies, n.d., WG/LAB/79, *circular*, 148, 4 August 1936, WG/VIS/10. D. N. Pritt, newly elected to the National Executive, remembered Gillies's control of all matters relating to refugees and socialist emigrés; when Pritt asked a question about Menshevik emigrés he was 'frowned down', Pritt, D. N. (1965), *An Autobiography of D. N. Pritt, Part One, From Left to Right*, Lawrence and Wishart, London, pp. 105-6. One of these tales, in July 1939, was of an imminent German invasion of Poland. *Dalton Papers, Diary*, 10 July 1939, I 2.1.

43. *James and Lucy Middleton Papers*, Attlee to Middleton, 24 August 1938, MID/60/41. Maisky to Middleton, 1 January 1937, MID/59/5; Middleton to Maisky, 5 January 1938, MID/60/6; Maisky to Middleton, 28 June 1939, MID/62/38.

44. *Dalton Papers, Diary*, 2 April 1939, I 20.30, *Diary*, I 20.41 and 42; 11 July 1939, I 21.50 and 22 August 1939, I 21.15. For the opinion that alliance with the Soviet Union was sound policy, the Red Army effective despite Stalin's progress, see Jukes, G. (1991), 'The Red Army and the Munich Crisis', *Journal of Contemporary History*, vol. 26, no. 2, April.

45. Donoghue, Bernard and Jones, (1973), op. cit., p. 263.

46. *National Emergency Conference on Spain Report*, April 1938.

47. Austrian socialist, then acting as Ambassador for Spanish Government. *Dalton Papers, Diary*, 12 April 1938, I 19.9. Buchanan's reading of this meeting, that Dalton opposed Deutsch, seems mistaken: the former's comment was applied to his colleagues. See Buchanan, Tom (1991), *The Spanish Civil War and the Labour Movement,* Cambridge, pp. 111/112.

48. 'Labour and Spain', official *Report* of the Emergency Conference of Labour Parties, 23 October 1938. *International Sub-Committee Minutes*, 23 January 1939. *Pollitt visits Spain* (1938), International Brigade Dependents' Aid Committee, London. Brockway, F. (1942), op. cit., pp. 267-8.

49. *Dalton Papers, Diary,* 29/5/38, 1-19-13. *Labour and Socialist International Papers, International Information*, vol. xv, no. 20, 31 May 1938.

50. *Dalton Papers, Diary*, 29 May 1938, I 19.13 and I 19.15, 20 September 1938, I 19.43., 22 September 1938, I 19.49. *James and Lucy Middleton Papers*, LSI letter to *Times*, 29 September 1938, MID/60/43.

51. Braunthal, Julius, (1967), op. cit., p. 490. *International Advisory Committee Minutes*, 30 November 1938.

52. *Labour and Socialist International Papers,* Gillies to Dalton, May 1938, LSI/22/2/7.

53. For LSI statutes see Braunthal, Julius (1967), op. cit., p. 266, citing *Protokoll des Internationalen Sozialistischen Arbeiterkongresses in Hamburg* (Berlin 1923).

54. *Labour and Socialist International Papers*, Gillies to Adler, 24 June 1938,

LSI/22/2/12, no theses requested, Adler to Gillies, 26 June 1938, LSI/22/3/3, shorthand note of meeting, Gillies to Adler, n.d., LSI/22/3/10.

55.   *Labour and Socialist International Papers,* Gillies to Adler, 11 February 1939, LSI/22/2/4.

56.   For the British position, see *International Sub-Committee Minutes,* 21 March 1939; *Labour and Socialist International Papers,* note of International Sub-Committee meeting, 21 March 1939, LSI/22/2/72.

57.   *Labour Party Conference Report* 1939, p. 34. As Naylor has written, NEC caution was excessive; if the Labour Party had led a popular front containing the Liberals and some Conservatives, communist influence would have been diminished. Naylor, J. F. (1969), op. cit., p. 269. *Philip Noel Baker Papers,* Churchill College, Cambridge, Zilliacus to Noel Baker, 9 June 1936, 2/23. *Dalton Papers, Diary,* 6 October 1938, I 19.62, Cecil to Dalton, 21 November 1938, IIA 5.2.20; Dalton to Cecil, 1 December 1938, IIA 5.2.18; *Diary,* 9 December 1938, I 19.72; Jay to Dalton, 20 February 1939, IIA 5.2.25; Dalton to Jay, 24 February 1939, IIA 5.2.26; Dalton to Jay, 24 February 1939, IIA 5.2.26. *Attlee Papers,* Churchill College, Cambridge, draft of autobiography, 1/16/1. As Braunthal wrote, the British Labour Party was the sole European party to preserve its independent outlook. In Sweden, Norway, Finland, Belgium, Denmark and Czechoslovakia, Social Democratic parties had collaborated with bourgeois parties, and in France and Spain with communists. Braunthal, Julius (1967), op. cit., pp. 483-4.

58.   *Dalton Papers,* 23 January 1939, IIA 3.1.27. *James and Lucy Middleton Papers,* Hugh Dalton's Report, March 1939, MID/62/18. *Philip Noel Baker Papers,* 2/41. Noel Baker received resolutions of support for Cripps from Hampstead Garden suburbs (7 February 1939); Acton (5 February 1939); Westminster St George's (6 February 1939); Canterbury District (31 January 1939); Beddington and Wallington (3 February 1939); Marylebone (30 January 1939); Westminster Abbey (5 February 1939).

59.   *Labour and Socialist International Papers,* Gillies to Adler, 4 April 1939, LSI/22/2/45.

60.   *Labour and Socialist International Papers,* Gillies to Adler, 21 April 1939, LSI/22/2/51. *International Sub-Committee Minutes,* 21 April 1939.

61.   *Dalton Papers, Diary,* 15 February 1939, I 20.11. (The TUC decided against going to the World Conference against Racialism and Anti-Semitism in Paris, Autumn 1939, probably because it was suspicious of communist involvement: *Trades Union Congress International Committee Minutes,* 25 July 1939. Hendrik de Man (1883-1953) was Professor at the University of Brussels; he had been secretary of the Youth International (1907); as a government minister 1939-40 he accepted the 'New Order' under the Nazis and was later convicted *in absentia* to twenty years imprisonment.

62.   *Labour Party Conference Report* 1939, pp. 264-65.

63.   *Labour and Socialist International Papers,* Adler's report, August 1939, LSI/22/4/4.

64.   *Labour and Socialist International Papers,* Labour Party Information Department Report, n.d., LSI/22/4/29, Adler's Report, August 1939, LSI/22/2/4.

65.   *Labour and Socialist International Papers*, Adler's Report, August 1939, LSI/22/2/4.
66.   *Labour and Socialist International Papers*, notes of meeting, August 1939, LSI/22/4/9.
67.   *Labour and Socialist International Papers*, memorandum of Northern Socialist Parties to LSI executive, 16-18 September 1939, LSI/22/4/12.
68.   *International Sub-Committee Minutes*, 13 July 1939.
69.   *Labour and Socialist International Papers, Memorandum* by Albarda, 26 August 1938, LSI/22/4/5.
70.   *Labour and Socialist International Papers,* International Solidarity Fund *Report* 1939, LSI/21/12/6.
71.   *Arthur Henderson Papers*, Dalton's notes, n.d., HEN/16/1/iv.
72.   *James and Lucy Middleton Papers*, Middleton to Katharine Bruce Glasier, 23 August 1939, MID/62/51.
73.   *Labour and Socialist International Papers*, Adler's report, LSI/22/4/44.

1 LSI Congress, 1923, postcard

A similar postcard was sent by William Gillies to James Middleton endorsed
'Unity is achieved! but I was not there at the great moment!'

Source: International Institute of Social History, Amsterdam.
Photograph by Peter Manasse, Sound and Vision Department.

2 LSI Congress, 1925, advertisement

Source: International Institute of Social History, Amsterdam.
Photograph by Peter Manasse, Sound and Vision Department.

3 LSI Secretariat, on balcony of a hotel in Paris, 1933, Kathia and Friedrich Adler to right

Source: International Institute of Social History, Amsterdam. Photograph by Peter Manasse, Sound and Vision Department.

**To honour the fallen
of the
BRITISH
BATTALION
INTERNATIONAL
BRIGADE**

NATIONAL MEMORIAL
MEETING EMPRESS
HALL EARLS COURT SUNDAY
JANUARY 8th, 7.30

Fred Copeman

**BARNET SILVER BAND   BATTALION PARADE
CLAPHAM ACCORDION BAND   TRUMPETERS...DRUMS
SPEAKERS FROM ALL PROGRESSIVE PARTIES
PAUL ROBESON   JOHN GOSS**

Tickets 1/-, 1/6, 2/6, 5/-, all seats reserved, from Charlotte Haldane, 1 Litchfield St., W.C.2

4 International Brigade Meeting, 1939, advertisement

Source: International Institute of Social History, Amsterdam.
Photograph by Peter Manasse, Sound and Vision Department.

Per
ruĝa savilo
proletoj
savas
la dronantan
verdan
stelon

5 *Sennacieca Asocio Tutmonda* postcard, n.d.

Source: International Institute of Social History, Amsterdam. Photograph by Peter Manasse, Sound and Vision Department.

6 Labour League of Youth, 1930s, advertisement

Source: International Institute of Social History, Amsterdam.
Photograph by Peter Manasse, Sound and Vision Department.

Text Jim Connell   Maryland

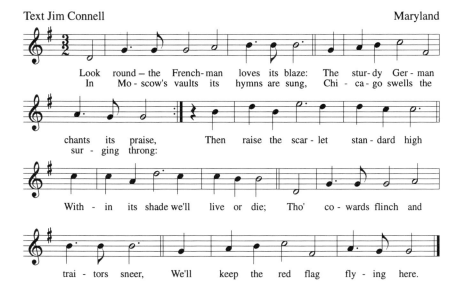

Look   round – the   French- man   loves its blaze: The   stur- dy   Ger - man
In   Mo - scow's   vaults   its   hymns are sung,   Chi - ca - go swells the

chants   its   praise,   Then   raise the   scar - let   stan - dard   high
sur - ging throng:

With - in   its   shade we'll   live   or   die;   Tho'   co - wards flinch   and

trai - tors   sneer,   We'll   keep   the   red   flag   fly - ing   here.

7 The Red Flag

Source: *Everyday Songs for Labour Festivals*, Labour Party, n.d.

Text from the French of E. Pottier

Degeyter's Air

A - rise! ye starve-lings from your slum-bers, A - rise ye cri-mi-nals of want, For rea - son in re - volt now thun-ders, And at last ends the age of cant. Now a - way with all su-per - sti-tions, ser-vile mas-ses, a-rise! a-rise! We'll change forth-with the old con - di-tions, And spurn the dust to win the

Chorus

prize. Then___ com-rades come ral - ly; And the last fight let us face; The In - ter - na - tio - nal___ U - nites the hu - man race, Then___ com-rades come ral - ly; And the last fight let us face; The In - ter - na - tio - nal U - nites the hu-man race.

8 The International

Source: *Workers' Song Book*, Workers' Theatre Movement, n.d.

Text Douglas Robson

Arr. R. Liebich

Whirl-winds of dan-ger are ra-ging a-round us O'er-whel-ming for - ces of

dark-ness as - sail Still in the fight, see ad - van-cing be - fore us

Refrain

Red Flag of Li-ber-ty that yet shall pre-vail! Then for-ward, ye wor-kers

free-dom a - waits you O'er all the world on the land and the sea:

On with the fight for the cause of hu-ma-ni-ty, March, march ye toi-lers and the

Coda

world shall be free! March March ye toi-lers and the world shall be free.

9 March Song of the Red Army

Source: *Sixteen Songs for Sixpence*, Lansbury's Labour Weekly, n.d.

Text W. T. M. Collective

Our en-gine's roar - ing, roar-ing to the bat - tle: High in the
But for the wage-slaves and the toil - ing mas - ses A song of

air a-bove the clouds we speed; Our bombs are rea-dy our ma-chine guns
hope in our pro - pel - lors whirled: We drop them leaf-lets, while we bomb their

rat - tle 'Gainst the world's im - per - ial - ist - ic greed. Fly
bos - ses; The first Red Air Fleet in the world.

high-er, high-er, and high-er; Our em-blem the So - viet

(shouted)
Star: And ev' - ry pro-pel-lor is roar - ing RED FRONT! de -

fen-ding the U - S - S - R.

10 The Soviet Airmen's Song

Source: *Songs of the People*, University Labour Federation, Cambridge, n.d.

Russian Air   Arr. R. Liebich

Com-rades, the bu-gles are   sound - ing   Shoul-der your arms for the   fray
Firm   in   our faith we shall   con - quer   Sla - ver- y's yoke we shall   break

Bold - ly   we'll fight for our   free - dom,   Brave - ly we'll hew out a   way:
Wel - com - ing death e - ven   gai - ly   Fight- ing for   Li - ber- ty's   sake:

Bold- ly we'll fight   for our   free - dom   Brave- ly we'll hew out a   way.

11 The Red Army March

Source: *Songs of the People*, University Labour Federation, Cambridge, n.d.

Text L. Woodward

J. H. Willcox, arr. Alan Bush

Round the world a new song's ring-ing, Li-sten wo-men of all climes! 'Tis the

mo-ther's song we're sing-ing tel-ling hopes of hap-pier times, We will

put all hate be - hind us, We whose hearts are sick and sore, Tired of

strife and emp - ty vic - t'ries, Bear the pangs of war no more.

12 The Mothers' International

Source: *Pioneer Song Book*, Cooperative Education Committee, 1944.

CHAPTER FOUR

The International Faith: Subject and Special Interest Groups

Previous chapters have indicated that a commitment to Socialist internationalism was more than the common philosophy of a handful of left European politicians. Rather, internationalism was a wide-ranging belief system with roots deep in the European Labour Movement. Arthur Henderson called on this faith in Britain when he made his 1933 appeal for resistance to dictatorship and his judgement was vindicated by the breadth of British support for the Spanish government and by mass membership hostility towards fascism. In Europe, the faith was reflected in Adler's prediction of 'the final triumph of the fighting prôletariat'. Such ideas were the inspiration for the creation of bodies such as the Labour and Socialist International and the International Federation of Trades Unions, but these formal bodies alone could not encompass the full statement of the International Faith nor could they be sustained without the wider participation of the Labour Movement in Internationalist ventures. There were any number of bodies and occasions at which British Internationalism could be expressed. Some subject based bodies operated as loose alliances of European socialists contributing an internationalist outlook in their own sphere, and this chapter begins with an overview of such groupings. In addition, a variety of special interest groups with wide-ranging memberships which broadened the base of international participation are considered below. Some of these specialist groups encouraged travel abroad; it was important for the vitality of the International Faith that ordinary Labour Movement members were willing to travel, to make their own cultural and political explorations.   Other groups focused on education, traditionally an issue of prime importance in the British Labour Movement, Sport was an effective proselytiser. Housing was a special interest that appealed to local councillors, making corrections at the level of local social policy, where greater knowledge of conditions abroad led to debate at home.

Subject-based Internationals

Among subject-based Internationals was the Socialist Anti-Alcohol Alliance, to which was afiliated the British Workers' Temperance League, president, Arthur Henderson; chair, Joseph Jones, Miners' Federation; treasurer, Arthur Salter, MP. Temperance had traditionlly been an issue of interest to the British Labour Movement, with its many non-conformist members. Among other affiliates, the

Finnish Social Democratic Party had an Abstainers' Union and there was a strong Belgian organisation. Vandervelde, when Minister of Food in the First World War, had prohibited alcohol; afterwards, as Minister of Justice, he failed to secure total prohibition but banned retail sales of alcohol and introduced high taxes on spirits, wine and beer: the sale and consumption of spirits in any public place was forbidden.[1] On the other hand, some groups aimed to control rather than ban the sale of alcohol, for instance, the Labour Campaign for Public Control and Ownership of the Liquor Trade. The latter's secretary, J.J. Mallon, was of the opinion that the example of United States' prohibition showed that banning alcohol was a class issue, as the rich could obtain drink at any time.[2] A second example of an international gathering dear to British hearts was that of the Protection of Animals; in addition to the many British affiliations were hundreds of French, Belgian, Swiss and Dutch societies and one in Colorado.[3]

The importance of organising the legal profession internationally had been recognised since Vandervelde's failed attempt to defend Social Democrat prisoners in the Soviet Union. In 1928 there was an attempt to create an International Association of Socialist Lawyers, with national secretaries and correspondents.[4] Adler summarised the position: Germany had an Association of Socialist Lawyers; other countries had lists of individual lawyers but no central organisation. By 1930 there were 13 national secretaries and 1,540 members and in 1932 the International Association was formally constituted. Although no British lawyers were affiliated, several received correspondence (Alfred Baker, Arthur Henderson junior, D.N. Pritt, H. Walter Samuel, Stafford Cripps). The moving spirits had been the German lawyers and many were forced to stop practising in 1933 when Hitler came to power. Thereafter, international organisation was weak, although the need was great, for instance in enquiring into the condition of political prisoners. Stafford Cripps was one of those who participated in stagings of the Reichstag trial. Blaming communists for firing the Reichstag had been one of the devices empowering the Nazi coup; restagings of their trials were organised as part of Münzenberg's 'front' activities, and were part of the campaign which succeeded in securing the release of some communist prisoners. Despite Münzenberg's activities, Justice Internationals were split between Social Democrat and Third International groups. In 1938 there was an attempt to revitalise the Socialist Lawyers' Association; Adler invited all lawyers who attended LSI meetings and those enquiring into the conditions of political prisoners to meet (a means of including those in 'front' groups) and offered to act as their administrative officer, with Vandervelde acting as president. The Labour Party considered recommending the Haldane Society as the British affiliate. The overall aim was given as: 'the imbuing of the judicial system with the socialist spirit', the protection of workers against class injustice, against persecution for political convictions, for the abolition of the death penalty and the right to asylum.[5]

Peripheral to the LSI but of use to socialist politicians was the Inter-Parliamentary Union, which held conferences where socialists formed a substantial bloc and organised their voting power. This first met in 1903 (Vienna) and was reformed in 1921 (Stockholm); the secretary general, Lange, swapped information with Adler on conference resolutions and memoranda, for instance on disarmament (1930). At the 1931 conference Dr Winter (Czechoslovakia) spoke about secret voting in Eastern Europe; the following year Tom Shaw welcomed the delegates, delivering his speech in both French and German. When fascist delegates tried to introduce organisational changes in 1936, the socialist bloc met daily and mounted a successful resistance. By 1939, however, the delegation of British Labour Members of Parliament numbered merely five; there were proposals for an Inter-Parliamentary Conference of Socialist Members to remedy the situation. Scott Lindsay (PLP chair) was in favour but feared the Spanish delegates' proposals might present problems, presumably by demanding support for the Spanish government which the Labour Party felt unable to promise.[6]

The *Union International des Villes et Pouvoirs Locales* was a similar organisation for local councillors. This was created in 1913 on Belgian initiative and was reformed in 1924 (Amsterdam). Local authority finance, structure and powers were examined, each country, including Britain submitting exhaustive information. Wibaut, the Dutch socialist, was a leading figure; the 1936 conference was due to be held in Berlin, which he refused to visit. The LSI considered sending its *rapporteur* on the Local Authorities Campaign against Unemployment, but finally advised its affiliates to join Wibaut's boycott.[7] British interest in local government abroad was reciprocated; for instance, following Labour succes in the 1933 municipal elections, telegrams came to Transport House from Hungary: 'Against the rush of the fashism (sic) and national socialism ... the glorious results of the British Labour Party ... Hurrah! the International Socialdemocratism! Hurrah! The British Labour Party!', and from Finland, Belgium and France. The International Workers of the World offered campaign speakers.[8]

Such peripheral Internationals, inspired by leadership figures, in some cases allowed the international faith to spread beyond leaders of the Labour Movement. Some Labour leaders were of the opinion that internationalism, if it were to become a powerful force, must be fuelled also by broader contacts. For instance, Harry Gosling, president of the Transport and General Workers' Union, believed that leadership contacts would fail in their aim unless they were underpinned by more widespread involvement: 'The general working class public must be at the back of the International Conferences if the latter are to realise their aims'.[9] In his view: 'The first step to perfect international understanding' was through 'the medium of travel abroad'.

Travel

Workers' interest in travel abroad was made possible by the advent of holidays

101

with pay and progress in motor vehicle transport. It was stimulated by war-time experience in Belgium and France, interest in the Soviet Union and the activities of various Labour Movement organisations commited to peace and disarmament. Understandably, as holidays were short, travel was restricted to Europe and the more accessible parts of the Soviet Union. Margaret Happold helped found International Tramping Tours (ITT), magazine *Pilgrim,* which advertised extensively in Workers' Educational Association publications. Its aims were:

> a movement to promote peace in international understanding ... enabling groups of people (British and others) to travel in lands other than their own at a minimum of cost, tramping or sharing single accommodation, thereby making intimate contact with the individuals who constitute the peoples of the world.

At first, the political situation allowed ITT to focus on enjoyment; by 1935 the need was felt to do more for 'informed pacifist opinion' and tours visited the places affected by the 1919 Peace Treaty. By 1938, the fascist advance had changed the emphasis: a refugee sub-committee was considered and its report stated that:

> a tour should not be regarded as successful unless every member of the party comes back with ... some insight into the political institutions, the legal system, the Health and Education services, the Press and the cultural life of the countries visited.[10]

Similarly, International Friendship Holidays operated in Belgium, France Norway, Germany, Spain and Austria and was advertised as: 'designed to promote international understanding. Education classes at many centres. Inexpensive excursions. PEACE THROUGH FRIENDSHIP (sic)'. Holiday Fellowships ran comparable tours.[11] WEA ran its own tours, including trips to the Soviet Union; the 1937 Soviet tour included visits to education and social welfare institutions. The Cooperative Wholesale Society Fellowship organised Red Triangle Tours to Europe. The Labour Party League of Youth attempted to arrange its own tours through the Socialist Youth International (SYI). Erich Ollenhauer, secretary of SYI reported in 1932 that there was many opportunities, youth festivals in the Netherlands, Switzerland and Scandinavia. He wrote that: 'we are sure there could be locally a lot of arrangements for us to give to comrades from abroad a chance to get a good insight into the work of the Socialist Youth'. Arrangements could be made for the British to stay in 'comrades' houses'. Peter Dockerty, when secretary of the Independent Labour Party Guild of Youth, suggested that he might set up a section 'devoted to organising holiday tours aboard' and that he could arrange tours for visitors to Britain.[12]

The biggest travel agency, the Workers Travel Association (WTA), occasional magazine *The Travel Log,* was formed as a result of a meeting called in 1921 by Cecil Rogerson, of the London Labour Movement 'in a back room of Toynbee Hall, where we had no equipment and no capital'.[13] A committee was formed to promote travel parties from 'the works, the forge, the mine and the garage'. The aim was 'a robust, self-governing cooperative movement of the workers themselves'; the committee contacted adult education, political, industrial and cooperative branches of the Labour Movement. WTA was adopted by the Labour Party, Trades Union Congress and Cooperative Party (1922) and eventually operated largely through trades union and Cooperative offices with a handful of agencies in major towns. However, it retained its independence and was registered by the Independent and Provident Association (1924). Ties to the Labour Movement leadership were stronger after 1931, when WTA moved to Congress House and Ernest Bevin became president (the presidency was first offered to Ramsay Macdonald, an impossible choice on the latter's expulsion from the Labour Party). WTA was a non-profit making organisation, shares were open to all in the Labour Movement and shareholders travelled at a discount.

There were three aims, variously but constantly expressed in WTA publications: to promote goodwill through direct experience of habits of life, social problems and culture abroad; to promote peace; and to serve ordinary people, appealing to the Labour Movement rank and file. For instance, Arthur Creech-Jones (Transport and General Workers'Union, clerical section) wrote in the WTA Staff Guild organ that WTA was: 'more than a travel agency or tourist organisation for workers'; it aimed at 'a spirit of friendliness and understanding' and a 'contribution to world peace'. J.W. Bowen (Post Office Workers Union), WTA chair, said in his address to the 1931 WTA conference that the aim was not: 'cheap holidays for the middle classes' ... 'ventures not commercially viable were undertaken, the main goal being the promotion of goodwill and peace'.[14] Although parts of WTA advertisements read much like later holiday brochures aimed at the mass market:

> You get all the advantages of the friendly spirit, the comradeship and good-natured fun of W.T.A. parties, which arrange things so that there is no hitch. Passports, foreign currency, languages - all these little troubles vanish when you decide to 'go W.T.A.'.[15]

Bowen wanted workers to use leisure wisely: 'we do not want our members to travel just to produce financial results or for the sake of sightseeing'. Had the holidays consisted of sea-and-sand entertainment solely, they would have failed to provide the desired experience.

WTA did offer holidays in Britain, but numbers did not match those for holidays abroad until 1928. Echoing war-time experience, Belgium and France were popular venues, followed by Germany and Switzerland. Tours were also arranged to the Soviet Union and Spain. In its first decade, WTA covered its costs and was able to increase services year by year. By 1931 WTA *10th Annual Report* was able to record 13,706 holidays. In 1931, and typically for the decade 1923 to 1933, the 'Continental programme' was the most popular (10,869 holidays) while special parties accounted for about a tenth of bookings

(1,780). Travellers were expected to show an intelligent interest in socio-economic and political issues; programmes included visits to places of interest (for instance, the Belgian trip included Ostend, Bruges, the Ypres battlefield, Ghent, Brussels, Antwerp, Waterloo). The 1932 trip to the Soviet Union may serve as an example; Herbert Morrison led a study of political institutions while Ernest Greenwood (WEA) led an inspection of educational institutions. The WTA brochure, *See Russia for Yourself* (1932) implied the expectation that the traveller would know of different attitudes to the USSR in the Labour Movement. Among other study initiatives, Ernest Bevin led the 1931 Rhine trip, while Women's Cooperative Guild special parties met women's organisations in Bruges, Brussels and Ghent. WTA fellowships, numbering 16 by 1933, continued education work with lectures, discussion and film shows. The amount of education work varied with the traveller; at least, s/he made a journey that would have been extremely unlikely a generation before; for the most enthusiastic, study could inform personal exploration of European culture and workers' organisations.[16] It would seem that WTA went some considerable way to meet its first objective, of promoting goodwill and understanding.

Whether WTA met its objective of serving ordinary people is more difficult to estimate because WTA did not categorise its clients, apart from gender and marital status. Women travellers outnumbered men by five to four; married couples formed 60 per cent of all clients and single women were the greater proportion of the remainder. The preponderance of single women is interesting; women had not achieved equal pay; if their ability to travel rested on employment in higher salaried sections of the labour force, it might be a comment on the interaction of gender and social class in the Labour movement rank and file. Women bereaved in the First World War may have felt the need to visit war graves. It might also be that travel offered freedom from prescribed gender rôles, more restrictive for women at home; there are numerous examples of women travellers who rejoiced in escaping such domestic constraints.[17] There is no record of travellers' ethnic background. It was not the case that bookings relied merely on repeated trips; WTA *11th Annual Report* (1932) recorded that a third of its clients were undertaking their first expedition abroad, an enviable marketing achievement. Bookings fell to 6,730 in 1932, possibly an effect of the depression; it may be inferred that workers with some excess income normally used WTA. Married couple's bookings fell to 21 per cent of the total and those of single men rose. Women were, of course, more likely to lose their jobs in a depressed labour market.

While Morrison, Bevin and later, Hugh Dalton joined WTA tours, leading politicians and trades unionists usually contacted the Labour Party International Department directly for travel advice. William Gillies held one WTA share; he arranged details of journeys for leading figures and used WTA to book hotels and arrange foreign currency for conferences abroad. WTA helped with journeys to the Hamburg conference (1923) at which the LSI was reconstituted. Thus it is hard to see to whom WTA, through Cooperative and trades union offices, sold holidays direct, if not to the ordinary Labour Movement member. Advertisements stressed the 'ordinary incomes' of clients; WTA *10th Annual Report* (1931) recorded that 70 per cent of bookings were for one week because of the moderate means of clients.

Looking back on the first decade, Bowen asked: 'But have we reached the workers?' and through examining the record decided: 'It is not unreasonable ... to assume that the bulk of these holidays were taken by working people'.[18]

WTA *11th Annual Report* (1932) noted: 'we should like to see our movement justify its faith in international travel as a contributor to International Peace'. This grandest of WTA aims certainly expressed a sense of internationalism but was hardly capable of achievement in view of the political situation. 1932 was the second year in which bookings for holidays in Britain outstripped those for Europe. However, 63,000 bookings by 1933 was evidence of WTA success; passport costs rose and holidays in Germany had to be cancelled that year, so that the venture seemed threatened. WTA ensured its survival and, indeed, consolidated its success by arranging sea cruises, but bookings soon picked up; married couples and single women's bookings again rose; overseas bookings rose in comparison to holidays at home and 1939 was WTA's highest turnover to date. WTA tourists to Spain (1936) and Czechoslovakia (1938) had to be rescued in the teeth of the fascist advance while the 18th *Annual Report* reported 3,500 travellers evacuated from Europe. Their persistence, despite the growing difficulties of travel, indicated that WTA tourists were motivated by more than the desire for a good time, that there was curiosity and interest, a willingness, physically and mentally, to cross national barriers.

Housing

Stefan Berger has written: 'The importance of housing for the emergence of a political working class identity should not be underestimated'. Workers' proximity to each other, together with their enjoyment of a degree of domestic comfort, both enhanced their ability to organise and contributed to the development of a working class hegemonic culture. From this culture the Labour Movement could draw. There was a gender, as well as a class component to demand for better housing; housing had long been one of the major interests of Labour Movement women. The Women's Labour League (1906-18) had contributed to war-time reconstruction schemes, its opinion influencing housing design in the building boom encouraged by government grants introduced in the1920s.[19] Labour Party subsidies, privileging public housing, spelt the introduction of the council housing programme, while Conservative policy favoured the private builder; competition between the parties on the issue was fierce and was the subject of an extensive Labour Party campaign. Margaret Happold, for instance, contributed to the project to clear Leeds slums and build the Quarry Hill flats in their stead. However, both parties concentrated on building small family homes; the miniature castle-and-moat design which feminists had questioned. The Labour Party failed to address these feminist concerns. The author Naomi Mitchison, working in an election where Labour was 'going all out on housing' expressed some of these:

> nice little home nests, brick houses with every convenience for the housewife and home lover, all separated ...(will) encourage the feeling of the close family group, the comfortable feeling of male ownership, the house pride of the woman, all of those things which those of us who hate ownership in all forms must be anxious about.[20]

Moreover, by encouraging the 'close family group', the Labour Party weakened associational class culture which relied on political activity within the community but beyond the family circle.

Housing in Europe seemed to have avoided some of these 'home nest' traps by providing tenement dwellings which incorporated common laundries and cafés. *Labour Bulletin* (December 1929) reported that in France 'great improvements have taken place in the type of working class dwellings built'. *Labour Magazine* (July 1925) lauded the housing programme of the Viennese socialist city council. The council was the largest property owner in Vienna; it both planned to provide more housing and controlled accommodation by fixing the number of rooms according to the size of the family and expropriating any spare space. *New Leader* (the Independent Labour Party organ) reported Poplar ILP's 1929 summer programme ending with a lecture and lantern slide show in which: 'scenes from Poplar streets were compared with the council houses and housing schemes in Vienna' (27 September 1929). On the same theme Minnie Pallister of the ILP wrote in *New Leader* (1 November 1929) of a block of flats in Vienna with a central courtyard, bathing pool, gardens, a kindergarten and communal washhouses which altogether 'made my mouth water'. An exhibition at the Workers' Educational Association 1936 conference contrasted British slum dwellings with European tenements. Discussion of this covered points such as the difficulties of carrying children upstairs and finding space for prams, one correspondent doubting whether there was sufficient support for this type of development in Britain and preferring 'garden cities' (landscaped estates built in suburbs). He wrote perceptively of the need to consider transport and 'community life' when planning housing, referring to 'the dreadful examples of some of our "new estates"'.[21]

Accounts of Vienna were generally laudatory. Apart from the municipal housing scheme there were public baths, crèches, assembly rooms, a centralised welfare service, sanitoria, homes for alcoholics and elderly people. The first municipal marriage consultation bureau in Europe was opened. Gas, trams, electric light were provided very cheaply and water free of charge. Viennese innovation perhaps reflected the strong representation of women in the Social Democratic Party; they called for a

> rationalised household ... not only the introduction of labour saving

technology.. They also advocated the avoidance of wasteful duplication through the construction of architecturally planned housing, the centralisation of facilities such as cooking and laundries and the engagement of professional cleaning and childcare services.[22]

The great European venture in the field of architecture was the Bauhaus workshop. Like the Vienna workshop (founded 1903), Bauhaus attempted to overcome artistic isolation and required artists and craftsmen to collaborate; its manifesto required: 'communal planning of extensive, utopian projects'; there was to be collaboration with trades unions and industry leaders and public participation through exhibitions; all Bauhaus design was to be capable of mass production.[23] German tenements, accordingly, deeply impressed a group of British local authority councillors who attended the 13th International Housing and Town Planning Congress in 1931. This group visited Berlin, Breslau, Dresden, Leipzig, Hamburg, Prague and Amsterdam. They reported satisfied tenants in homes usually built by public utility societies with state assistance; shops and beer halls were incorporated into the tenement blocks, staircases were clean and electrically lit and flats usually contained two bedrooms, a bathroom, kitchen, scullery and living room; poorer houses might lack the bathroom, but what most excited the councillors was that all dwellings had an open-air balcony where workers ate and which served as social space.[24] In the field of housing, connections were being made at the level of local social policy and interest in conditions in Europe was leading to discussion at home. As with workers' travel, it was the rise of fascism in Europe which sundered these ties, making contact difficult and putting an end to experiments such as those of the Viennese city council and the Bauhaus workshop.

Education

In order to appreciate issues such as town planning, local authority finance, architecture, education was needed. Greater claims have been made, that education, use of information, thinking about social and economic problems can militate against fascism, which relies on the success of demagogues propounding propaganda. Hannah Arendt, of course, has written extensively about this. Some hints of her argument can be found in contemporary accounts, for instance, the pages of *Highway*; John Brown, 'an ex-Ruskin student' wrote (April 1936) of a visit to Italy and the reasons why fascism might prove attractive; he argued against an easy belief in the probability of resistance to Mussolini: 'the enfranchised prôletariat has expressed itself in some peculiar ways ... the W.E.A., as part of the intellectual vanguard, must do its bit'.[25] New initiatives in education between the wars were studied; for instance, Austrian reform of the education structure and curriculum, backed up by an education research body. One of the proclaimed successes of the Spanish popular front government was improvement in the state education system and the campaign against illiteracy, which included forming a Cultural Militia for army education.[26] However, proposals exceeded national schemes. There were plans to organise teachers internationally; to implement international adult education; and to provide some international experience for young people and children.

To organise teachers, a preliminary conference was held in Brussels in August 1922 and a Teachers' International was founded in October 1923, with representatives from Germany, Austria, the Netherlands and Belgium. The Teachers' 1923 conference drew up rules for the Socialist Education International which had been founded the previous year; this was awarded a small subsidy from the Labour and Socialist International and in 1924 set up headquarters in Vienna (chair, Max Winter, secretary Jalkotzy). This seems not to have won British approval; in the opinion of Gillies it was 'not a workers' education institution in all senses of the term'.[27] There were difficulties in fostering links between teachers; W.H. Marwick, British educationalist wrote that while in Britain, France and Denmark the workers' education movement had a philanthropic base in the broad Labour Movement, in Sweden, Germany and the Soviet Union there was a stronger public tradition of adult education linked to trades unions. The major problem was that perceptions of the rôle of education and the responsibilities of teachers and students differed in the reformist and revolutionary wings of the International Labour Movement. Marwick hinted at this when he wrote of the difficulty in accommodating bodies which privileged teaching on class struggle, such as the Plebs League in Britain, Écoles Marxiennes in France and the institutions in the Soviet system.[28]

While the LSI and IFTU wrestled with these problems, an Education Workers' International (EWI) had developed - organ, *Teachers International.* This body remained outside the fold of LSI/IFTU or the Third International; its affiliates were from both reformist and revolutionary wings. They were listed thus: France (RILU), Soviet Union (RILU), Portugal, Spain (both IFTU), Belgium (IFTU), Luxemburg (IFTU), China (Kuomintang). In addition, Italy and Britain were in membership; in the former the affiliated body was, of neccesity, anonymous; the position of the British was ambivalent. EWI's coverage was broad, and its journal carried news from the United States, Canada, New Zealand, the Phillipines, China and Japan as well as Europe.[29]

EWI was contemptuous of a failed IFTU attempt to set up an international trade secretariat for teachers. To this end, a meeting was held (1924) in Britain at Ruskin College (the trade union college). Seventy delegates from 21 countries attended. A committee was formed to draft a constitution and make arrangements to discuss first, exchanges of students and tutors, languages, including the use of Esperanto, and finance; second, the establishment of an international college. Finance was a problem: whether to set up a central fund or restrict contributions to trades unions involved in exchanges; but the major problem related back to wariness of communism. The Trades Union Congress, the Workers' Education Association, the Cooperative Movement and Ruskin

College favoured education 'in the sense it was normally understood', in other words broadly cultural; the Plebs League Movement and Labour Colleges which sprang from it, organised in the National Council of Labour Colleges (secretary, J.P.M. Millar), and the Scottish Labour League wanted to educate workers 'in the class struggle'. The WEA accepted state aid; the NCLC insisted on 'Independent Working Class Education'. Sanderson Furniss, the Ruskin principal was of the opinion that the meeting: 'was a most unsuitable place for pursuing a quarrel which is, in the main, a British quarrel' ... the TUC was 'wholly opposed to the Marxist system of thought'.[30] This was, of course, disingenous as the relative influence of socialism and communism was an international question, but the plan foundered on the rocks of these disputed seas. It was agreed that working class education should be under working class control.

Against this background, British international education links were problematic, but reasonably vigorous. The National Union of Teachers did not support the proposed IFTU body because of its trade union bias; IFTU, for its part, would not attend the EWI, to which RILU delegates could not get passports. At their 1926 conference, The Education Workers proposed affiliation to the Anglo-Russian trade union committee, which would have reflected their political philosophy; however, one of the British delegates (Capper) rightly reported that such an affiliation was an impossibility, as the Anglo-Russian was an *ad hoc* committee. EWI therefore affirmed its sympathy with this attempt to build bridges between reformists and revolutionaries. British delegates to EWI, in addition to Capper, included Redgrove, secretary of the Teachers' Labour League.[31] The position of the Teachers' Labour League was indicative of the problems faced by British teachers in international affiliation; Redgrove provided a history for *Teachers International* (1927): at its 1917 conference, the NUT considered affiliation to the Labour Party but this was rejected in a referendum of members; the Teachers' Labour League was created as a result. At the latter's first large post war conference (Bethnal Green, 1924), there were 46 delegates, plus representatives of 28 Labour Parties and Trades Councils, 14 representatives from nine trades union branches, two from Trades Council women's sections, four from the National Council of Labour Colleges, four from the Cooperative Party, two from the Labour Esperanto Association, 16 from the TLL, 17 school managers and councillors and 12 visitors. By the time Redgrove's article appeared, the TLL 'has been disaffiliated by the Labour Party'. Its communist connections had rendered the TLL suspect; in fact, the British delegates left the 1927 EWI conference early because they were going to Russia.[32]

Despite the difficulties of organising teachers, international adult education remained of interest to the British Labour Movement. The existence of the Plebs League, National Council of Labour Colleges, Ruskin College, the Workers' Education Association, was evidence of the traditional commitment of British Labour to adult education; each political party ran its own classes. The

WEA had links with Scandinavian counterparts and participated in Scandinavian English Speaking Schools. *Highway* reported: 'The schools abroad have arisen from the growth of the friendly contacts between ourselves and the WEA movement in Sweden, Denmark and Norway, and it is important that this relationship be strengthened'.[33] Subjects studied included Scandinavian economic and social problems and the WEA movement. WTA made travel arrangements. Ernest Green (WEA general secretary) reported on the 1936 school: 62 students attended, from Britain, Sweden, Denmark, Norway, Finland, The Netherlands and 12 African American delegates from Chicago, then unusual enough to receive special mention. Lectures were in English; one group studied international problems, another trades unions. The students stayed in a hostel and all wore blue uniforms. Further schools were planned for Denmark (1937), Norway (1938), Sweden (1939), Britain (1940).[34]

The British contributed advice to the International Peoples College founded in Denmark in October 1921 'on the idea of fostering internationalism and idealism'.[35] Aided by voluntary bodies, with state and local authority support, this had an advisory committee of British (George Lansbury), German and American contacts. By 1939, the WEA represented Britain and WTA and the Cooperative Society offered scholarships.[36] IFTU, marginally less sensitive to the dispute between socialism and communism than the LSI in the 1920s, went furthest to achieve international education by developing the Elsinore college. Foreign students (mainly British and German) attended in the summer months; the three official teaching languages were Danish, English and German. Esperanto was studied. Summer schools were frequently held in conjunction with conferences of trades unions so that students could listen to debates and delegates could participate in classes. The Reuben George fund was to be used for summer school scholarships.[37] In addition to the Elsinore project, there were links between education movements in various countries with student exchange schemes and IFTU summer schools, helped by the Worker's Travel Association. WEA, for instance, was interested in the French Centre for Workers' Education inspired by Jouhaux and Professor and Mme Lefranc; this held a summer school in London in 1933.[38] WEA also provided scholarships to ILO summer schools.[39] WTA funded scholarships for members of its fellowships to WEA summer schools. By 1939, 300 trades union scholarships were offered by 27 trades unions for summer schools.[40]

The International Cooperative Alliance also ran international summer schools, designed to provide education on a world economy: 'aspirations ... to satisfy all ... physical and intellectual needs under a system of just distribution'.[41] Syllabi included building large societies, attracting individual savings, centralising purchasing in a wholesale society, trading between consumers and agriculturalists. The British Cooperative Union had been the inspiration for the scheme and provided the sole students at the first schools in 1929; in 1930, 150 students from 21 countries participated and the British ran a special school for advanced students.

University students organised their own International, that of Socialist Students and Worker Students (ISS), organ *L'Etudiante Socialiste*. This had developed from an organisation founded in Belgium (1890), whose first conference (1891) was chaired by Vandervelde. Dr Otto Friedlander was the moving spirit behind its reformation in 1926, at Amsterdam.[42] ISS was a small campaigning body, seeking to promote socialism within the universities and to provide a contact point for 'worker' students; the number of British affiliates was around three hundred. ISS had tried without success to extend its reach beyond Europe; United States students had once affiliated but withdrew. However, during the Spanish Civil War, ISS began to attract a larger membership, which altered its nature and made discussion of relationships with communist student organisations necessary; British affiliation rose to 2,000. The fifth ISS congress that year was held at St Michael's Hall, Oxford, with an evening dance at Ruskin College arranged by the trade union summer school then meeting at that venue. British delegates included John Cornford, poet and political activist. Laski spoke on the international position of socialism. A coordinating committee had been working with communist students and recommended uniting the two groups. Cornford's proposal that the communist committee be present at the discussion was accepted for the reasons that fascism 'avait maintenant gagné du terrain' (had now won territory), and that there was French and Spanish enthusiasm for united action. The coordinating committee became a unification commitee with the object of calling a united conference the following year: 'Le congrès d'Oxford sera un grand pas en avant dans l'histoire internationale des travailleurs'. (The Oxford Congress will be a big step forward in the international history of the workers.)[43] There are no records of the united conference; Cornford's death in Spain has been widely lamented. Talks (see chapter six) about merger of socialist and communist youth organisations in general illustrate the difficulties.

Other international academic institutions included the International Institute of Social History (IISH) founded (1935) by Prof. N.W. Posthumus at Amsterdam from his existing social history archive, with support from the Centrale insurance company, which helped fund 'cultural purposes on behalf of the Labour movement'. The LSI was notified of the Institute's existence. Although IISH was 'neutral' there were several socialists on its committee; it had a well-stocked library of socialist and labour publications and gradually collected the papers of some of the leading socialists. The IISH Guide notes that there was 'a rescue function ... an assiduous, sometimes breathtaking search for documents, books, pamphlets, leaflets all over Europe, often threatened to be destroyed by the fascist action'.[44] There was a great need for such a collection, the LSI's archives having been damaged by war and split between several places: 'there is no need to describe in detail the wanderings of these archives' wrote Adler in 1928, having attempted to gather them together.[45]

The International for Socialist Youth (Berlin headquarters), the International Socialist Federation for Sport and Physical Education (Prague) and the Socialist

Education International (Vienna) met in 1928 to assess the position on education; an exhibition of the work of the three Internationals was held during the conference; LSI delegates were invited. Otto Gloeckel, director of the Austrian education system, spoke about the impact which labour movements could have on elementary education and Kurt Lowenstein (Berlin) on socialist education for workers' children. The Socialist Education International had developed not so much as an organisation to foster links between teachers or workers, but rather to provide education in the broadest sense, at school, home and community level so that children would grow up 'fit for the class struggle'. Gillies's comments that it was not a workers' organisation should be understood in this context. SEI provided excursions, Sunday schools, sports, summer schools, ran its own 'homes for children' and 'kinder-gardens' (sic) and worked in schools and juvenile courts. Some British educationalists were in touch with SEI, but its strength was in Central and Eastern Europe; Germany had 350 local groups reaching 200,000 children, in Poland, Jewish groups were also formed, Austria had 361 groups with 300 professional helpers, Czechoslovakia 84 branches, Hungary 26 branches, Latvia 25 organisations; of other sizeable groups, Denmark had 62 divisions.[46]

The natural affiliate to SEI would have been the Woodcraft Folk, noted in LSI files as 'a credit to the organised Cooperative and Labour Movement', an educational and entertainment organisation for young people that consciously provided both an alternative to the militarist-oriented Scout movement and a taste of a 'green' environment. However, there were two counts for British reluctance about SEI involvement; on the one hand, activities were uncomfortably similar to those of the Hitler Youth and on the other, it was difficult to separate education 'for the class struggle' into socialist and communist wings. One of the Woodcraft Lodges, indeed, at the time of the Spanish Civil War, made the suggestion that the Young Communist League and the Labour Party League of Youth should merge. In 1936 SEI held a children's camp in Britain, assisted by the Woodcraft Folk which welcomed a thousand British children from the age of ten and a thousand from the Red Falcon youth (affilited to LSI) of Czechoslovakia, Switzerland, Belgium, France and Scandinavia. Gillies asked for a list of patrons and the Trade Union Education committee decided not to be associated with the camp, but to give help if there were any difficulties with the British authorities. There were fears that the Public Order Act of that year would prohibit children from wearing uniform, but the Home Secretary, did give permission for the camp. A particular concern of Gillies, then in his 'communazi' phase, was the involvement of Ben Greene, a prospective parliamentary candidate who was acting as organiser. Greene favoured a popular front and was suspected of Nazi sympathies following a visit he had made to Germany. There were rumours that leaders of the Reich Youth executive and the Reich Führer school attended the camp.[47] In any event, the Woodcraft Folk thereafter emphasised entertainment to escape the trammels of the public order legislation.

That international education in Britain was more oriented to adults than children was a function of the British Labour Movement's focus on the representation of working people. Nevertheless, engagement in summer schools abroad and in trades union and cooperative adult education was evidence of willingness to learn about European cultures and Labour Movements. For instance, WEA offered translations of *Mein Kampf.* In April 1939, the WEA was still trying to maintain contact with Czechoslovakia and advertising the International Summer School planned for August that year at the Czech Academy of Labour, Prague.[48] The formal organisation representing education workers, the International of that name was constrained by its refusal to opt for either the socialist or communist wing of the international movement. This latter split was a constraint on the development of both national and international education.

Sport

International sporting movements had also to overcome the presence of conflicting socialist and communist groups. Additional hindrances to British participation were that, on the one hand, some perceived sport as a distraction from political activity, while on the other, such sport as existed tended to be about either individual performance or club/team competition and reward; the massed drill which characterised European sporting meetings was unfamiliar to the British. The Women's Labour League had been keen on activities such as swimming, but both in Britain and Europe sport was a gendered activity, young men predominating; the European approach may have encouraged women's involvement. Cuts in working hours in Europe between the wars allowed greater participation in leisure activities in general.

There were a number of left sporting groups in Britain, such as those linked to the *Clarion* newspaper, Labour football clubs (including the Guildford Cooperative Ladies football team), the Scottish Labour Sporting Federation, the parliamentarians' cricket club, but nothing to match the German Sports and Gymnastic League founded in 1893. G.D.H. Cole wrote in *New Leader* (2 March 1923): 'I am still looking forward to the day when Cup finals will be eclipsed in public interest by Labour's own sporting events', calling for a National Labour Sports League. The Independent Labour Party called a meeting on 5 April 1923 to establish a British Socialist or Workers' Sports Federation.[49] It was Tom Groom (chair of the Clarion Cycling Club) who inspired participation in international sport, claiming:

> the future pacification of the world will be won, and held, on the democratic sporting fields of the Workers International Olympiad.

Arguing that the British could enter team and individual athletic events, Groom gave the opinion that involvement would:

develop and propagate among the workers of all countries, and more particularly among the youth of both sexes, the taste for, and the practice of, physical education and sport ... to work for international peace, which is not possible except by a strenuous anti-militarist campaign.[50]

His appeal was successful, the British Workers' Sports Federation being founded in 1923, supported by the Clarion Cycling Club, Labour Party and Trades Union Congress.

The Workers' Sport International was set up in Ghent in 1913. Its first meeting after the war (1919) was attended by delegates from Britain, France and Belgium; in 1920 at its Lucerne conference, with nine nations represented, the International was formally reconstituted. Henceforth it was often known as the Lucerne International or (Socialist Workers) Sports International; the formal title was International Federation for Physical Education and Sport. Jules Devlieger (Belgium) was secretary, later succeeded by Rudolf Siaba with Julius Deutsch as president. Tom Groom attended the 1913 and 1920 conference and BWSF affiliated to the Sports International. By its 1925 Paris conference there were 18 affiliated federations with 1,500,000 members. Two years later the Helsingfors conference reported 1,600,000 members of whom 956,446 were men, 126,459 women, 257,802 youths and 244,103 children. Germany accounted for the majority of these (913,786 members) and there was sizeable membership in Czechoslovakia (153,188) and Austria (141,016). Delegates came from sporting organisations across East and West Europe, including Britain, and also from America and Palestine. Britain was noted as one of the 'weaker' affiliates. The Sports International covered all kinds of activity, including bicycling, skiing, mountaineering, aviation, chess and radio. It aimed at 'spiritual and ethical development' in order to 'create a new humanity' and to act as 'the guard of defence of the working population against fascism'. Until 1927 the Sports International was 'neutral', following the policy adopted by the German organisation to avoid domestic conflict; that year the LSI Bureau was invited to send delegates to its meetings and the body affiliated to the LSI. The TUC formally recognised BWSF.[51]

As the trade union International mirrored the International Labour Office created by the Paris peace treaty, so the Sports International reflected the development of the Olympic movement. Sporting events began in 1921, when the Czech Workers' gymnast association entertained the athletic societies of Belgium, France, England, Germany, Switzerland, Austria, Yugoslavia, Bulgaria, and the Ukraine. Meetings were also held in Czechoslovakia in 1927 and 1934; the Clarion Cyclists attended the 1927 meeting; Vandervelde represented the LSI in 1934. In 1922 the Leipzig Workers' Gymnast club entertained 3,000 athletes. The Swiss meeting in 1923 was the occasion for Tom Groom's plea. In 1926 the Vienna Sports Festival was held. Frankfurt, in 1925, hosted the first workers' Olympiad which was repeated at Vienna in 1931, a Wintersports Olympiad also being held; 1,000 athletes from 26 countries attended (compared to 1,408 from 37 countries at the 1932 Olympic games). In protest at the site of the 1936 Berlin games, a Workers' Olympiad was due to be held in Barcelona but had to be abandoned because of the Spanish Civil War.[52] British teams were sent to these international meetings and the Olympiads. A British socialist football team toured Germany and football and tennis teams toured the Netherlands. In 1934, Belgian, Austrian, Czech, Polish and Swiss sports teams were welcomed to the Tolpuddle Martyrs celebrations in Dorset. Tom Binet, a British athlete at the 1936 Olympiad expressed some of the spirit of the Sports International and of the commitment which enabled the formation of the International Brigades: barricades were put up, his car was fired on and his hotel doors bolted, but Binet wrote: 'with our Scottish pipers at our head, we, with the teams of all the other nations represented, marched in procession, escorted by armed cars, to the Sports Stadium'.[53]

Despite such enthusiasm, British participation was limited by socialist/ communist conflict. The effects of this division had been noticeable from the start. A Moscow-based Red Sports International had been founded in 1921: 'in order to make the toiler ... physically capable of the efforts demanded by the prôletarian class struggle'. The Sports International had maintained contact until 1927, although of the opinion that the Moscow body was 'the starting point of all conspiracies against the Lucerne International'. The Communists insisted on the right to participate without committing themselves to unity of organisation. A BWSF football team toured the Soviet union in 1927; the following year marked the start of the Third International's period of greatest hostility towards social democracy. Communist tactics to influence sports organisation were successful in Britain; communists George Sinfield and Walter Tapsell were elected to the BWSF executive, Sinfield ejecting Tom Groom as general secretary. The TUC withdrew its recognition of BWSF and Labour's leaders set up a National Workers' Sports Association in 1930 to counter the communist move, building on London Labour sporting groups. In 1931 the British Workers' Sports Association had 6,000 members, but the situation was reversed as united and then popular front policies succeded; BWSF was dismantled and NWSA recovered lost ground, recruiting 9,000 members, mostly from large industrial areas. NWSA organised sport for the Labour League of Youth. The communist period had been successful in recruiting more women, although these remained less than a fifth of the membership; BWSF had women's sections, netball being the most popular sport.[54]

An attempt to achieve a sporting united front by inviting Soviet organisations to the reconvened 1937 third Workers' Olympiad at Antwerp failed, because the Communist International insisted that all its affiliated organisations should be admitted and the Sports International would accept only a limited number. The LSI had supported this Olympiad, but IFTU had not; Adler wrote that since the last Olympiad: 'the international Labour Movement has lived in the hollow of the wave ... in historical development the hollow of the wave is often followed by the crest'.

He was unsure whether the crest would be the triumph of the workers or of the fascists. In the face of such foreboding, the third Olympiad was a great success; all affiliates attended, the procession was huge and those countries whose sports organisations had affiliated to neither socialist or communist International (France, Norway, Spain, Sweden) came as guests. Some BWSF members joined the International Brigade; Walter Tapsell was killed in Spain, as were Tom Darban and Ray Cox of the Clarion Cycling Club.[55] The spirit of the sucessful Workers' Olympiads is, perhaps, best conveyed by surviving film footage, which show the marches on the final day of the games, athletes parading bearing banners in many languages, all demanding peace.[56]

Conclusion

The Sports International was unusual in its relatively long period of 'neutrality' and tolerance of tension between socialist and communist international perspectives. This, combined with the success of the CPGB in 'capturing' the British Workers' Sports Association, may help explain British 'weakness' in sport in the 1920s. In the next decade, Britain was able to participate more fully, as Tom Binet suggested and as contemporary film shows. Such differing organisations as the Woodcraft Folk and the Socialist Students were also willing to minimise socialist and communist division.

The paralysing potential of socialist/communist conflict is evident from the difficulties of adult educators. One of the reasons why the young sportspeople, the travellers, campers, investigators of housing, the lawyers staging the Reichstag fire, were able to be more tolerant may have been the active nature of their international engagement. Fritz Wildung, of the German group, emphasised this at the 1922 SI meeting: 'Our International differs from the political and trades union Internationals in that it brings its members together in action'.[57] Two factors seem to have heightened activity; one was the Spanish Civil War: students, sportspeople, socialist lawyers were all especially active in 1936. The second, obviously related, was that fascism had 'gagné du terrain' (won territory); this was a spur to resistance, rather than resignation; travellers were rescued up to and during the outbreak of war, educators planned the Prague summer school for August 1939.

Such activity substantially spread international participation beyond the confines of the bureaus of LSI/IFTU. Many activists; town councillors; lawyers, were middle, even upper-middle class, but workers also were involved. Bowen (WTA) asked, have we reached the workers? and concluded 'yes'. International participation was not, overall, a gendered activity; in education, sport, men activists preponderated but in travel, the majority of participants were women, while in the field of housing women displayed keen interest. The ethnic grouping of participants is not recorded. By their nature, it is difficult to identify these people, to trace a career in a footnote; one must be content with, for instance, 'John Brown, ex-Ruskin student'; it is thus not possible to measure the length of individual involvement, to trace whether this was confined to one summer school, one Olympiad, or was a repeated experience. We do know that there were many first-time travellers.

We know also that at any one time, there were several thousand sportspeople, travellers, animal protectors and local councillors, who chose to make international links through Labour and socialist, class-conscious organisations. This choice of class-oriented political membership marks the rank and file from the working class at large. Of course, all these bodies were headed by their own small vanguards, but their administrative work was merely the tip of the organisation. LSI meetings, on the other hand, were themselves, in a sense, the purpose of political party international cooperation. One inhales, reading the travel, sporting and education archives, the scent of a socialist supra-national community. That there was a domestic working class associational community at this time is generally accepted;[58] the socialist community drew from this but was also peopled by middle class adherents to Labour and socialist politics and was distinguished by its international perspective.

It seems, from examples of sporting involvement, the education of children, the children's camp, that in some instances the British may have been challenged by this sense of cultural community which differed from the home-grown male - breadwinner model of Labour representation. In some cases, for instance London, Labour leaders capitalised on community building; Stephen Jones has written that Herbert Morrison 'built a reputation for ... cultural outlets' including classes, a legal advice bureau, a choral union, dramatic federations; the Northern Labour clubs were similarly pervasive.[59] In general, other European parties, notably the Germans, were more comfortable with all-embracing organisation. It was, of course, the similarity to fascist corporate ideas and Nazi communities that rendered broad organisation suspect. However, as has often been inferred from accounts of women travellers' freedom from restrictive gender identities, escaping into a foreign community can be empowering, creating space for questioning values, challenging models of behaviour. This questioning was an important aspect of resistance to fascism; debate is an essential facet of democracy. International participators were curious, did wish to learn. The strength of the CPGB may have been its orientation towards a non-British model, which encouraged breadth of organistion; this may account for its success in organising sport. Alun Howkins noted that CPGB isolation in its 'class against class' phase 'created the foundation at least of a visible revolutionary and oppositional culture' with its own press, cafés, dances, film society, bookshops, a culture that was noted for its anti-racism and greater commitment for gender equality.[60] Britain, in fact, was not at the centre of this international world. If there were such a central reference point, it was provided by Adler and his secretariat. For British participants, however, Gillies's rôle did remain important, in documenting, storing, disseminating information.

The motive for the foundation of many of these international bodies was the preservation of peace. Founded in the decade following the First World War, they sought fellowship. Adler's files full of letters in several languages, the ideals expressed, the mundane minutiae of the regular and extensive travel arrangements and hotel bookings across Europe, for all sorts of gatherings, by their principles and practice make the Second World War seem inconceivable. The dark war - winter, when it covered all Europe, ended this culture. There were some twisted legacies; Galleon Travel succeded WTA; housing tenements were built; international sports events continue: but these are pale reflections of expressions of 1920s and 30s international socialist faith. To understand that faith, we need to look at socialist activities, as well as the committees of the formal organisations.

Notes

1. *William Gillies Correspondence,* Labour Party Archives, Manchester, Workers' Temperance League to Gillies, n.d. (1934); Press Service of International of Socialist Abstainers, n.d. (1934) WG/TEMP. August Dewinne (ed. *Le Peuple*) (1925), 'Temperance Reform in Belgium', *Labour Magazine,* vol. iv, no. 6, October. See also Polasky, Janet (1995), *The Democratic Socialism of Emile Vandervelde,* Berg, Oxford, ch. 5.

2. Mallan, J.J. (1923), 'America - a Temperance Utopia', *Labour Magazine,* vol. i, no. 4, August.

3. *William Gillies Correspondence,* List of Socialist attitudes to the International for Animal Protection, 1932, WG/20/7.

4. *William Gillies Correspondence,* WG/IL.

5. *Sozialistische Arbeiter Archives,* Amsterdam, Adler to LSI affiliates, 1.3.28, SAI 2949; Adler to all affiliates 6.1.38, SAI 2951.

6. *William Gillies Correspondence,* WG/IPC/20/1. *Sozialistische Arbeiter Archives,* Lange to Adler 17.9.30,SAI 3064; Adler to all affiliates, 14.8.31, SAI 3067; Adler to all affiliates 12.6.36,SAI 3069.

7. *William Gillies Correspondence,* WG/ULA/3; *Congrès Internationale des Villes et Pouvoirs Locales,* (1939) Barcelona.

8. *William Gillies Correspondence,* WG/ELE/1-14.

9. Gosling , Harry (1923), 'Foreign Travel for Workers', *Labour Magazine,* vol. ii, no. 3, July.

10. Standing advertisment, WEA *Highway; Pilgrim* (1935) no.9, Autumn; (1938) no. 15, Autumn; Obituary of Margaret Happold, 1900-1988, WEA teacher, housing researcher, Leeds City Councillor 1946-1966, *Independent* (1988) 13 September.

11. *Highway* (1936), April, flyleaf and standing advertisements.

12. Cooperative tours, *Highway* (1937), March p. 166-7; (1937) April p. 179. Youth, *Sozialistische Jugend Internationale archives*, International Institute of Social History, Amsterdam, Ollenhauer to Windle, 1 March 1932, SJI 742/16; Dockerty to Ollenhauer n.d., (?1930) SJI 750/17.

13. *Workers' Travel Association Records,* Trades Union Congress, London and included in *William Gillies Correspondence* WG/WTA. See also Cross, Gary

(1989), 'Vacations for all in the era of the Popular Front' *Journal of Contemporary History* 24, pp. 599-621. Cecil Rogerson was killed in a mountaineering accident in Switzerland in 1926; he did not enjoy good health and although his relations with WTA staff remained amicable, he left WTA as soon as it was firmly established to set up Friendship Travel; *Travel Log,* (1926) new series no.1, December.

14. For WTA objectives, see inside front cover of WTA *Annual Reports* 1923-1939; *18th Annual Report* (1939) emphasised the importance of 'direct and immediate experience'. Creech Jones, Arthur (1924), *Echo* no.2, December; Bowen, J.W. (1931), *Address to the WTA National Council.*

15. *Stepney Cooperative Citizen* (1936) May; for other examples, see *Wheatsheaf Holiday Guide* (1925).

16. WTA programmes are described in *Annual Reports* and advertisements; Herbert Morrison's tour, *12th Annual Report* (1933); Bevin's tour, *10th Annual Report* (1931); Women's Cooperative Guild, *13th Annual Report* (1934). Morrison's biographers, Donoghue Bernard and Jones, G.W. (1973), *Herbert Morrison: Portrait of a Politician,* Weidenfeld and Nicolson, London p.254 are of the opinion that Morrison's opinions of the Soviet Union were formed by this trip.

17. Clarissa Campbell Orr (ed.) (1996), *Wollstonecraft's Daughters: Womanhood in England and France, 1780-1920,* Manchester University Press, pp. 31-2 for brief discussion of women travel writers. Anne Louise Strong was one of the contemporary travel writers.

18. Bowen, J.W. (1933), *Address to the WTA National Council* (typescript). *William Gillies Correspondence* WG/VIS has details of assistance given. *Sozialistische Arbeiter Archives,* details of 1923 journeys, WTA general secretary to Tom Shaw, 1.5.23, LSI 65/1.

19. Berger, Stefan (1995), 'European Labour Movements and the European Working Class in Comparative Perspective' in Berger, Stefan and Broughton, David (eds), *The Force of Labour,* Berg, Oxford p. 257. Collette, Christine (1989), *For Labour and For Women, The Women's Labour League 1906-1918,* Manchester University Press, pp. 161-3.

20. Mitchinson, Naomi (1934-5), 'The Reluctant Feminist', *Left Review,* vol.i, p.306. For earlier feminist attacks on castle-and-moat design see Dolores Hayden (1987*), The Grand Domestic Revolution,* MIT. Berger, Stefan (1995), op. cit., pp. 257-9.

21. Pateman , G.H. (1936), *Highway,* March, pp. 143-4.

22. For praise of Vienna, see Pollac, Oscar (1925), 'A Socialist City', *Labour Magazine,* vol. iv, no. 3, July, p. 127. Women's influence, Lafleur, Ingrun (1978), 'Five Socialist Women: Traditional Conflict and Socialist Vision in Austria 1893-1914', in Boxer, M. and Quataert, J. (eds), *Socialist Women: European Socialist Feminism in the 19C and early 20C,* New York, p. 22.

23. Wingler, Hans (1969), *Graphic Work from the Bauhaus,* Lund Humphries, p. 18, citing Bauhaus manifesto.

24. 'Tenement Houses in Germany' (1931), *Labour Bulletin,* September, p. 203.

25. For a useful summary of Hannah Arendt's work, see Nye, Andrea (1994), *Philosophia* (Routledge). Brown, John (1936), 'Foreign Affairs and the W.E.A.' *Highway,* 1936, pp. 152-4

26. Gloeckel, Otto (director of the Austrian education system) (1924), 'Education Reform in Austria', *Labour Magazine,* vol. ii, no. 9, January, p. 404. Stewart, Margaret (1938), *Reform Under fire: Social Policy in Spain,* Gollancz, London.

27. *Labour and Socialist International Papers,* Labour Party archives, National Museum of Labour History, Manchester, note on file cover, n.d., LSI/21/10/4.

28. Marwick, W.H. (1927), 'International Adult Education', *Labour Magazine,* vol. v, no. 9, January, p. 402.

29. *Teachers International,* (1926) 5th year, no. 1, October, IFTU and RILU affiliates.

30. Sanderson Furniss, H. (1924), 'A New Renaissance', *Labour Magazine* vol. iii, no. 5, September, p. 207.

31. British delegates included Mabbs, Bell, Coleman, Williams, Miss Clarke, Moore; visitors Dr Kay, Miss Murray, Hicks; *Teachers International* (1926), 5th year, no. 1, October p. 3, NUT refusal to attend IFTU conference; p. 4, IFTU refusal to attend EWI conference; p. 14, proposed affiliation to Anglo-Russian Committee; 6th year, no. 1, October 1927, p. 27, British delegates.

32. *Teachers International* (1927), 6th year, no. 1, October, Teachers Labour League history; p. 19, British delegates leaving for Russia.

33. *Highway* (1936), March, p. 138, report by Ernest Greene.

34. *Highway* (1937), April, p. 187, report by Ernest Greene.

35. 'Labour Abroad' (1924), *Labour Magazine,* vol. ii, no. 10, February.

36. *Highway* (1939), January, p. 99

37. *Highway* (1938), November, p. 16.

38. *Highway* (1936), March, pp. 142-3

39. *Highway* (1936), March, p. 138

40. *Highway* (1936), April 1936, p. 160; ibid. (1939) February, p. 120

41. International Cooperative Alliance (1930), papers presented to Special Conference, Vienna, 22 August 1930 (ICA).

42. *Sozialistische Arbeiter Archives,* SAI 2946, Belgian branch ISS to Cher Camarade, n.d., Jean Alland to Cher Citoyen, n.d., typewritten notes on SSI, n/d.

43. SAI 2947, report of International Socialist Students, 5th congress, 1936. British delegates: Howell, Jones, Hewett, Miller, Hamilton-Russell, Helen Jeger, H. Katyenellenbogen, Shield, Collins; observers included Toynbee. John Cornford joined the Young Communist League in London in 1933 and edited *Student Vanguard.* He was an active communist while at Cambridge. See Heinemann, Margaret (1979), 'Three Left Wing Poets' in Clark, John *et al.* (eds), *Culture and Crisis: Britain in the 1930s,* Lawrence and Wishart, London, pp. 115-25.

44. Van der Horst, A. and Koen, E.(eds) (1989), *Guide to the International Archives and Collection at the IISH, Amsterdam* (IISH), pp. ix, x. *William Gillies Correspondence,* notification of founding of IISH, 25 February 1936, WG/IISH

45. Labour and Socialist International (1928), *Report: 3rd congress.*

46. *Conference Report* (1928), International Socialist Youth, International Socialist Federation for Sport and Physical Education, Socialist Education International, August.

47.   *Labour and Socialist International Papers,* LSI/21/10; comment on Woodcraft Folk, Woodcraft Folk to Gillies, 3 December 1936; suggestion on merger, Miss K. Neale, Rebel Lodge to Labour Party, 10 July 1936; Information on camp, SEI to Labour Party, 6 December 1936; patrons requested, Gillies to SEI, 23 December 1936; Trade Union Education Committee Minutes, 18 January 1937. Ben Greene, *Dalton Papers,* British Library of Political and Economic Science, part II 5, Stevenson (*Daily Herald*) to Gillies, 26 April 1936, Gillies to *Daily Herald,* 20 April 1936. Jones, Stephen (1988), *Sport, Politics and the Working Class,* Manchester University Press, pp. 115-6.

48.   *Highway* (1939), April.

49.   *New Leader,* 30 March 1923. Jones, Stephen (1988) op.cit., p. 75 ff.

50.   Groom, Tom (1923), 'Labour and Sport', *Labour Magazine,* vol. ii, no. 1, May, p. 7 ff.

51.   *Sozialistische Arbeiter-Internationale Papers,* Devlieger to Cher Camarade (Adler) 15 May 1925, SAI 2955; Adler to all LSI Bureau, 13 July 1927, SAI 2955; *Conference for Education Questions,* Brussels, 6 February 1928, p. 4, weakness of British, p. 213, hopes of 'spiritual and ethical development'. Delegates to 1927 conference from America, Belgium, Great Britain, Finland, France, Holland, Yugoslavia, Latvia, Luxembourg, Austria, Palestine, Poland, Roumania, Switzerland, Czechoslovakia, Hungary, Lithuania. TUC recognition of BWSF, Jones, Stephen (1988) op. cit., p. 76. Steinberg , David A. (1978), 'The Workers' Sports International, 1920-1928', *Journal of Contemporary History,* 13, p. 236, *passim.*

52.   *Sozialistische Arbeiter Correspondence*, advertising leaflets for 1926 and 1931 Olympiads, printed in German and Esperanto. *William Gillies Correspondence,* notification from LSI of 3rd Workers' Olympiad, 14 September 1936, WG/SPO/1. Jones, Stephen (1988), op.cit., p. 93, p. 107. Polasky, Janet, op.cit.,Vandervelde's attendance, p. 34.

53.   Binet, Tom (1936), *Stepney Citizen,* September.

54.   Jones, Stephen (1988a), 'The European Workers' Sports Movement', *European History Quarterly,* vol. 18, no. 1, January, p. 6; *Conference on Educational Questions* (1928), Brussels, pp. 2-3. *Sozialistische Jugend Internationale Papers,* Windle, Labour Party League of Youth adviser to Ollenhauer, 1 February 1932: 'NWSA organises the sports side of League activities', SJI 742/11. Jones, Stephen (1988), op. cit., pp. 78-81. Jones estimates that 18 per cent BWSF members were women; there was one woman on the NWSA executive.

55.   1937 Olympiad, *William Gillies Correspondence,* memorandum from Gillies to Citrine, 30 November, 1936, WG/SPO/4; Adler's publicity leaflet, 28 July 1937, WG/SPO/5. Jones, Stephen, op. cit., p. 186, death of Tapsell in Spain.

56.   For example, Tanskanen, Petri (1990), *Finnish Labour Heritage,* Labour Heritage, Helsinki.

57.   Steinberg, David A.(1978), *The Workers' Sports Movement,* op. cit., p. 236.

58.   Williams, Chris (1996), 'Britain', in Berger, Stefan and Broughton, David (eds) op.cit., p. 109, pp. 120-1.

59.   Jones, Stephen (1988), op. cit., p. 106.

60.   Howkins, Alun (1980), 'Class Against Class: the Political culture of the

CPGB, 1930-1935', in Gloversmith, Frank (ed.), *Class, Culture and Social Change,* Harvester, Sussex.

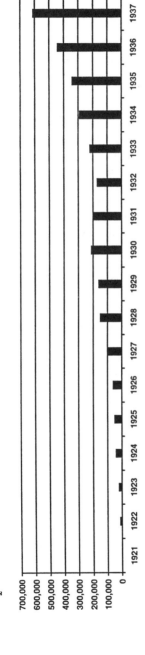

£

Source: Workers' Travel Association Annual Report 1953

Figure 4.1 Workers' travel association annual turnover, 1921–39

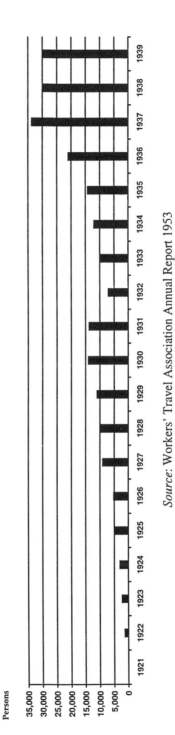

Persons

Source: Workers' Travel Association Annual Report 1953

Figure 4.2 Workers' travel association overseas bookings, 1921–39

CHAPTER FIVE

'Arise ye Starvelings': The Language of Internationalism

As the title of this chapter suggests, the language of internationalism was frequently extravagant, emotive and inspirational and, taken in its broadest sense, extended beyond speech. Arthur Henderson called for 'the international solidarity of the workers'; massed choirs sang 'Arise ye starvelings from your slumbers; arise ye criminals of want'. Three major means of Labour Movement international communication were Esperanto, music and art. Its willingness to use a variety of media was important, because the British Labour Movement was largely monolingual. French critic Romain Rolland justly observed in *New Leader* (3 August 1923): 'the obstacle of obstacles (to internationalism) is language'. International Department records reflect British linguistic incompetence; it is possible to read them entirely in English, because translation was a matter of course. In addition, a translation service was provided notably not by William Gillies, who was no linguist, but by his assistant Christine Howie.[1] The membership had more need to experiment with alternative forms than the leadership. English was an international language and leaders could rely on its acceptance in communication with the Labour and Socialist International and the International Federation of Trades Unions. The leadership aimed to report, to instruct, to negotiate; its means were print, typescript, shorthand, the formalities of reported speech, platform rhetoric. The membership, if it aimed to make personal contact with European workers, could rely neither on ready comprehension, nor translation, nor the services of a secretariat. Use of Esperanto was a possible way to meet some of the membership's needs. Esperantists indeed claimed that use of their language was 'practical internationalism'. Music was not merely accessible but encouraged the expression of intensity of feeling, the articulation of extravagant goals. It could be used to attract recruits, to inform and to entertain.[2] Art could be used to explain events and arouse opinion.

Esperanto

There were serious attempts to use Esperanto to overcome the 'little trouble' of inability to speak foreign languages. As has been stated, it was not essential for the leadership to develop linguistic skills. The willingness of some of the ordinary Labour movement membership to learn Esperanto is, therefore, the more remarkable. At one level, the function of Esperanto was simply to allow people of different nationalities to communicate. Jean Jaurès had recognised this when he called Esperanto: 'le latin de la démocratie' (the Latin of democratic countries). Henri Barbusse was among international socialists giving support, referring to Esperanto as: 'the ABC of the International'... 'it will enable him (the worker) to get in touch with comrades in every country in the world, and to understand their international differences, their hopes and struggles'.[3] The British League of Esperantist Socialists (*Brita Ligo de Esperantistag Socialistoj, BLES*) echoed Gosling in affirming that rank and file contacts should underpin those of the leadership: the latter had the benefit of translation services at conferences but Esperanto could serve the former:

> In the past, Conferences have been field days for Labour leaders ... That helped to contribute to the international weakness of our organisation ... the rank and file all over Europe and America ... Japan and China ... must come into personal contact; and Esperanto gives them the means of doing this.[4]

Barbusse made the same claim as the Workers' Travel Association that war was caused by the lack of this contact: 'wars are caused largely because workers of different countries are ignorant of each other'.[5] BLES asserted that Esperanto could assist international socialist organisation: 'For us workers ... existing differences of language hamper all our attempts at international organisation'. As employers had formed international organisation, so must workers: 'as members of the world wide working class, we are members one of another in a very real sense'.[6] The *Manifesto of Anationalistes* stated that 'les anationalistes estiment désirables et possibles, l'unification des peuples, la complète disparition de tout ce qui est national' (Anationalists consider the unification of people, the complete disappearance of everything with a national identity, both possible and desirable) and that such an organisation in effect created a new international class of people ('En fait, il s'est créé dans la société une nouvelle classe d'hommmes: les dirigeants de la classe ouvrière').[7]

Some Esperantists made a more extensive claim: that using Esperanto was, in itself, socialist international activity. Romain Rolland (*New Leader* 3 August 1923) wrote that: 'the universal language is the most peaceful and the most active ... it transforms the very spirit of man'. The Esperantist journal *La Socialista* explained:

> the hydra heads of national chauvinism are not lopped off by moral slogans about internationalism and the unity of the workers. A common language is practical internationalism, a weakening of the arrogance of great nations who impose their language on other peoples.[8]

Tonkin, the historian of Esperanto, has called this claim of practical internationalism: 'the sacred, grand and important idea that an international language contains in itself ... brotherhood and justice among all peoples'.[9] As is implied here, an homogenous language has been widely accepted as one of the criteria illustrating the existence of a nation state (second in importance perhaps, only to minting a single currency). Identifying language as a factor of

125

nationality between the wars was complicated by changes in the jigsaw pattern of nation states; Hobsbawm, for instance, reminds us that plebiscites between the wars: 'revealed significant bodies of those who spoke one language but opted to join the state of those who spoke another'.[10] Nevertheless, nations protect their languages and, at this deeper level, use of Esperanto challenged one of the bases of the concept of nationalism. Intended as a method of communication at home and abroad, Esperanto replaced the connection of language and location with freedom of expression across territorial borders. In its use at home, Esperanto may have had the additional benefit of overcoming the class connotations of differences in English style and accent.

Esperanto speaks directly of hope. Invented in 1887 (by Ludovic Lazar Zamenhof because of the linguistic and social challenges he faced as a Jew in Poland) it was politically controversial from the outset. Zamenhof believed his language illustrated that: 'We all feel ourselves members of a single nation'. However, the Esperanto Movement split at its first conference into 'neutrals' who eschewed politics and the politically committed.[11] Esperanto was banned in the Third Reich; the Zamenhof family was arrested and Lidia (Zamenhof's daughter) died in Treblinka. Socialist Esperanto groups were formed in France (1905), Britain (1907), Hungary (1909), the Netherlands and Czechoslovakia (1911), China (1913) and Finland (1923). Initially, Esperanto was favourably received in the Soviet Union where a group founded in 1921 evolved in 1929 into the association *Sennacieca Asocia Tutmonda* (SAT) which published *Sennaciulo*. SAT was a broad umbrella organisation to which many socialist groups affiliated. As SAT proved itself insufficiently ready to further Soviet policy, the Third International founded the International of Proletarian Esperantists (1932). Esperantists from both groups were arrested under Stalin's later purges. The Radical Workers' Esperanto Movement was founded in Western Europe.[12]

While the number of international organisations implies popularity it also makes it difficult to quantify Esperanto speakers. The variety of groups was reflected at national level and these were organised on a somewhat anarchic basis; participation was important, not formal membership. The Labour Party conference of 1922 was informed of the post-war re-establishment of the British League of Esperantist Socialists (BLES) that year. BLES advised its members to join SAT and vice-versa. Some members favoured merger of the two bodies. BLES grew quickly from a dozen members in 1922 to an organisation with a respectable number of affiliates; by its 1926 Annual General Meeting these included Independent Labour Party branches and League of Youth, Socialist Sunday Schools, the Workers' Esperanto Club in London and groups in Sheffield, Bradford, Birmingham, Bournemouth, Leeds and Dundee. The Secretary was C. W. Spiller, like WTA's Bowen, of the Postal Workers' union; Mark Starr of the Builders' union was a prominent section head, as was A. Atherton of the Railway Workers. Meanwhile SAT continued to grow and by 1933 had huge lists of members, individual and affiliate, with several groups in each major city including 14 in Manchester. The Socialist Party of Great Britain had its Esperanto group. A Workers' Esperanto Society was set up in Manchester in 1927 and had its own organ, *The Worker Esperantist*. The British Labour Esperanto Society had branches in Stepney, Paddington, Harrow, Watford, Southend, Islington, Sheffield, Gateshead, Edinburgh and Glasgow. Despite its name, the British Labour Esperanto Society, which published its own magazine, *Contact*, was affiliated to the International of Proletarian Esperantists.[13]

Contact differed from other socialist Esperanto publications. It aimed to facilitate private Correspondence between speakers of different languages, arranging translation into Esperanto where necessary but publishing the letters in English; the content was important rather than the use of Esperanto. *Contact* was very obviously under the control of the Third International and carried extensive news of the Soviet Union, although its remit was global (China, the United States, New Zealand, Canada). It was distinguished by the authentic voice of contemporary communist publications; for instance: 'From its inception ... Esperanto has been the plaything of all sorts of dilettantes ... the Workers' Esperanto Movement has rescued the language from the hands of Philistines and turned it into an instrument for the workers' struggle'.[14] In the same issue there was a report that the editorial board of *Pravda Severa* 'notes with satisfaction the model work of the British worker - Esperantist'. Advertisements for *Labour Research* were carried.

The British Labour Movement press abounded with advertisements for courses of study and with Correspondence indicating the attraction of Esperanto. For instance, a *Daily Herald* correspondent (2 January 1925) wrote that after short study he was able to write to people in several European countries. The British League of Esperantist Socialists reported that there were regular Esperanto features in *Plebs, Workers' Dreadnought, Bradford Pioneer* and several trade journals and that there were speeches in Esperanto at Hyde Park: 'it provides a neutral means of communication for people of differing national tongues'.[15] At the British League of Esperantist Socialists' annual general meeting (1926) it was reported that advertisements for lessons had been printed in various trades union journals, for instance *Railway Review:* 'almost every Labour, socialist, trade union and Cooperative journal has Notes and Articles and the *Daily Herald* for some months past has made a regular feature of Esperanto Notes'.[16] The ILP Guild of Youth was especially keen on Esperanto. It adopted a letterhead *La Guildo de Junaluro uzas oficiale Esperanti* (The Guild of Youth uses Esperanto as its official language). Guild of Youth secretary Tetley explained this passion in 1925, writing:

> The various national movements are linked up internationally, but that is not sufficient because only the leaders meet each other ... Those of us who know only one language will be like dumb animals, only able to transmit our thoughts by a glance, a nod of the head or a shake of the hand.[17]

127

The TUC in 1926 voted in favour of adopting Esperanto as the official international language and recommended its use in trade union assisted education. At Ruskin College and by the National Council of Labour Colleges, Esperanto was included in the curriculum in 1926.[18]

Mark Starr used the occasion of the TUC vote to suggest to Adler that LSI adopt Esperanto in Correspondence and encourage national sections to use Esperanto; he offered to put LSI *International Information* into Esperanto journals.[19] There was no record of a reply. Adler's office, as a matter of course, made English, French and German translations of most material received, indicating that it was the British Labour Movement which most benefited from an international language; others of Adler's correspondents commonly spoke their own language and English. In August 1930 SAT sent conference admission cards for LSI visitors but there was no indication that these were used. The League of Nations was more receptive. Its 1922 *Report* compared Esperanto favourably to other international languages (Ido, Esperantide, Occidental) as a 'living language' which was beginning to attain style and was capable of development. The International Labour Office, created by the 1919 Peace Treaty to compliment the League of Nations and initially organised by the French socialist leader Albert Thomas, printed an Esperanto version of its bulletin.[20]

Spiller aimed at 'close and cordial relations with other Esperanto Labour organisations'.[21] This, unhappily, seems to have been the reason why Esperanto fell out of favour with the Labour Party and trades union leadership. The latter was wary of collaboration with communists, openly or through the agency of communist 'front' organisations and Esperanto associations came under suspicion of promoting such collaboration. The official record of connections with Esperanto associations is one of repression, rather than the use of Esperanto; this, again, makes it difficult to estimate numbers involved. Ironically, in view of Stalin's later opposition, because the British Labour Esperanto Association affiliated to the International of Proletarian Esperantists it was perceived as a gateway to the Communist Party of Great Britain. The latter's *Workers' Life* conference in 1927 aimed to:

> bring before the workers of London the necessity of giving full support to the International language Esperanto as a means of breaking down the artificial class barriers which keep workers of the world divided.

The Labour Party and Trades Union Congress leadership were wary of collaboration. *Workers' Life* denounced Marion Phillips for her refusal to read Soviet greetings written in Esperanto to the 1927 Labour Women's conference, implying that she was prejudiced against both Esperanto and the Soviet Union and therefore a poor socialist on either count.[22]

The Esperanto Movement, for its part, showed little enthusiasm for the Labour Movement leadership. Delegates from the Universal Esperanto conference failed, in 1926, to attend a specially convened meeting of the TUC;

Pugh, chair of the TUC General Council was among those who waited in vain for an hour. In 1928 the TUC remitted to IFTU an invitation to attend a conference on Intensification of Workers' Culture, including the use of Esperanto. TUC interest thereafter was limited. Thus, in 1934 Edinburgh trades unionists were warned not to attend meetings of the British Labour Esperanto Association because of communist involvement.[23] However, Sir Walter Citrine sent £10 and greetings to the 1936 SAT Manchester conference from: 'British trades unions, sharing the common aim of friendship and understanding through the development of a strong working class movement throughout the world'.[24]

Citrine's 1936 gesture reflected the greater tolerance of the popular front period and the urgency of the struggle against fascism. Esperanto's claim to represent practical internationalism can be best sustained by its evident utility among the polyglot forces defending the Spanish government; socialist, anarchist and communist groups joined in producing a stencilled *Informa Bulteno* of five to six pages and by late 1936 this had an International Press Service heading.[25] Illustrating communist commitment to the Spanish cause, *Contact* featured Spain regularly from its October/ November 1936 number, when the middle pages were devoted to a report on the defence of Barcelona (July 1936):

> it was indeed a magnificent sight, only comparable to those days of the great French revolution or those of 1917 in Russia. On the streets, soldiers, policemen and workers armed with rifles and machine guns were seen fraternising together.

Contact (June 1935, no. 18) had already reported: 'The Hell of Bayenberg - Truth about Germany's Concentration Camps'. The suppression of Esperanto by Hitler and Stalin illustrated that there was some basis to its claim of 'practical internationalism' because its use was seen as treachery. Its use proclaimed a faith that peoples of different nationalities were able to share not only communication, but a peaceful purpose. As a means of communication it was, perhaps, superseded only by one which needed no words: music.

Music

Music and song can be performed by one or more people to individuals or groups, speaking across language barriers; they are conversations of infinite possibility. Between the wars left-wing musicians were experimenting with notation and re-thinking the relationship of artist and society; new technology such as the gramophone and wireless made it possible to replace sheet music as the means of disseminating musical sound. There was much debate about which type of music was appropriate for socialist communication. Some, such as communist activist and historian Angela Tuckett Gradwell, preferred 'folk' or human music, to 'art' or classical music; other musicians, such as Sidney

Finkelstein, preferred classical, 'truly great "universal music"'; Rutland Boughton wrote that folk music was particularly appropriate to a workers' movement because it derived from working people: 'the sailors' chanties, the sowing, milking, weaving, spinning, shrinking songs spread by the journeyman tramping'. The composer Alan Bush, a founder of the Workers' Music Association, rejected concert music, opera and BBC light music; he sought an alternative notation for a new style of proletarian music.[26]

Sidney Court, conductor of the Deptford (London) Labour choir, wrote with some justice that each civilisation produced its own music. It was, of course, the limitations of a Western, classical inheritance which Angela Tuckett Gradwell sought to escape by insisting on 'human' music. Court illustrated the dangers of musical racism when he wrote that Western melody showed a higher mental development than 'the mere rhythmic beating of drums among the lower races'. Negro spirituals were well known in Britain, performed in 'blackface'and depicting a stereotypical feckless Black cotton worker; related to 'folk' work songs, these were collected in Labour Movement songbooks. Afro-American blues and jazz and African music was beginning to be heard in Britain. The American New Deal included a Federal Arts Project which provided public relief work for unemployed cultural workers. This went some way towards reclaiming the status of Black music; in addition, the American Music League, from 1936, collected Negro songs of protest. This challenge to Western tradition was germane to Bush's argument.[27] Jazz was, of course, among the music banned by the Nazis ('Jazz is vulgar: atonality is insane') and included under the heading 'cultural Bolshevism' by which progressive music was labelled deviant, in contrast to melodic *Reichmusik* which was firmly entrenched in the Western tradition.[28]

The League of Coloured Peoples was set up in Britain in 1931 to recognise the skills of Black musicians but met with opposition from the Musicians' Union and Actors' Association and work permits were hard to obtain. Roland Hayes had been one of the first African Americans to visit Britain and his repertoire included Swahili songs. He was followed by Paul Robeson, who became a popular actor and concert performer in London between the wars. Robeson was a left sympathiser and, to an extent, part of the London Labour scene; he met Labour MPs at the House of Commons in November 1928, lunched next to Ramsay MacDonald and had tea with Ellen Wilkinson and Jimmy Maxton. An early biographer (Marie Seton) records that Robeson equated the class issue in Britain with that of racism in America; that he was politicised by the journalist Frederick Kuh's reports of the Reichstag fire and by a trip to Moscow which involved a day's wait in hostile Berlin. She alleges that Robeson found the station guards reminiscent of the Klu Klux Klan.[29]

Paul Robeson challenged Labour Movement racism by his presence. In his London concerts he sang Negro spirituals arranged by his accompanist Lawrence Brown; he also collected the folk songs of the countries he visited and was a considerable linguist. Robeson sang at the 1937 Spanish Civil War demonstration at the Albert Hall when Attlee reported from the International Brigade. Robeson visited Spain the following year. Robeson acted *Plant in the Sun* for Unity Theatre, an evolution of left theatre groups and the Workers' Theatre Movement and gave a benefit performance of *All God's Chillun,* arranged by Lord Marley's committee, for Jewish refugees.[30] At Sheffield Robeson 'adopted' a hundred Spanish children referred by the Foodship council. These are good examples of the way music entertained, informed, inspired political action. The political content of Robeson's songs was not complex but conveyed important basic points.

Daniel
Didn't my Lord Deliver Daniel
And why not everyman?

All Men are Brothers (to the choral section of Beethoven's ninth symphony)
Build the road of peace before us
Build it wide and deep and long
Speed the slow and check the eager
Help the weak and curb the strong
None shall put aside another
None shall let another fall
March beside me oh my brother
All for one and one for all.

Part of the power of musical language is that it allows expression not merely of opinion, but of emotion, visions and dreams. This allows for full participation, which can heighten a sense of community. The attraction of music had, of course, long been recognised by the British Labour Movement. Its earliest pioneers used music to inform, entertain and recruit members; as Sidney Court wrote: 'Most great reform movements have been helped to success by a song, sometimes light in character and soon forgotten'. Court recommended all Labour Party branches start their own choirs, for entertainment and interest and to broaden their local community base. The Labour Party agreed to sponsor a choral union in 1925. Tom Thomas, of the Workers' Theatre Movement, has written about the universal use of song in the Labour Movement. Angela Tuckett Gradwell remembered: 'singing, dramatic poetry and dancing' in the lively Bristol Labour Movement, which had its own songbook. Her sister (Joan Tuckett) became a founder member of Bristol Unity Theatre.[31] Between the wars, numerous songbooks were available which could draw on this legacy and music continued to inspire gatherings, examples including annual conferences of the trades unions and the Labour Party.

Red Flag was the song most identified with the Labour Party. Written by Jim Connell, Irish Republican socialist, this was conceived as an international song, inspired by the Paris Commune, Irish Republican Movement and the execution of anarchists in Chicago. The second verse, referring explicitly to

131

internationalism, was given in Labour Movement songbooks until the Second
World War:

> Connell, *Red Flag*
> Look round - the Frenchman loves its blaze
> The sturdy German chants its praise
> In Moscow's vaults its hymns are sung
> Chicago swells the surging throng.

Music was less Eurocentric than many other communication media. This was
partly due to connections with African American musicians such as Paul
Robeson, but also due to the unique contribution of the music of the
International Workers of the World (IWW - Wobblies), a group otherwise not
much in evidence as an influence on the British Labour Movement (although
IWW had helped British war resisters). IWW songbooks ran into 50 editions
between the wars, indicating their popularity. These gave expression to socialist
and internationalist sentiment. Examples were the songs written by Joe
Hill(ström), to whom convention generally ascribes the role of IWW organiser
executed in 1915 for his part in the strikes on the United States East Coast.

> Joe Hillström: *Scissor Bill*
> Scissor Bill the foreigner is cussin
> Scissor Bill he says 'I hate a coon'
> Scissor Bill is down on everybody
> The Hottentot, the Bushman and the Man in the Moon.[32]

Joe Hill's death inspired the well known poem by Alfred Hayes set to music
by Earl Robinson in 1936. Paul Robeson sang *Joe Hill* at the 1939 Earl's Court
memorial concert for International Brigaders killed in Spain. Historian Archie
Green has discussed the meaning of the song at length; it commemorates
martyrdom and glorious defiance and has been hugely successful. Green is
wary of mythologising Joe Hill and thus losing sight of the reality of workers'
resistance; he is of the opinion that the IWW split, some members becoming
communist, spread the song; Hayes was a communist when he wrote the poem.
Noting the power of the song, Archie Green asks: 'Why does Hill's cultural
role as a songwriter elevate him above fellow labour organisers and socio-
economic analysts?' It is this power to inspire which made music such a useful
tool of Labour internationalism; socialist songs were the liturgy required to
engage in expressing the faith.[33]

> Hayes / Robinson, *Joe Hill*
> From San Diego down to Maine
> In every mine or mill
> Where working men unite to fight (some versions - defend their rights)
> Its there you'll find Joe Hill.

Questions of dogma did creep into music. Rutland Boughton, for instance, left the London Labour choir for *revolutionary* mass singing. The communist-oriented Workers' Music League warned of *Red Flag:* 'its uneven rhythm tends to cause the marchers to fall out of step'.[34] It preferred *Whirlwinds of Danger, Red Army March* and *Songs of the Workers' Air Fleet.* A communist Red Troupe which toured the coalfields in 1932 gave a programme of songs and sketches which included *Air Fleet*; Angela Tuckett Gradwell (admittedly a biased witness) remembered that after Red Troupe stopped in Bristol: '(they) had us all singing lustily "and every propeller is roaring RED FLAG" for many a long day'.[35] Hans Esler, forced into exile from Germany, wrote *United Front Song,* words by Berthold Brecht, which was first performed by the London Labour Choral Union (8 March 1933, Westminster Theatre, London) conducted by Alan Bush.[36] The *Internationale,* however, while supplying the Soviet Union with its anthem, was sung by all sections of the Labour Movement. Written by Eugene Pottier at the time of the Paris commune and set to music by Paul Degeyter (1888), translated into several European languages, this was performed at the 1910 Second International conference and then adopted by the Third International.

> Degeyter/Pottier, *Internationale*
> Arise ye starvelings from your slumbers
> Arise ye criminals of want
> For reason in revolt now thunders
> And at last ends the age of cant ...
> Then comrades come rally
> And the last fight let us face
> The Internationale
> Unites the human race

The *Internationale* was popular in the Spanish International Brigade. The latter had its own songbook, *Canciones de las Brigadas Internationalas,* although the singing sometimes degenerated to such as *Nellie Dean. Highway* reported a similar mix of popular and revolutionary songs at the Scandinavian English speaking summer school:

> there is plenty of time for ... song. Only a free and happy democracy *can* sing as the Scandinavians sing ... the welkin rang with ... 'Pack up your troubles' etc. ... the babel of tongues, songs of all nationalities and none ... united in one International fraternity.[37]

Harry Pollitt (CPGB secretary) described the many languages at the camp fires of the Republican Army in Spain and how the *Internationale* was 'sung in a medley of every language under the sun'. Despite Pollitt's obvious bias in its favour, its omnipresence in songbooks confirms his claim. Pollitt gave a moving account of hearing the *Internationale* after the Spanish government victory at Teruel: as the troops came back from the front line to be greeted by the local townspeople: 'the fog was so great that the impression given was of a cheery throng of ghosts'; the next morning there were: 'Spanish soldiers' songs, the Italian *Bandiera Rossa*, and German, English and American revolutionary songs. In very truth, it seemed the workers of the world had united'.[38]

Parodies were notable examples of the use of music to inform. They could be enjoyed by those with knowledge of the international situation and could both educate the committed and win converts. Parodies did rely on the audience sharing a common Western musical inheritance to make their point. Given this constraint, Rufus Hogg rightly wrote in *Peoples' Parodies*: 'experience has shown and continues to show, that there is no better method for driving home a point to an audience than by means of a jingle'. An example was his song in support of the League of Nations. Organising the London East End garment trade in the 1920s, the communist Sam Elsbury had perfected the use of parody, together with women strikers who improvised words to music hall songs.[39] In *Proletarian Parodies* Elsbury included a defence of the Soviet Union.

> Rufus Hogg, *Peoples Parodies,* to the tune of *Three Blind Mice*
> Three blind states
> Three blind states
> Fear makes them run
> Fear makes them run
> But if they'll abandon the gun and knife
> And call on the League to abolish strife
> These people will work for a happier life
> In these blind states.

Sam Elsbury, *Proletarian Parodies,* to the tune of *Bring Back my Bonny to me.*

> I've heard all your tales about Russia
> Of the terror that's on over there
> I'm inclined to believe they are mush, Sir
> For to lie you are not particular.
> Please tell, please tell,
> Please tell the truth for a change, a change.

An obvious point is that either gender could sing. It had been the tradition in the Labour Movement that women concerned themselves with entertainment. How to value this has been problematic for historians; en-gendering the rank and file in the context of music might be enlightening. The subject matter of many songs was fighting/dying/organising, but songs that have survived written by and addressed to women include those of the Women's Cooperative Guild, in which the call to arms gives way to the call for peace and there is a conscious link of women's rôles as mothers and carers with internationalism.

> *The Mothers' International*, tune *Faber*, words Mrs. L. Woodward
> Round the world a new song's ringing,
> Listen: Women of all climes
> Tis the mother's song we're singing
> Telling hopes of happier times:
> We will put all hate behind us

We whose hearts are sick and sore
Tired of strife and empty victories
Bear the pangs of war no more.

Similarly, the Socialist Sunday Schools, which were organised on a national basis by Lizzie Glasier Foster and Clarice McNab (Women's Officer of the Scottish Labour Party), used a hymn book whose precepts replaced biblical commandments; nine and ten were:

9. I do not think that those who love their own country must hate and despise other nations, or work for war, which is a remnant of barbarism.
10. I look forward to the day when all men and women will be free citizens of one fatherland and live together as brothers and sisters in peace and righteousness.[40]

Music and song, as part of the language of internationalism, fulfilled several functions; information, entertainment, inspiration. Perhaps, more importantly, they allowed participation, the expression of emotion and opinion. Although we cannot tell how many people sung, it is interesting that some of the songs have survived in performance while speeches and journalism have faded; an indication that rank and file participation, while anonymous, might be more deeply felt and rooted than high profile politics; music helped empower the rank and file internationalist dream.

Wireless

To disseminate Labour Movement music a new medium was available, radio transmission. There was much interest in how socialists could make use of radio. In Britain, the government vested the right to broadcast in the Post Office and from 1922 issued licences. Marconi had bought up international broadcasting rights and socialists feared a Marconi news monopoly.[41] The British press in general (with the exception of the Labour *Daily Herald* and, more surprisingly, the *Daily Telegraph*) were opposed to Post Office ownership partly, in the opinion of the Labour Movement, because many proprietors, including Marconi, belonged to the Empire Press Union. Marconi had created companies abroad to exploit broadcasting patents; for instance, Swiss Marconi gained a 30 year Swiss monopoly in wireless, telegraphy and telephones (1921-2); in Austria, Marconi had 65 per cent of broadcasting rights (1922); in Portugal and Sweden, Marconi had 30 year licences. Marconi had formed the Radio Corporation (Amsterdam); the *Telefunken* Company, Berlin; the *Telegraphie et Telephone Sans Fils*, France. A commercial Radio International company was created to allocate spheres of influence through these. In order:

to safeguard the interests of the Socialist Working Class in respect of wireless and of ensuring that the Workers' Cultural Movement shall have due influence in the further development of wireless in respect of organisation, technique and culture

135

a Wireless International (Arbeiter Radio Internationale) was formed following an International Radio conference (September 1927).[42] Denmark, Germany, Austria, Czechoslovakia and the Netherlands had been represented at the conference and, together with Danzig, Yugoslavia, Luxembourg, Switzerland and Russia formed the branches; Julius Novotny became secretary and headquarters were first, Vienna, then the Netherlands. Arbeiter Radio had its own news sheet which gave technical advice and encouraged the use of radio for socialist propaganda.[43] Although the Labour Party initially 'took the view that in the current circumstances in Britain a socialist organisation of radio hams "would not lead to any productive or appropriate field of activity"', *New Leader* asked for an article on the 'significance of workers' radio international' but failed both to print the article and to carry an accompanying advertisement.[44]

Gillies wondered whether the Labour Party should not buy radio time and 'address the British Working class from Belgium or Holland'.[45] The wisdom of this seemed greater after the loss of the 1931 election. Arbeiter Radio commented that the microphone had been used by Labour's opponents, whereas in Europe there were social democratic listeners who contributed a ready-made platform at election time.[46] No advertising of commercial products was allowed, otherwise the respective social democrat parties had free use of their broadcast time subject to the supervision of a state commission. In the Netherlands, for example, Arbeiter Radio had the use of the transmitter three and a half days a week. Belgian socialists were allocated one evening a week and in Czechoslovakia there were 'Labour hours'. Gillies was favourably impressed until a possible source of controversy became clear; Arbeiter Radio was considering a united front approach and the Third International might want to broadcast to Europe, either separately or under the aegis of Arbeiter Radio. The Soviet Republic had a transmitter in Leningrad and possible designs on another in Luxembourg, where the LSI was also negotiating to buy time.[47] The Belgians had been cautious about this possibility; they refused to join Arbeiter Radio until it was exclusively socialist:

> D'après les décisions provisoires de l'organisation du radio qui englobe aussi moscou nous ne pouvons ... pas tenir compte de l'adhésion des camarades belges (sic).[48]

> (After the provisional decisions of the radio company to include Moscow as well, we cannot count on the Belgian comrades joining.)

Gillies discovered that broadcasting time at Luxembourg was one hundred pounds an hour; in addition there would be speakers' travelling costs and expenses; he therefore told James Middleton: 'my advice is: keep on the right side of the BBC'. The Luxembourg transmitter began broadcasting in November 1932, a Luxembourg Broadcasting corporation having been formed on French initiative. Gillies was of the opinion that although the aim was to create '"a Peace Transmitter" it will probably be little else than an advertising transmitter selling its sending time to anyone'.[49] On Gillies's advice, the Labour

136

Party refused to send a delegate to Arbeiter Radio executive committee meetings.[50] The market was quickly growing; for instance, WEA raised money to supply wireless sets to South Wales unemployment centres.[51] Nevertheless, it seemed Gillies' fears had been prophetic There were arguments about the use of air time before the Nazi coup d'état. Afterwards, Philip Noel Baker wrote: 'the French armament firms will *now* be glad to allow German socialists to use the station in order to criticise and inflame the German government still further'.[52] Meanwhile, the *Volkradio* in the Third Reich preserved its listeners from decadence by lacking 'superfluous frequencies'.[53] Gillies wrote to ask the Luxembourg Party Ouvrier about the new station. In 1936 Arbeiter Radio wrote to ask what May Day broadcasts the Labour Party had made; Gillies had to reply none.[54] Labour caution, due to costs and fears of communist influence, meant that Labour lost a chance of capturing a home audience and an opportunity of influencing the development of an international working class culture. By 1939 conditions were impossible and Arbeiter Radio seemed a lost cause.

Art

Arnold Hauser has written: 'The artist can only become an artist by entering the relations between man' ... 'The artist unfolds these forces in the service either of a ruler ... or of a particular community, rank in society or social class'.[55] In common with musicians, left artists were rethinking their role in society and benefiting from technological inventions which encouraged visual experimentation. The art market was changing, private exhibitions by groups and individuals enabling direct sales to the public. The identity of artist, of audience and appropriate content were issues. While left artists in their professional capacity were not, in the ordinary sense, members of the Labour Movement rank and file, creating rather their own vanguard, it was the potential and existing broad Labour Movement membership which they addressed. They worked at the junction of worker/ proletarian/ vanguard.

Left artists who sought to serve the rank and file had an international perspective; their political commitment dictated both client group and subject matter. In so serving, they contributed to the idea of internationalism by providing it with images; making the vision visible. David Mellor is of the opinion: 'One of the key themes of British cultural history in the 1930s, in its relation to British painting, is the tension between internationalism and nationalism'. Left artists were reacting to what Mellor has termed 'cultural nationalism', which they identified with the 1931 National government.[56] Serving the different imperatives of a national or international vision was, in fact, a matter for resolution by artists throughout Europe between the wars. This was made clear by the 1995/6 Council of Europe exhibition *Art and Power* which recreated the 1937 Paris exhibition. The latter 'concentrated public attention on the tensions of a confused and deeply divided Europe'...'German and Russian pavilions confronted each other, symbolising the ideological battle between Fascism and Communism' while the Spanish pavilion publicised the Republican Government's struggle and the Italian pavilion paid 'tribute to an Imperial past and an Imperial future'.[57] Hobsbawm has commented: 'Art has been used to reinforce the power of political rulers and states since the ancient Egyptians', by glorifying power, creating a 'public drama', providing education and propaganda.[58] International art sought rather to subvert the powerful, to visualise connections between people; but also, of course, to educate and publicise.

Artists and artists' groups

The rôle of the artist in society has, of course, been a matter of discussion and propaganda at least since Vasari's *Lives of the Artists*. The Vienna workshop (since 1903) and the Bauhaus movement (from 1919) were contemporary groups requiring social involvement. Critic Stanley Cusson wrote: 'Only in the last two centuries have some artists, by being segregated, created an aesthetic of their own that excludes the client and presupposes that an artist can create in private for the pleasure of no-one but himself'.[59] F.R. O'Neill wrote that: 'Art is a social activity'; he sought to discover 'the different ways in which the artists of the world have been of value, or benefit to mankind'.[60] Some workers, such as E. Davison, the Glasgow rail worker, created a proletarian atelier:

> Their pleasure is to be regarded as that of worker artists whose art is the free expression of experience and idealism arising from personal service to one noble cause

as *Labour Magazine* reported in unusually visionary language.[61] *New Leader* (12 April 1929) reported the foundation of an ILP Artists' Guild.

Painters such as Paul Nash and Edward Burra formed Unit 1 which had 'Labour Party sympathies' and in which 'the International Creed was ... reasserted'.[62] Artists' International, formed to honour the Russian revolution, was the longest lasting and is the best known of groups addressing working people and promoting an international perspective. Some of the original organising group were communists but, adding Association to its title, AI soon extended its reach by moving, simultaneously with the Communist Party, from the extremes of political correctness to extend its reach. Artists in membership in the earlier years worked mainly for London advertising agencies. AI did not elect its members; it was able to grow, as Katy Deepwell has written, because the organisation 'defined their professional class of artist members through their art school training and participation in recognised forms of professional exhibitions'. Deepwell is of the opinion that whereas in general, trends in the art market did not favour women, AIA's political commitment attracted women (a tiny minority in the Royal Academy). Women formed roughly 40 per cent of AIA membership and were active at all levels, organising and exhibiting; working class artists in membership were, however, overwhelmingly male.[63] Although AIA remained 'gender blind'[64] in that artists tended to depict men in heavy industry and women at home, it has helped to provide a record of women's experience in left activity; for instance Pearl Binder's *Chalking Squad* which portrays a women marking a wall to exhort workers to 'unite against fascism,' while her male companion stands guard. AIA account books, kept since March 1937,[65] show a large and varied membership which included well-known artists such as Vanessa Bell, Augustus John, Nan Youngman, Pearl Binder, Graham Bell, the cartoonists Gabriel and James Boswell, societies such as that for Industrial Artists in addition to the Society for Cultural Relations with USSR. AIA's orientation remained left and Russophile; several of its members visited the Soviet Union.

AIA defined its aims through a process of discussion and debate. Representing artists, campaigning for better pay and conditions was its first object although it had a special idea of artistic work and identity: 'The days when the artist was regarded as a Romantic individualist are over' stated AIA when calling a congress in 1937: 'he has proved himself a vital asset in our industrial and social life'. The artist could not be separated from 'the life of the people' and 'industrial production'.[66] In its travelling exhibition catalogue for 1939 AIA repeated that its inspiration came from 'the life and work of the people'.[67] AIA's constitution was built up from fundamentals - peace, democracy, cultural development - and these were plausibly linked to artistic needs; peace was a necessity for artistic production; democracy was essential if people were to follow their own tastes ; social values should privilege 'the vigour and vitality of culture'.[68] The further connection was then made that: 'the freedom of artists to carry out their work is seriously threatened by the spread of Fascism and the preparations for war'.[69] Building on these fundamentals, the AIA News Sheet of September 1938 framed a draft constitution and announced arrangements for electing a committee.[70] These proposals were made after AIA representatives had attended the International Peace conference and the decisions of the latter were also recorded as AIA aims: they included the withdrawal of all foreign troops from Spain and the restoration of the trading rights and loan facilities of the Spanish government; a ban on the sale of material used in air raids by aggressor states; the evacuation of civilians from threatened areas; protection of food ships; a world commission for victims' aid and help for Spain and China. These various aims, artistic, political and international, were drawn up in a preliminary draft for a meeting on 14 October 1938 at which they were adopted.[71] The heads of the constitution were 'roughly classified' in a flyer as first, 'exhibitions, paintings, drawings, sculpture and engraving to demonstrate the unity of artists holding the most diverse of aesthetic opinions in support of the aims of AIA'; second, fundraising; third, attending foreign exhibitions and showing foreigners' work at home; fourth, work with the Peace Propaganda Bureau; fifth, political activity on issues such as the situation in Abyssinia and in Spain and participation in the International Peace Campaign.[72]

These activities were not to be pursued solely by the central body; AIA was keen to recruit local support. These included Ashington, the Working Men's College, Sheffield, which had a 'particularly effective May Day greeting card which was sold and used extensively'.[73] Once it had defined its aims, AIA gave detailed instructions for the creation and maintenance of these local branches. These instructions emphasise the political activity expected, including propaganda, letters to local papers, affiliation to local peace councils, Spain and China committees, and Left Book Club groups. The artists' work, including this political activity, was to be the focus and organising principle of the groups.[74] Of course, AIA aims were defined and local groups instructed at a time of popular front activity, when political activity at local level was at its broadest.

Content and methodology

Art was less participative, more propagandist than music, but the debate on content was similar. That on realism *versus* surrealism replaced that on folk music *versus* classical. Camille Huysmans, secretary of the pre-war Second International favoured the former; he wrote in *Labour Magazine* of Meunier, 'the sculptor of modern industrial labour'.[75] The Soviet Republic gave its patronage to realist art. Cliff Rowe, one of AIs' founders, had spent 18 months in Moscow and was among those influenced by the Red Army's patronage.[76] Realism had a substantial body of support among the group of left intellectuals and critics who debated style and content of art, its social meaning and the role of the artist in the 1930s. For instance, Montague Slater praised the Red Army painter Dmitri Tsalpine whose work was 'a step forward in our knowledge of what socialist art is going to look like', a craftsman who has beaten 'the old world artists at their own game'. F.D. Klingender, however, was of the opinion that Tsalpine had been in the West for too long and showed the influence of its outdated mode. Marxist intellectual Alick West wrote: 'the fight between socialism and fascism is the reality'.[77]

Surrealism, on the other hand, was thought by Herbert Read to illustrate dialectic materialism, thesis, reproduction of experience; antithesis, internal workings of the artist's mind; synthesis, surrealism. He wrote that revolutionary art was not 'an injunction to paint pictures of red flags, ... factories or machines' but that:

REVOLUTIONARY ART IS CONTROVERSIAL
REVOLUTIONARY ART IS INTERNATIONAL
REVOLUTIONARY ART IS REVOLUTIONARY
(*sic,* Read's emphasis).[78]

The growing strength of the surrealist camp in the late 1930s was, in Brigitte Libmann's opinion, to the detriment of women artists because the surrealists' ideology of sexuality, which privileged the pursuit of passion to discover 'truth and dreams', was matched by an ideology of gender which perceived woman as child or muse. The *Living Art in England 1939* exhibition provided funds for refugees and was a focus for the distribution of anti-fascist literature: Libmann notes that Lee Miller, the woman surrealist, broke ranks to use realist photography in order to record her anger.[79] The leaflet the surrealists group produced, at the time of the Artists International congress against non-intervention in Spain, ended with a call for the united front and an expression of political and artistic commitment:

> we demand ... the vindication of the psychological rights of man and the liberation of the intelligence and imagination ... we intervene as poets, artists, and intellectuals by violent or subtle subversion and by stimulating desire.[80]

As musicians used parody, so artists used posters, cards and cartoons to inform and entertain, also expecting a degree of knowledge in their audience. Examples were the postcards designed by the Catalonian *Commissariat de Propaganda* and distributed in Spain, and Christmas cards bearing scenes from the civil war. These used simple devices so that their meaning was immediately apparent. Each daily paper had its cartoonist; although their productions were designed for immediate consumption, they often required relatively sophisticated political knowledge from their audience. Cartoons, therefore, tended to bear an explicatory, blunt inscription that paraphrased the whole drawing and a note that showed its derivation. Examples of cartoonists were Gabriel, and James Boswell[81] from the *Daily Worker;* Geza Szörbel, a refugee from Czechoslovakia and Michael Biro, 'a socialist cartoonist startling Europe' whose work was shown in *New Leader* from 8 February 1929. *Teachers' International* featured Anton Hansen, a Danish artist: 'his language is that of the great revolutionary artists ... intense pity for the poor'.[82] Most moving were the drawings Spanish children sent to the International Solidarity Fund. These took the form of illustrated postcards and little booklets printed by potato cut on thin, poor quality paper, cardboard and wrapping paper, with essays on 'How the soldiers for the Republic are fighting' and drawings, collated into booklets tied with Republican ribbon.[83] Each bore the child's age range. They are a reminder that the language of art does not depend on professional artists for expression and that it can convey visions and dreams.

A chief method of AIA operation was the big exhibition. *No More War* and *The Social Scene* (1934) were the earliest. Tom Wintringham thought the former showed more acquaintance with working class political movements than with the working class itself, while the latter was 'something between a demonstration and a national gallery'.[84] Klingender, whose opinion was that art should be 'primarily a revolutionary agent for the transformation of (that) reality', would, of course, have approved this orientation.[85] At *Artists against*

Fascism and War (1935), 350 artists showed 600 works. AIA also produced posters for the 1935 general election and others critical of the Royal Jubilee. One exhibition was devoted to Spain (1936). The 1937 exhibition included a section on peace posters and leaflets from Britain, France, the Netherlands, Spain, and the United States, in addition to examples of press advertising and broadsheets issued by the Peace Publicity bureau. AIA matched epistemology and methodology; the 1939 exhibitors were asked to provide mounts without frames and to give an account of the underlying idea and method of production; the exhibits were thus accessible.[87] Easel painting was described as a thing of the past; the future was lithograph and political comment.[88] The 1939 catalogue advertised lithograph and graphic art so that originals could be sold cheaply, to reach a wide audience.[89]

Activities

With the proceeds of mass exhibitions, cabarets and subsidised portraiture, AIA provided an ambulance for use by Republican troops in Spain. Paul Robeson flew from Moscow to attend the meeting at which the ambulance was dedicated. AIA also arranged international exhibitions and AIA artists exhibited in Paris (1935), the Soviet Union (1934/5) and the Netherlands (1936).[90] AIA established contacts with French and Belgian groups and the John Reed clubs in America. That some of these activities did have an impact was illustrated by a reported attack made by Hitler on modern art and, in particular, the exhibition of works by German emigrés,[91] AIA reported this as an attack on 'those who think truth, those who see truth, those who speak truth'. *See truth* is a striking phrase indicating the way in which art could make visions visible. Its popular front approach and commitment to making political art accessible was shown by AIA's participation at the Aid Spain demonstration at Trafalgar Square in September 1938. Local authorities would not allow a planned public showing of work in the Square and surrounding streets, so blank banners were taken on which artists pinned drawings made of the crowd; a collection was taken and the drawings auctioned off in the following week. Seven hundred artists, actors and writers signed the AIA petition.[92] AIA perceived May First preparations as 'the greatest demonstration against Reaction and the inevitable development of Fascism and War ... an awakener not only for our pro-Fascist government but for the irresponsible Die Hards of Transport House'. AIA operated its own refugee committee. To James Fitton of the AIA, 'Art seemed to be the only international language that made sense in those days'.[93]

Picasso, in an interview in 1945 insisted that: 'Painting is not done to decorate apartments. It is an instrument of war for attack and defence against the enemy'.[96] An artist connected to AIA, Felicia Browne, was killed in Spain. Her sketches show a strength and confidence that perhaps indicate she had reconciled her special skills and her socialism; she was making the struggle visible, as AIA artists attempted to do in their exhibitions. Hauser's insistence on the necessity of artistic commitment is clarified by Browne's oft-quoted description of the paralysis she had experienced before going to Spain:

> You say I am evading things by not painting or making sculptures ... I cannot make it ...I can only make out of what is valid and urgent to me. If painting and sculpture were more valid and urgent to me than the earthquake which is happening in the (Spanish) revolution, or if the two were reconciled so that the demands ... didn't conflict ... I should paint or sculpt.[95]

Conclusion

Felicia Browne's tragedy reminds us that the people who formed the Labour Movement membership were not passive bystanders to their leadership's international activity but had their own concerns and their own methods of expression. Esperanto, music and art met the needs of the membership, rather than the leaders; the latter had their own means of communication, not least the services of the Labour Party International Department.

Labour Magazine reported the pleasure of 'worker' artists in expressing their 'experience and idealism'. Esperanto, music and art served the purpose of entertainment for the Labour Movement membership; exhibitions and concerts seem to have been well supported. The importance of this function has been often overlooked and might supply the answer to Archie Green's question ('why does Hill's cultural role ... elevate him?') about the legendary labour organiser who achieved posthumous fame in song. An entertaining approach may have made the international scene more accessible; after 1933, it may have been one way of dealing with the 'sensational tales', the fears and horrors of fascism.

Esperanto, music and art were ways of making contact with other peoples. It is interesting that musicians and Esperantists were able more easily to reach beyond Europe than the Labour and Socialist International or the International Federation of Trades Unions. In the field of music, in particular, connections were maintained with American Labor when more formal channels had broken down. It was not unconnected that musicians dealt with racism more effectively than, for example, Ernest Bevin denouncing the use of 'Moors' in Spain. Joe Hill's *Scissor Bill* tackled racism direct, while Paul Robeson made a living challenge. The Labour membership learnt from songs and cartoons how to deal with issues such as racism, the activities of the League of Nations or the situation in Czechoslovakia. Although the writers of parody and the cartoonists had their own bias, they helped balance opinion so that there was some justice for Artists' International claim that people were helped to 'see truth, speak truth'. As Rufus Hogg wrote, there was 'no better method ... than a jingle' for driving a point home.

At a deeper level than the communicative and educative function of these means of expression, lay that of inspiration. Music and art appeal to the emotions through choice of melody, use of a rousing chorus, words that appeal to the senses ('shrouded ... our martyred dead', 'Whirlwinds of danger are raging around us', 'For our eyes have seen the vision'), representation of scenes of battle. Hence the 'Call to Arms' of national armies, the use of flags, banners and pictorial ephemera that Michael Billig has called 'Banal Nationalisms'.[96] Internationalism needed also its 'Call to Arms' ('We'll keep the Red Flag flying', 'Arise', 'Come rally' 'March beside me'); a demand that the concerns of other peoples be addressed, that class interests be espoused across national and linguistic barriers. Internationalist music and art met this need because they encouraged engagement. In common with Esperanto, they were participative forms of communication; not only were they dialogues between exponent and audience, but they assumed group participation. Thus Esperanto developed, lived as a language; in music new forms were discussed and style fiercely debated; left artists experimented with big exhibitions, lithographs, street portraiture. In the camps of the Spanish civil war one could see the zenith of such participation.

All three media were affected by the split of international socialism into communist and socialist wings. Esperanto was the biggest sufferer, under suspicion during the hostile 'class against class' phase. Communists were cautious about using *Red Flag,* Gillies mistrusted Radio Luxembourg and Artists' International added Association to its name to signify a more open approach. Yet all three also offered a meeting ground for the broad Labour Movement membership. One could not proscribe a song in a democracy; but the continuing strength of diverse international communication was exemplified by the actions of the dictators in banning Esperanto and by the Nazi racist condemnation of 'degenerate' music and art and promotion of '*Reichsmusik*' and '*Volkradio*'.

Esperantists made the further claim that by use of an international language they practised internationalism. Esperanto societies outlasted the LSI and IFTU; internationalist art also survives and is exhibited, the reverse face of the 'Art of the Dictators'; the International was heard in Tiannamen Square and the *All Men are Brothers* accompanies international events as varied as the fall of the Berlin Wall and European football matches. Felicia Browne's comments about creativity are germane; that the international faith needs to be freshly experienced and that this must be an individual, as well as a group phenomenon.

Notes

1. *International Department Records, William Gillies Correspondence,* WG/TRANS, *passim.*
2. The importance of making space for entertainment within the Labour Movement has been underestimated. This is a gendered issue, because women so often volunteered, or were conscripted into the role of entertainment

provider. Collette, Christine (1991), 'New Realism, Old Traditions', *Labour History Review* 56 (1), Spring.

3.   *Socialismo,* Esperanto Centre archives, London, E335; Jean Jaurès, cited in *La Socialista,* August 1931, E335 (05); Henri Barbusse, cited British League of Esperantist Socialists executive committee, 1 April 1923, E335 (06).

4.   British League of Esperantist Socialists (1923), *Esperanto and Labour,* July p. 617.

5.   Henri Barbusse, op. cit.

6.   British League of Esperantist Socialists (1923), *Esperanto and Labour,* July p. 4.

7.   Avid, L.G. and Waringheim G., (1931), *Manifeste des Anationalistes,* Paris pp. 4-5.

8.   *La Socialista* (1931), August, Esperanto Centre, London E335 (05).

9.   Tonkin, Humphrey, et al. (eds & trans.) (1933), Janton, Pierre, *Esperanto: Language, Literature and Culture,* New York, p. 35.   I am indebted to Deborah Chirrey (Edge Hill University College) and Stephen Revell (Glasgow University) for discussion of these points.   For the importance of currency, witness the current debate about European coinage and national sovereignty. On language, cf. the conscious development of the Russian language at the end of the eighteenth century and Hebrew in the twentieth century.

10. Hobsbawm, E.J. (1991), *Nations and Nationalisms,* Cambridge, p 134; see also ibid., p. 165, American concern over hispanophone immigration and the 1980 movement to declare English the offical spoken language; p. 140 for the use of Spanish, rather than Catalan, by anarchist republicans seeking to avoid bourgeois/nationalist connotations.   See also Smith, A.D.(1988), *The Ethnic Origin of Nations,* Blackwell, Oxford, p. 27 for opinion that language is 'irrelevant and divisive for the sense of ethnic community';   Anderson, Benedict (1971), *Imagined Communities,* Verso, London 1991, p. 67 for importance of a 'national print language' to developing countries.

11. Tonkin, Humphrey, et al., op. cit., Zamenhof cited p. 29.

12. Heller, Wendy (1985), *Lidia: The Life of Lidia Zamenhof, Daughter of Esperanto,* George Ronald, *passim* and p. 236, persecution; Large, Andrew (1985), *The Artificial Language Movement,* Blackwell, Oxford, p. 102 ff. on SAT/SEU;   Tonkin, Humphrey, et al., op.cit., p. 33 ff. persecution. Noltenius, Rainer et al., (1993), *Ilustrita Historio de la Laborista Esperanto Movada* Dortmund, includes a full explanation of the different groups.

13. *Socialismo*, British League of Esperantist Socialists, Esperanto centre, London, E335 (06) (42); SAT 335; SAT *Jarlibro* (year book) 335 (06) (52). Affiliation to Proletarian International, Large, op. cit., p. 109.

14. *Contact,* 15 March 1935.

15.   BLES, (1923), *Esperanto and Labour,* op. cit.

16. *Socialismo,* British League of Esperantist Socialist Annual General Meeting, 1926, Esperanto Centre, London E335 (06) (42).

17. *Sozialistische Jugend International Papers,* International Institute of Social History, Amsterdam, Tetley to Dear Comrade, 13 October 1925, SJI 745/12.

18. Trades Union Congress Records, Modern Records Centre, Warwick University, *Esperanto* MSS 292 903 (i); F. Smith, secretary of Ruskin College to Citrine, 17 February 1926; Millar, National Council of Labour Colleges to Citrine, 1 March 1926.

19. SAI 2954 Starr to Dear comrade (Adler) n.d. 1926.

20. *Informservo de Internacia Labora Oficejo* 1922-7; *Bulteno de ILO* 1926-32, E331 (06), Esperanto Centre, London.

21. *Socialismo,* British League of Esperantist Socialists secretary's report 10 March 1933 E335 (06) (42), Esperanto Centre, London.

22. *Workers' Life,* 20 May 1927.

23. Failed delegation, Frith, TUC secretariat, to R. Kreuz, Secretary to International Committee of Esperantists, 25 July 1926, Trades Union Congress Records, *Esperanto*; refusal to attend 1928 conference, Citrine to Mark Starr, 28 February 1926; Isa Davison, secretary of Edinburgh branch of NUASA to TUC, 24 May 1934, reply, 30 May 1934, Trades Union Congress Records, *Esperanto.*

24. Telegram from Citrine to Esperanto congress, 13 July 1936, Trades Union congress Records, *Esperanto;* 16th SAT Congress, Manchester 1936, *Socialismo* Esperanto Centre, London.

25. CNT/AIT/FAI *Informa Bulteno.*

26. Tuckett Gradwell, Angela (author, worker for civil liberties, historian, journalist, aviator, hockey player, folk musician), interview with author, unrecorded, 23 August 1988; Finkelstein, Sidney (1924), *Composer and Nation: The Folk Heritage in Music,* Lawrence and Wishart, London; Boughton , Rutland (1923), 'The Arts as Part of the Workers' Life', *Labour Magazine,* vol. ii, no. 7, November, Bush, Alan (1935/37), Music and the Working Class Struggle', *Left Review,* vol. II, p. 646. Use of gramaphone, Williams, J.R. (1936), 'Gramaphone Notes', *Highway,* April, p. 176.

27. Court, Sidney (1924), *Labour Magazine,* vol.ii, no.10, February. Pickering, Michael (1990), 'A Jet Ornament to Society', in Oliver, Paul (ed.), *Black Music in Britain,* Open University Press, Milton Keynes, p. 38 ff. Rye, Howard (1990), 'Fearsome Means of Discord: Early Encounters with Black Jazz' in Oliver, ibid., p. 51.

28. Programme notes (1995/6), *Entartete Musik* exhibition, Royal Festival Hall, London. Exhibition created by Dumling, Albrecht & Girth, Peter, cited, Hans Pfitzner, 1933.

29. Seton, Marie (1958), *Paul Robeson,* Dobson, London. Seton wrote to support the campaign for the restoration of Robeson's passport after its confiscation for alleged UnAmerican activities and glosses over Robeson's political position but her style is that of the communist journalist portraying the communist hero and the stages by which he acquired revolutionary consciousness. Southern, Eileen (1982), *Biographical Dictionary of Afro-American and African Musicians,* Greenwood, Connecticut & London, p. 232. Southern, Eileen (1983), *The Making of Black Americans,* Norton, New York & London, p. 404 ff.

30. Seton, Marie (1958), ibid. Chambers, Colin (1989), *The Story of Unity Theatre,* Lawrence and Wishart, London.

31. Tuckett Gradwell, Angela (n.d.), 'The People's Theatre in Bristol', *Our History,* no. 72, p. 2.; Tom Thomas (1972), 'The Workers' Theatre Movement: Memoirs and Documents', *History Workshop Journal,* no.4 includes reference to NEC sponsorship of choral union. See also Court, Sidney (1924), op. cit. See also Yeo, Stephen (1977), 'The Religion of Socialism' *History Workshop,* 4, Autumn, pp. 34-5. A recent example is given

by Nelson Mandela of the contribution music can make to a political movement: Of African music, Mandela (1995) writes: 'It can ignite the political resolve of those who might otherwise be indifferent to politics ... Politics can be strengthened by music, but music has a potency that defies politics, *Long Road to Freedom*', Abacus, London, p. 209.

32. For IWW war resistance, see Weller, Ken (1985), *Don't be a Soldier,* Journeyman, London. *Scissor Bill, IWW Songs,* 23rd edition, 1928.

33. Green, Archie (1993), *Wobblies, Pile Butts and Other Heroes: Laborlore Explorations,* University of Illinois, Urbana and Chicago, p. 78 ff. Joe Hill, Wobblies' split p. 82, songwriters' fame, p. 91. The text for *Ballad of the Americans* was by John Latouche, Paul Robeson made the first radio broadcast. Richards, Sam (1983), 'Joe Hill: a Labour Legend in song', *Folk Music Journal,* vol. 4, no. 4, pp. 307-84 traces the song in Britain; Richards writes that Robeson first sang Joe Hill at Earl's Court in 1949, but this seems to be a reference to the 1939 concert described by Seton. Richards's opinion is that Seton had 'little time' for Robeson's politics (p. 372) but he appears not to have read between the lines of her work (see n. 28 above).

34. *Workers' songs no 1,* Workers' Music League (nd.). Boughton, Rutland (1923), 'The Arts as Part of the Workers' Life', *Labour Magazine,* vol. ii, no. 7 November, my emphasis.

35. *March Song of the Red Army,* words by Douglas Robson, arr. R. Liebich to *Vichrey Vrazhdyebuye, 16 Songs for 6d,* Lansbury's Labour Weekly, nd; *Soviet Airmen's Song,* text WTM Collective, *Workers' Song Book,* WTM, nd. Tuckett Gradwell, Angela, *The People's Theatre in Bristol,* op. cit., p. 4.

36. Esler, Hans, *Entartete Musik,* op. cit.

37. *Highway* (1937), April, p. 190.

38. *Pollitt visits Spain,* (International Brigade Dependants' Aid Committee, February 1938) p. 18, p. 8.

39. Hogg, Rufus (1938), *Peoples' Parodies* distributed by Collett's bookshop; Elsbury, A.B. (nd.), *Proletarian Parodies,* see also *Rego and Polikoff Strike Songs* (1983), United Clothing Workers' Trade Union, published in facsimile by Centreprise, London.

40. Curtis (ed.), *New Songs for Cooperators,* (Birmingham, n.d.). Liddington, Jill (1989), *The Long Road to Greenham,* Virago, London.

40. *Socialist Sunday School Hymnbook* (1910), Socialist Sunday School Union.

41. Ammon, C.G. (1923), 'A Bid for the Worldwide Wireless Monopoly', *Labour Magazine,* vol. ii, no. 8, December.

42. *William Gillies Correspondence,* Arbeiter Radio handbook, 1927, WG/LW; *Sozialistische Arbeiter-Internationale* papers, Conference Report 5.9.27 sent to Adler SAI 2932.

43. Arbeiter Radio *Nachrittenblatt,* no. 1, nd.

44. Ibid.

45. *William Gillies Correspondence,* Gillies to Middleton, 2 December 1931, WG/LW.

46. *William Gillies Correspondence,* Arbeiter Radio to Gillies, 12 November 1931, WG/LW.

47. *William Gillies Correspondence,* Gillies to Adler, 24 October 1932, note from Arbeiter Radio, November 1932, WG/LW.

48.   *Sozialistische Arbeiter-Internationale papers,* Van Roosboeck (?) to Adler, 6 June 28, SAI 2933.

49.   *William Gillies Correspondence,* Gillies to Middleton, 2 December 1932, WG/LW.

50.   *William Gillies Correspondence,* Gillies to Arbeiter Radio, 18 May 1932, WG/LW.

51.   *Highway* (1936), March.

52.   *William Gillies Correspondence,* Philip Noel Baker to Gillies, 29 June 1933, WG/LW.

53.   *Entartete Musik,* op. cit.

54.   *William Gillies Correspondence,* Gillies to Arbeiter Radio, 16 April 1936, WG/LW.

55.   Hauser, Arnold (1971), 'Propaganda, Ideology and Art' in Meszaros, Istvan (ed.), *Aspects of History and Class Consciousness,* Routledge and Kegan Paul, London, p. 128.

56.   Mellor , David (1980), 'British Art in the 1930s' in Gloversmith, Frank (ed.), *Class, Culture and Social Change,* Harvester, Sussex p. 186.

57.   Exhibition notes, XXIII Council of Europe Exhibition, *Art and Power under the Dictators 1930 - 1945,* Hayward Gallery, London, 26 October 1995 - 21 January 1996.

58.   Hobsbawm , E.J. (21 October 1995) 'Art of Darkness', *Independent.*

59.   Cusson , Stanley (1933), *Artists at Work,* Harrap, London p. 16.

60.   O'Neill, F.R. (1939), *The Social Value of Art,* Psyche Monograph, no. 12, Kegan Paul, Trench, Tubner and Co., London.

61.   'Socialism and Art' (1923), *Labour Magazine,* vol. I, no. 10, February, p. 461.

62.   Mellor, David, op. cit.

63.   Rickaby, Tony (1978), 'Artists International', *History Workshop Journal,* 6, Autumn; Morris, Linda and Radford, Robert (1983), *The Story of Artists International Association 1933-1953,* Oxford, cited, Fitton p. 10; Deepwell, Katy, 'A Fair Field and no Favour: Women Artists working in Britain between the Wars' in Oldfield, Sybil, op. cit. pp. 150-151. Deepwell, Catherine (1991) 'Women Artists in Britain between the Two World Wars', Phd. thesis, University of London.

64.   Deepwell , Catherine (1991) op. cit., p. 354, p. 353 ff.

65.   *Artists International Association Archives,* Tate Gallery, London, AIA account books 7043.11.1.

66.   Ibid, Catalogue for 1937 exhibition 7043.3.3.

67.   Ibid, Catalogue for travelling exhibition 7043.3.4 Jan 1939.

68.   Ibid, Catalogue for 1937 exhibition 7043.3.3.

69.   Ibid, flyer for Nov., 1935 exhibition 7043.4.1.

70.   Ibid, *Artists News Sheet* September 1938, 7043.19.1.

71.   Ibid, Constitution 7043.18.1, 7043.18.2.

72.   Ibid, flyer nd. (1938) 7043.17.3.

73.   Ibid, catalogue for 1937 exhibition 7043.3.3, AIA news sheet 7043.19.2.

74.   Ibid, AIA news sheet 7043.19.3.

75.   Huysmans, Camille (1924), 'Meunier', *Labour Magazine,* vol. ii, no. 2, June.

76.   Morris, Linda and Radford, Robert (1983) op. cit.

77.   Slater, Montague (1934/1935), *Left Review,* vol. I, p. 236 and (1935/1937) vol. ii, p. 83; Klingender, F.D. (1935/1937), *Left Review,* vol. 2, p. 38. See

Chambers, Colin (1989), *The Story of Unity Theatre*, Lawrence and Wishart, London, p. 132 for account of Klingender and others addressing Unity Theatre weekend and summer schools on Marxism and its relationship to cultural and political events.

78. Read, Herbert (1936), 'Surrealism', *Left Review*, vol.ii, July supplement and (1935), 'What is Revolutionary Art?', *Five on Revolutionary Art*, Lawrence and Wishart, London, cited, p. 22.

79. Libmann, Brigitte (1994), 'British Women Surrealists - Deviants from Deviance?' in Oldfield, op. cit., p. 156 and p. 166.

80. *Artists' International Association Archives*, surrealists leaflet 7043.17.1.

81. Lucas , John (1978), 'James Boswell' , *The 1930s*, Harvester, Sussex.

82. *Teachers International*, sixth year, no 2, November 1927.

83. Spanish Children's Books, National Museum of Labour History, Manchester.

84. *Left Review*, vol. 1 1934-35, p. 40 and vol. 2 1935-1937, p. 161. Tom Wintringham was an author and communist activist.

85. Klingender, F. (1935), 'Content and Form in Art', *Five on Revolutionary Art*, Wishart, London.

86. *Artists International Association Archives*, Catalogue 1937 exhibition 7043.3.3.

87. Ibid, Catalogue 1939, travelling exhibition 7043.3.4.

88. Ibid, AIA news sheet, June 1939, 7043.19.2.

89. Ibid, Catalogue, January 1939, 7043.3.4.

90. Ibid, AIA flyer, 1936, 7043.17.3.

91. Ibid, AIA leaflet, n. d. (1938), 7043.17.2.

92. Ibid, Artists News Sheet, 7043.19.1.

93. Ibid, AIA News Sheet n. d., 7043.19.3, AIA News Sheet, June 1939, 7043.19.2.

94. Picasso, cited, XXIII Council of Europe exhibition, op. cit.

95. Felicia Browne (1936), *Drawings by Felicia Browne*, Lawrence and Wishart.

96. Billig, Michael (1995), *Bizarre Nationalisms*, Sage, London.

CHAPTER SIX

'Matters affecting Women': International Contacts between Women, Young People and Cooperators

The history of Labour Movement contacts with the Labour and Socialist International and the International Federation of Trades Unions has been largely that of men. Not only was the 1918 Labour Party led almost entirely by men, but the new people who came to the fore in the 1930s were also masculine; chapter three records the 'new men' advisedly. The trades union leadership was male to an even greater degree; while the voice of such women as Beatrice Webb and Ellen Wilkinson can sometimes be discerned in Labour Party debate, that of trades union women is muted. This gender exclusivity applied particularly to formal contacts. Outside the mainstream of the Labour Party and trades unions, in special interest groups such as the Sports International, evidence has been found of women's participation. Consideration of broader methods of communication has revealed active internationalist women among the Labour Movement membership. This chapter completes the study of internationalism by balancing the account of male LSI/IFTU contacts with that of formal women's and youth international organisations. It enquires whether in this formal context, women and young people had a distinct experience and philosophy of internationalism. As women frequently organised in the Women's Cooperative Guild, this chapter includes an account of International Cooperation.

Women's organisation and international contact before 1918

Before the First World War it was usual for British women to organise in separate political and trades union bodies. For instance, British women concerned with issues of female employment were members of the International Congress of Working Women, founded in the United States in 1882. Participation in this international body diminished as national organisations developed, such as the Women's Labour League, the Women's Trade Union League and the National Federation of Working Women. The Women's Social and Political Union, which took direct action to campaign for women's enfranchisement, had been formed by Mrs Pankhurst in response to her local Independent Labour Party's exclusion of women from their meetings.[1] Socialist international women's contacts were inspired by an international women's conference held prior to the 1907 Socialist International meeting.[2] This conference gave rise to the British Socialist Women's Bureau in which Social Democratic Federation women's circles representatives played a prominent part. Heralding the later division between reformists and revolutionaries, the Women's Labour League later ran a rival Women's International Council from its offices, which in time assimilated the Women's Bureau.

These bodies remained extant during the war. *Labour Woman,* the organ of the Women's Labour League, never stopped printing its column 'Our Sisters from Abroad' and included reports on German women. League women and ILP women were among those who signed, in late 1914, an open Christmas letter 'to the women of Germany and Austria'. The International Conference of Socialist and Labour Women in March 1915, attended by delegates from Britain, France, Germany, Russia, Poland, Italy, the Netherlands and Sweden, issued a manifesto: 'To the Women of the Warring Nations', demanding a just peace. Women from various party and suffrage organisations organised a conference in May 1915 in order to form an International Committee of Women for Permanent Peace at the Hague, although Women's Labour League representatives were unable to travel to the congress because the government refused passports. The International Congress of Working Women publicised the Hague meeting; Margaret Bondfield, trades unionist and Women's Labour League organiser, was a member of the Hague Committee. Women worked also for peace at local level; Helen Crawfurd in 1916 formed a Women's Peace Crusade in Glasgow, which socialist women activists joined. This made contacts throughout the North of England. It brought to prominence Agnes Dollan of the Women's Labour League, whose husband Pat Dollan was later to concentrate LSI minds on peace.[3]

In Britain, the experience of working more closely with male colleagues during the war in groups such as the War Emergency: Workers' National Committee, helped persuade women to renounce their separatist organisations. The Women's Labour League merged with the Labour Party, its leader Marion Phillips becoming Labour Party Women's Officer, while the Women's Trade Union League merged with the Trades Union Congress. The Standing Joint Committee of Industrial Women's Organisations (SJC), representing Party, trades union and Cooperative women was formed in 1916 to advise the Labour Party on women's issues.

International Federation of Working Women

The International Congress of Working Women was one of the first bodies to resume meetings after the war. Its 1919 Washington meeting was held a little before the Berne conference of the Second International rump. British delegates, Marion Phillips, Gertrude Tuckwell (Women's Trade Union

League) and Susan Lawrence (London County Councillor) proposed a resolution on behalf of the Standing Joint Committee which demanded women's equality of treatment at work, irrespective of their family responsibilities. This implied rejection of gendered protective legislation, an issue which had been much debated by the women's movement in Britain. Mary MacArthur (National Federation of Working Women) had championed trades boards to regulate pay and conditions while others had preferred free negotiation.[4] The issue continued to be controversial at home but the British resolution was accepted at Washington. The Congress met again in New York in 1920, now titled the International Federation of Working Women. Mrs Raymond Robins (USA) was elected president and Mary MacArthur, vice-president.[5]

IFWW next met at Geneva in 1921 with delegates from Belgium, Cuba, Czechoslovakia, France, Italy, Norway, Poland, South Africa, Switzerland, the United States and a group from China, in addition to the British delegation of nine women, the largest present. Mary MacArthur had died suddenly; the Labour Party and Trades Union Congress appointed the British delegation, which included Marion Phillips. Oudegeest, Fimmen, Jouhaux and Mertens were fraternal delegates from IFTU. Mrs Raymond Robins retained her position; Marion Phillips was elected secretary and Mrs Harrison Bell (formerly of the Women's Labour League) treasurer; each country nominated a vice-president, Margaret Bondfield acting for Britain. The British delegation accepted the invitation of the congress to act as IFWW's Bureau. Mirroring IFTU discussions at the time, the main business was 'war against war', and action against unemployment.[6]

British women were thus well represented in international trades union organisation. However, the women's international body obviously had to sort out a *modus vivendi* with IFTU. As chapter one has shown, Britain was not in a leading position at IFTU. This may account for some of the difficulties that were to be experienced between IFWW and IFTU. Marion Phillips travelled to Amsterdam for consultations and attended IFTU's conference in 1922, where it was resolved:

> The International Trade Union Congress considers it urgently necessary that the Trade Unions in all countries should give their fullest attention to the organisation of women's labour. Unorganised women workers constitute a danger to the conditions of labour for the whole mass of workers.

IFTU was instructed to encourage the organisation of women, 'the most efficient form of ... trade unions is that which comprehends both men and women'. However, there were two stings in the tail of the resolution. First, 'special organisations of women workers' were to be affiliated to national confederations. Second, 'the objects and composition' of IFWW were 'not sufficiently clear', and IFTU was to report further on this, meanwhile maintaining friendly relations.[7] Women's organisations were thus signposted as subordinate, at both domestic and international level.

IFWW remained unbowed, and suggested that IFTU affiliate to its sister organisation and pay fees according to the number of women active in each national centre. Work was started on an investigation of the conditions of labour of women and children in the textile trade and a report made to IFTU in 1923. Monthly supplements on women's work were to be published with IFTU press reports. Further investigations covered sweated work at home and family allowances. Marion Phillips followed the Labour Party line that international bodies were advisory only, but also demanded rank and file involvement in international conferences, writing that

> delegates come to exchange and discuss information rather than pass a binding resolution, to find out about a subject and see it from each nations' point of view and discuss its treatment.[8]

Despite these modest ambitions, IFWW continued to meet resistance. Some unions with large female memberships stayed aloof. Marion Phillips then employed an old Women's Labour League tactic, mixing charm and confrontation by holding the 1923 IFWW conference at the same time and place as IFTU's summer school (Bruhl castle, Cologne). Delegates and students were able to participate in each others' activities and a thorough debate could be held between IFWW and IFTU officers.[9]

The TUC, despite the prominence of British women at IFWW, seemed concerned to keep women's organisation under its control and was concerned that 'matters affecting women' should be dealt with: 'in a manner unrelated to other departments', so suggestions that there be a Women's Secretariat and Congress at IFTU were dropped. British delegates obediently pushed at the 1923 IFWW Congress for closer collaboration between IFTU/IFWW. On the one hand women's activity was being promoted, nationally and internationally, while on the other hand an autonomous women's organisation was treated with extreme caution. It was not surprising that the report on progress to the 1924 Labour Conference was ambiguous:

> so far as Great Britain is concerned the management of the Federation (IFWW) affairs now lie with the General Council of Trades Unions though it is hoped, through their representatives upon the Standing Joint Committee, to keep in close touch with it.[10]

At IFWW's 1924 Conference the British delegates promoted a Women's Section at IFTU, to replace IFWW. This happened the following year, Mary Quaile (Transport and General Workers' Union) being appointed British representative.

British women had by no means lost interest in international affairs. One instance was a trip to the Soviet Union made in 1925 in order to address what women felt were inadequacies in the report of the 1924 trade union visit headed by Albert Purcell.[11] The women set out to discover: 'conditions affecting the work, health and general conditions of women and children in

153

Russia'. They were very favourably impressed by workers' participation in factory management, that factories were 'light and spacious', with on-site medical and dental care and crêche provision. Whether the visitors appreciated that they saw model factories is difficult to judge; they were concerned to praise good practice but were not without criticism. It was noted that the 'new economic policy' had cut crêche numbers (1,308 in 1924 from a height of 2,509 in 1922) and cost some women jobs, because they were less well organised than men (forming about 25 per cent of trades unionists) and because their labour was costly, given the generosity of maternity leave. On the other hand: 'women at work on treadle machines and other occupations in which work during the menstrual periods are unhealthy have two days off with pay during this period'. There was equal pay and sickness insurance covered dependents. Common dining rooms and children's corners lightened domestic drudgery and freed women to participate in political debate.

However, IFTU's Women's Section, now called the International Committee of Women's Trades Unionists, held only three conferences: Paris 1927, Brussels 1933, London 1936. The 1927 Conference dealt with women's right to work. Professional women were described as vital to the economy, but handicapped by the opposition to working women, which kept wages low. The position of domestic workers, largely women, was considered: the Conference resolved that domestic workers should have at least the average industrial wage. In implicitly acknowledging that women's unpaid work in the family impacted on women's wage labour; in this case women domestic servants; international trades union women made a contribution to a debate still current. Other topics discussed were protection for women workers, an eight hour day, regular inspection, sickness insurance, the right to belong to a trades union, minimum wages, maternity leave, the prohibition of night work.[12] By 1933 international trades union women were remarking on the 'feminisation' of the contemporary labour force: in light engineering, electrical apparatus, textile, food and chemical trades, the number of male employees was falling and that of women rising. This trend was said to be encouraged by factory organisation and the subdivision of labour; war had also shown that women could be effective, for instance in motor engineering work. In non-regulated trades, women were working fifty to sixty hours a week and suffering fatigue; night work was permitted because the International Labour Office directive prohibiting this had been amended in 1934. The right to work was again discussed, as a marriage bar had been placed on married women civil servants in Germany on 30 June 1933. In Austria and Italy also, fascist governments banned married women's work. In Yugoslavia, Belgium, France, Luxembourg and Britain, there was a similar tendency and attacks had been made on married women workers in the Netherlands and the United States.[13]

At the 1936 Conference, women trades union turned their attention to

154

women's nationality rights; they planned to lobby the League of Nations to achieve equal nationality rights for women. A Women's Committee of the League of Nations, or a correspondence bureau was suggested. However, women trades unionists here faced a paradox of their own making; it was difficult on the one hand to request special protective legislation for women, on the grounds that women had special needs, and on the other hand, to argue for equal citizenship. Jeanne Chevenard (France) wrote that women demanded citizenship: 'although ... it cannot be accepted by the Labour Movement, as it could allow for an interpretation which might exclude protection for women'.[14]

Women's international trade unionism had fallen hostage both to a philosophy that emphasised their weakness, rather than empowering them to seek equality, and to a practice of persuading women that autonomous gender organisation was inappropriate. The politics of international relations were also to their disadvantage; British women ran IFWW's organisation at a time when Britain was seeking a higher profile at IFTU and would not risk hiving off women's trades unions. At home, male leaders were building the Trades Union Congress so that the politics of caution again applied. During its brief existence, IFWW had identified areas where women could have made a special contribution, not least the textile trade which remained (and remains) poorly organised, to the detriment of 'the whole mass of workers', women and men, as IFTU had foreseen in 1922.

Women at the Labour and Socialist International

In contrast to IFTU, the LSI recognised the need for a woman's section from the outset. Austrian women pushed for a Women's conference and Adler may well have been in favour; certainly, he later worked amicably with LSI women organisers. LSI women did not operate from a basis of equality; but they did maintain their organisation and activity throughout the inter-war period.

The International Congress of Labour and Socialist Women met at Hamburg in 1923, a few days before the LSI was officially reinstituted. Delegates from Britain were Marion Phillips; Ethel Bentham, a medical doctor and Women's Labour League organiser; Beatrice Webb; Susan Lawrence. LSI accepted the women's proposal to convene regular Women's Congresses, although it did not fully implement the women's demand that the LSI executive committee should contain at least one women. The LSI asked instead that a representative be sent to meetings to take part in discussions 'although without voting rights'. Beyond these demands, the Women's Congress had resolved to work for women's enfranchisement; to consider an International Women's Day; to promote education and peace; to promote the welfare of mothers and children. Five presidents were elected: Marion

155

Phillips, Adelheid Popp (Austria), Frau Bang (Denmark), Frau Juchacz (Germany) and Frau Tilanus (Netherlands).[15] Adelheid Popp was chosen to attend LSI executive committee meetings and, in fact, became known as the executive women's representative, so LSI women went a long way towards fulfilling their 1923 demands.

As agreed, the LSI called the first International Conference of Labour and Socialist Women together with its own Congress at Marseilles in August 1925. The SJC arranged the Labour Party delegation. IFWW experience was put to use by including Mrs Harrison Bell and Marion Phillips. The latter deputised for Adelheid Popp at LSI meetings. Agnes Dollan, who represented the Labour Party, Mary Carlin (Transport and General Workers' Union), and Mary Bell Richards (Boot and Shoe Operatives) were the trades unionists, Ethel Bentham and Rose Smith - Rose represented the Fabian Society. The Independent Labour Party sent Margaret Bondfield, Dorothy Jewson and Minnie Pallister.[16] At this conference it was proposed that a Socialist Women's Advisory Committee of LSI be formed.

Tom Shaw was wary of reversing the trend against autonomous women's organisations, as was Jeanne Chevenard. Adelheid Popp, in proposing the Women's Advisory Council, had made it clear that women were not suggesting autonomous organisation.[17] Adler notified all affiliates of the Council's existence and asked for names of representatives to be notified to him. He confirmed that the LSI secretariat would carry out the administrative work, in conjunction with the International Women's Committee. Provisionally the Committee included British, German, Austrian, Belgian, Slav and Balkan representatives. Eventually, Britain was represented by Agnes Dollan, Dorothy Jewson, Marion Phillips; Germany had three representatives, Belgium and Austria two, and the remaining countries one each. Susan Lawrence was elected to the praesidium. Table 6.1 indicates the countries in membership. Edith Kemiss was the first committee secretary, followed by Martha Transk (1928) and Alice Pels (1934). Support from Adler was important in allowing women to maintain an international profile. For instance, in August 1926 Adler asked affiliates for information on how many women were represented in national parliaments, how women had voted in the last general election, whether there was a Labour Movement women's press and what women's trades union organisation existed.[18]

That the Women's Committee profile was not higher was largely due to British Labour leaders' caution about women's organisation, first displayed in debate on the constitution of IFWW. The Labour Party International sub - committee opposed the creation of a separate Women's Bureau and the proposal that the political wing in each country should elect its women's representatives 'in conjunction with women's organisations'.[19] British delegates accordingly voted against these proposals, which were dropped. Although SJC women were, in practice, consulted about representation, this was very different to empowering women to elect their own representatives directly.

The resolutions for its 1928 Congress set the pattern of the Women's Advisory Council agenda throughout the inter-war years. Topically, the Polish proposal was to oppose the mobilisation of women in war times. Other resolutions addressed the position of women at work and in the home. There were proposals for a public medical service open to all, for state care of sick and physically disabled people and the prevention and cure of illness. The ILP resolution covered women in all aspects of life: 'for the sick', non contributory national insurance; 'for women in industry', a living wage, public ownership of land, mines, transport, power, housing and equality at work; 'for the mother and child', the abolition of unemployment and low wages, full maintenance for six weeks before and six weeks after birth, a children's allowance payable to the mother and, more controversially 'scientific methods of family limitation'.[20] This resolution was interesting for the way in which it specified low wages and unemployment as problems for women bringing up a family and because it dealt with birth control.

The latter was much debated within the women's British Labour Movement at this time and there was a sizeable body of female opinion in favour. Pamela Graves has traced the British debate which started with the dismissal of a maternity and child welfare clinic health visitor for giving birth control information.[21] The health visitor was defended by Labour women but their plea was rejected by John Wheatley, Labour Minister of Health (1924). Left political women formed the Workers' Birth Control group in which Dorothy Jewson was active. Labour Party women's conference gave annual support for birth control but this was not debated by Labour Conference except in one year, 1926. Having supported miners in the lock out, women were that year rewarded by some trades union support, although the birth control resolution was still soundly rejected. At the International, the Austrian resolution to Women's Congress was also in favour of birth control: 'we consider the threat of penalties against artificial abortion to be objectionable'. The only complaint about the Congress was not on the subject of the controversial resolutions, but that while the full LSI Congress benefited from shorthand transcripts in three languages, the Women's Congress did not.[22]

For the 1931 conference, the British resolution was on domestic work and again mixed concern for women at home and at work, including domestic service. Scientific organisation of housework was demanded; housework was described as highly skilled and of value to the community, deserving high pay.[23] At this conference progress was made on women's suffrage. It was one of the weaknesses of women's international organisation that women were politically disadvantaged. Even where women were enfranchised, for instance in Weimar Germany, their election to political office was subject to the patronage of male-dominated political parties. Weimar women found that party discipline was restrictive; and cross-party meetings of women were disliked, despite the fact that proportional representation in European social democracies often resulted in coalition governments.[24] In Britain, it took arduous rehearsals of the suffragist arguments to win in 1928 the reduction of the age at which women were enfranchised to 21. In other social democracies, including France and Belgium, socialists participating in coalition governments feared to upset the balance of power by enfranchising women. Sara Huysmans of Belgium deplored the situation in *Labour Magazine*, noting that socialists feared that women would vote conservative and that catholic parties were, therefore, generally in favour of women's enfranchisement.[25] Socialist distrust of the suffrage movement had been indicated when IFWW sent a telegram to the International Suffrage Alliance, reminding that body of working women's needs.[26] Vandervelde had been opposed to women's suffrage on the grounds that it would delay universal manhood suffrage; his first wife (Lalla) had agreed this position. It was, therefore, a major success when the Women's Council persuaded Belgian delegates to the 1931 LSI conference to support women's enfranchisement; the French agreed to expedite their campaign for votes for women.[27]

The Women's Advisory Council began, in 1931, an ambitious programme to investigate, compare and portray statistically conditions of life, including the cost of living, of women in European countries. The British were among the most conscientious in supplying statistics, but these were never wholly reliable and the project remained incomplete. Other issues dealt with included women's nationality on marriage, the Women's Council being concerned that women should not become aliens in their country of birth.[28]

Resistance to fascism had the effect of submerging gender politics. Johanna Alberti has written that fascism 'shifted the perspective' because although fascism was a direct threat to feminism, resistance was class-based; women's resistance was subsumed in the general response of the Labour Movement.[29] We might add that channels for presenting women's separate opinion, nationally and internationally, were restricted; both the SJC and Labour women's conference were advisory. Socialist women did join feminist and other left political women in the Six Point Group which affiliated to the World Committee against War and Fascism; but these included Communist women and united front work was susceptible to proscription. Individual women, of course, made huge contributions to resistance, but there was no single female organisation capable of making its voice heard. Internationally, women's organisation was particularly badly hit by the rise of fascism since, Britain aside, women's strength derived from the large German and Austria Labour Movement membership (see table 6.1). Belgium, Denmark, Sweden, Czechoslovakia, Hungary and the Netherlands had respectable numbers of women in political parties and trades unions, but these could not compare with the 800,000 women in German trades unions. This was double the number of women in British unions, although 700,000 women were organised politically in Britain compared to about 230,000 in Germany. The loss of the

German Labour Movement in 1933 was therefore keenly felt at the Women's Council.

Attention paid to issues of gender thus diminished as the focus of international organisation became the struggle against fascism, with one curious exception. For reasons the files do not explain, the 1935 LSI Congress expressed the opinion that 'women seem to be too little concerned with questions of doctrine' and the LSI 'considered it urgently necessary' for the women leaders to 'see where they stood'. A long-postponed study week was therefore convened at the Belgian Labour College in 1936 on the theme 'Economic and Political Democracy and Women'. This study week had originally been devised by the Women's Council as a ten day conference for rank and file women, funded by women parliamentarians who would each donate a day's pay. Now, the leaders of the women's parties attended a programme of lectures and seminars, outings and discussions. Maria Mahler, speaking on 'Trades Unions under Fascism' noted: 'we are looking here at the ground work for a fascist war'.[30] Taking a leisurely approach, prioritising discussion, with relatively low-level expectations, the women deemed their week 'a brilliant success' although we do not know if LSI objectives were met. The LSI, of course, was at this stage coming to terms with its inefficacy and this year prepared its pessimistic report listing fascist successes. LSI women continued to demand a rank and file conference. Mary Sutherland (secretary of the SJC after Marion Phillips's death in 1932) successfully proposed that an International Women's Week replace the conventional Women's Day, to spread the international spirit in face of 'the growth of fascism and menace of war'. The Women's International secretary was to provide information on each country and national parties were urged to attract visits from women comrades in other countries and to make group visits in return.[31]

The Spanish civil war had the same huge impact on women's work as it did on LSI work in general. The 1937 report of the Women's Committee reported women's activity and 'enthusiastic support to the efforts of the workers' parties to help Spain' in all countries. To contribute to the international 'spirit', and meet Mary Sutherland's proposal, the secretary was collecting reports of a day in the life of a woman in each affiliated country; a qualitative, rather than quantitative attempt to provide this information. Making use of both this data and the statistics collected, two enquiries were being pursued, one on the needs of working class households and the second on the health of children and adolescents. However, it had proved impossible to contact the Women's committee of IFTU (as we have seen, by then almost non-existent) and the Women's Committee attached to the League of Nations 'has a phantom existence'. Information on women's employment and women's rights in each affiliate was therefore requested. The approach of war had re-politicised the birth control debate; the Danish representative of the International Women's committee (Naina Anderson) condemned the dictators' purpose and method in seeking population increase. She called for the reasons that people practised birth control to be attacked rather than contraception itself and demanded social legislation for this purpose.[32]

The final constraint on women's organisation was the policy of some LSI affiliates, notably Britain, to reject any united front work. Both Communists and Cooperators organised outside the mainstream of the British Labour Movement and there was no reason why they should not, on occasion, collaborate. This rendered Cooperative activities, including those of the strongly pacifist Women's Cooperative Guild, suspect. When the latter proposed an International Women's Congress for Peace and Democracy supported by the World Committee against War and Fascism, LSI women were of the opinion: 'This Congress should have been attended by national and international women's organisations of all tendencies'. They were unable to instruct affiliates to attend because national women's movements had to accept the discipline of national parties. The problem, although it was not specifically stated in the record, seems to have been the involvement of the united front World Committee. British Labour women got as far as choosing Jenny Adamson of the Labour Party national executive and Mary Sutherland as their representatives, but these two were strongly advised by William Gillies to have nothing to do with the Congress and to work for a substitute gathering restricted to LSI, IFTU and Cooperative delegates. Both submitted and decided to give priority to work with refugees.[33]

Thereafter, women's organisation was increasingly difficult in the face of the fascist advance. Numbers dropped throughout 1938. Plans for a further study week to be held in the Netherlands were postponed until 1939 because the Dutch government had objected to criticism of its foreign policy, so that there were fears of Soviet police supervision. The event was then further delayed to 1940 and Britain was chosen as the venue. The inquiry on the cost of living continued but only Britain and Belgium were able to contribute information. The campaign to protect Spanish children and provide food intensified. It was proposed that women operate a boycott of Japanese goods. Resolutions were taken against the Nazi annexation of Czechoslovakia and horror expressed at the disappearance of people in both Spain and Czechoslovakia. Solidarity was expressed with women exiles and pledges were made to help refugees. Women's unremitting attempts to understand daily life in other countries, unique in formal international organisation, should be remembered; women had sought to become familiar with the countries where atrocities now took place. Norway joined the LSI and its Women's Council and Czechoslovakia left both. To complete the catalogue of disasters, Adelheid Popp died in 1939.[34]

Women's organisation had been powerless in the face of fascism. The Women's Committee had, however, remained active and useful throughout the LSI's history. Women had acted with dignity despite the constraints of subordination within the mainstream organisation, denial of united front work and falling numbers. By 1939, with war imminent, women won greater involvement in LSI decision making: the right to send representatives to the executive in proportion to the female membership of affiliated parties.[35] Although this was granted too late to be of any practical use, it was, nevertheless, a tribute to women's efficiency in international organisation.

International Cooperation

We have seen that Cooperative women were more likely to countenance united front work than were women members of the Labour Party and trades unions. This greater tolerance was a function of the nature of international Cooperation, which maintained a neutral attitude towards both the LSI and the Third International. It is convenient to consider international cooperation here, because so many women were organised in the Cooperative Guild

The Cooperative Movement had a long tradition of internationalism. The International Cooperative Alliance was formed in 1895. Disruption of trade caused by the war made its revival problematic. However, as Honora Enfield, secretary of the Women's Cooperative Guild, wrote: 'as a trading movement it (Cooperation) depended for its very existence upon daily contact with foreign countries'.[36] The first post-war conference was held in 1921 at Basle, where H. J. May was confirmed as general secretary. At this conference the International Cooperative Women's Guild was formed; Guilds in Austria, the Netherlands and Switzerland joined the British women.[37] By 1925, 30 countries and 74 organisations, representing 85,000 societies and 40,000,000 individual members, attended the ICA Ghent Congress, where the British supplied the largest national delegation.[38]

The International Cooperative Wholesale Society was formed in 1924, forbidden to undertake trading but charged with its promotion. Mr Golightly and Mr Lancaster of the British Cooperative Wholesale Society were elected chair and secretary respectively and headquarters were fixed at Balloon Street, Manchester.[39] Two hundred societies affiliated. The Women's International Cooperative Guild held a two day conference in 1924. Cooperators were represented at the World Economic conference in Geneva in 1927 by their Wholesale and Women's groups and by the secretary of the International Alliance.[40]

International Cooperative Alliance relations with Soviet Cooperatives differed fundamentally from those of LSI/IFTU with the Third International/RILU. Centrosoyus, the Moscow Cooperative Association, tabled a resolution for the 1925 Congress that the International Cooperative Alliance should enter into negotiations with the Third International and its affiliated trades unions. The Soviet delegation also asked for Russian to be the fourth international language (after English, French and German). The ICA agreed to allow Soviet associations a place on the International

Executive, but did not meet the Soviet request for authority to send substitutes for accepted nominees. To resolve the question of international affiliation it was decided, on the recommendation of the British delegates, to remain neutral.[41]

That this neutrality was prized was indicated in the progress of Cooperative relations with trades unions. In 1922 the Cooperative Alliance met trades unions to consider, among other issues, creation of consumers' councils with Cooperative and trades union representatives: 'to exercise a vigilant oversight of the sources and methods of production and supply in the interests of the consumer'. A Cooperative and trades union bank was also to be investigated. However, while resolving that good relations with trades unions were important and should be safeguarded, the Alliance decided priority should be given to preserving inviolate its neutrality. No formal joint committees were created; guidance for joint action when required was to be left to *ad hoc* meetings.[42]

Alliance neutrality did impact on the wider Labour Movement. Trades unions, who had, of course, pursued their own attempts at working with the Soviets, had good relations with Cooperators. Reports were exchanged, trades unionists advised to shop in Cooperative stores and Cooperators asked to check the trades union credentials of candidates for Cooperative office.[43] Third International trades unions had argued that the Alliance should be a closed organisation, trading through workers' organisations; the Anglo-Soviet Cooperative Wheat Exporting Company, formed in 1923, was a case in point.[44] When Soviet diplomats exploited the opportunity of Cooperative trading negotiations to make trades agreements with the 1924 Labour government the result was not so happy.[45] The Labour Party was possibly damaged at the polls and negotiations were not pursued until the election of the second Labour government.

In using its international connections for domestic advantage in this way, the Soviet Communist Party was not so different from the Labour Party, which always had an eye to the domestic impact of its international policies. For Cooperators there was no real problem with the Soviet attitude so long as it furthered trade. Indeed, in 1927, when the Soviet Trades delegation (ARCOS) was expelled from its London office, accused of espionage, British Cooperative societies were instructed to continue trading despite the 'alarming proceedings' and the Cooperative conference sent greetings to Moscow.[46] At the twelfth International Cooperative congress that year the central committee report was condemned as communist propaganda; the secretary's defence was to point to the attacks in the Soviet press on the neutrality of the Alliance.[47] Cooperative neutrality was restated by a commission in the early 1930s which defined the seven basic principles of the Rochdale pioneers, point five being neutrality in politics and religion.[48] International Cooperation was extremely good at fulfilling its prime purpose, world trade on an alternate model to that of capitalism, and its neutrality enabled it to convene broad-based meetings on peace and disarmament. However, it could not export that neutrality to the wider Labour Movement.

Women, cooperators and peace

As we have seen, Labour Movement women were involved in international feminist pacifist organisations from 1915, while there were pacifists throughout the Labour Movement, from George Lansbury to Fenner Brockway. Peace and disarmament had been the first goals of both IFTU and the LSI and the strike-for-peace policy was reiterated until the outbreak of the First World War. As the French Popular Front Premier Blum wrote to Gillies, peace was convenient for most regimes, but socialism and peace were indivisible:

> En effet, la paix est l'aspiration non pas seulement des pays de démocratie, non pas seulement de l'U.R.S.S., pour qui la paix est indispensable, mais elle est a même temps l'aspiration des mouvements populaires dans les pays où le fascisme est en pouvoir.

> L'organisation de la paix ne peut être séparée de l'organisation de la liberté et au bien-être des grandes masses populaires. Elle ne peut être donc séparée de la lutte socialiste.[49]

> (In effect, peace is the hope not only of democratic countries, not only of the Soviet Union, for which peace is indispensable, but is also the hope of popular movements in countries where fascism holds sway. The organisation of peace cannot be separated from the organisation of freedom and is for the well-being of the great mass of working peaple. Peace cannot therefore be separated from the socialist struggle.)

Despite the desire for peace, we have seen that Labour Movement leaders moved towards a militarist position in the 1930s. In this policy switch they were not supported by Cooperators, and women of the Cooperative Guild were the most persistent single group to privilege peace above all other internationalist positions. Jill Liddington has identified three over-lapping strands of anti-militarist feminism; maternalism, equal rights and the belief that 'maleness = violence'.[50] Cooperative women belonged to the maternalist category; we have seen that their anthem 'The Mother's International' expounded this theme; they also worked for equal rights and if they did not typify men as violent, believed in female pacifism. Naomi Black has questioned whether Women Cooperators were necessarily feminist, but, dividing feminist organisations into two types, equal rights and maternalist, places Cooperators in the latter category. Black records that some socialist feminists believed that women were incapable of violence and war, while others wrote that women were socialised into non-war-like behaviour.[51] On either count, this would place Women Cooperators also in the category of

163

'maleness = violence' pacifism. Ceadel has usefully differentiated Labour Movement pacificists, who chose peace as the best option but one which might have to be foregone in certain circumstances, from the more rare, true pacifist for whom no other choice was possible.[52] Women Cooperators were the genuine article. Margaret Llewellyn Davies, the leader of the Women's Cooperative Guild, wrote that the cause of peace made the strongest appeal to International Cooperative Guildswomen: 'For the brotherhood of nations is the religion of Cooperators'.[53]

Cooperative and Socialist women, including Marion Phillips, attended the IFTU Peace Congress at the Hague in December 1922. The International Federation of Working Women thereafter set up an organisation of women, educationalists and young people to educate the latter about the international Labour Movement's commitment to disarmament. George Lansbury wrote at this time that socialist women discussed contraception as a strike-for-peace'.[55] When IFWW floundered, Labour and Socialist International women did not take over specific responsibility for promoting peace. Women's peace groups continued, such as the Women's International League for Peace and Freedom (WILPF), which had grown from the Hague Congress and had its headquarters at Geneva, a symbolic reminder of female pacifism to the League of Nations. Tom Shaw was invited to the WILPF meeting at Washington in 1924, but it seems he did not attend. In 1931 the LSI women's praesidium refused a second invitation to a WILPF conference writing that they would give priority to a simultaneous mixed meeting held on disarmament by LSI/IFTU in Brussels. Internationally, therefore, Cooperative women were the only women's group in the Labour Movement to remain committed to female pacifism.[56] However, boundaries between groups could fluctuate: Agnes Dollan of the LSI Women's Advisory Council was a WILPF member.

The International Cooperative Women's Guild continued to work for peace. Its meeting in Stockholm in 1927 called for 'Total Universal Disarmament'. Women Cooperators demanded the use of an international language, preferably Esperanto, and, as we have seen, encouraged foreign travel and visits. They objected to school Officer Training Corps and promoted the Woodcraft Folk in place of the militarist Baden-Powell Scout and Guide movement. They criticised militarist school textbooks and films. It was, of course, the Women's Cooperative Guild which promoted, in 1933, the white poppy, an emblem of suffering in the First World War which aimed to escape the militarist connotations of the red poppy.[57]

The Cooperative movement took up the helm of the peace movement in 1933. Palmer, Secretary of the National Cooperative Authority, replied to the Labour Party and Trades Union Congress statement *Disarmament and Fascism* by launching an immediate campaign under the slogan 'Peace and Freedom', with a demonstration in the Albert Hall and meetings in 15 centres throughout Britain.[58] The Cooperative Movement promoted peace within the framework of the League of Nations, proposing voluntary contacts between countries to settle disputes with referral to the International Court of Justice if necessary. Eleanor Barton of the Women's Cooperative Guild declared herself an unashamed pacifist.

The Cooperative executive met more frequently with the Labour Party/TUC National Joint Council in 1930s and was thus more engaged in its policy decisions and exposed to the slow but steady acceptance of a militarist position. However, Cooperators avoided acknowledging that armed resistance to fascism was inevitable. They instituted imaginative methods of resistance, such as the 1934 International Cooperative Alliance grant of £4,000 to fund a ten per cent discount in Austrian Cooperative stores. Cooperators helped with relief work and prisoners defence.[59] To support the Spanish Republican government, ICA received help and pledges of support from representatives in the Soviet Union, Japan, Sweden, Netherlands, Finland, India, America, Iceland and Palestine. The Cooperatives launched the 'Milk for Spain' campaign in 1937; lorries carrying dried milk were driven into Barcelona and Madrid. Gillies, Middleton and Dalton met the secretary of the Cooperative Union to see if arrangements could be made for people to donate at local stores to credit the Cooperative Wholesale Society for the milk.

Male Cooperators may be said to have moved to a pacificist position when Barnes, the British delegate to the ICA insisted on a statement denouncing non-intervention in Spain. Even the Women's Cooperative Guild maintained its pacifist position by a mere 897 votes to 623 at their 1938 congress. However, Cooperators maintained the debate on peace. *Stepney Citizen* (February 1936) for instance, opined that a Cooperative commonwealth in Britain was the only hope for peace and (October 1936) that 'Munitions work will end in mustard gas', the eventual outcome being the destruction of the world population. *East Ham Citizen* (April 1937) warned that babies could not wear gas masks. *Cooperative Party Citizen* (July 1937) announced a 'big push' in the peace campaign, conferences, demonstrations, pamphlets in support of a League of Nations Peace contract. *Pioneer* (September 1937) warned 'war menaces us all - we must put the Party's peace message across'. In October 1937 *Pioneer* claimed: 'The Peace Campaign goes with a swing', with massive popular support: 'although many members of the Women's Guild have reservations on the policy of collective security', being totally pacifist and opposed to all armaments. In November 1937 *Pioneer* wrote of the cenotaph ceremony that: 'The ghosts of a million war dead cry: "Put an end forever to war"'.

Cooperators could not go all the way with the Labour Party and TUC move to rearmament. By condemning non-intervention in Spain, they also implicitly challenged the policy of opposing united and popular front work. When Eleanor Barton led the Women's Cooperative Guild, she issued a regulation which banned communist Guildswomen from holding office, but, as we have seen, Cooperators joined the Peace Alliance with Liberal and Communist representation, thus losing their influence with the mainstream Labour leadership. It was within the Cooperative wing of the Labour Movement, where women were strongly represented, (numbering around 87,000 by 1939) that the peace policy was most persistently and vehemently articulated.[61] Through their links with Cooperative women, Labour Party and trades union women, when free of leadership discipline, were included in this statement of the pacifist position. Women in the Labour movement did have a distinctive voice and philosophy; that of peace.

Youth

Young people were organised in the International of Socialist Youth, also formed at the inaugural 1923 Hamburg meeting of the Labour and Socialist International. The Youth International claimed 190,000 members in 23 European and Scandinavian countries and the United States. Secretary was Erich Ollenhauer (Germany), chair Karl Heinz (Vienna), vice chair Joseph de Grave (Ghent). The International Federation of Socialist Students (4,250 members) and the Jewish Socialist Youth Guild (9,052 members) were affiliated. British relations with the Youth International were a series of spurts of interest, the ILP making the most effort until 1932. It was the arrival on the scene of Ted Willis in 1934 that raised the profile of Labour Party youth in Europe, but Willis favoured united front work and therefore fell into disfavour with William Gillies. Youth organisation became a prime example of the way in which fears of communist infiltration at home and abroad interacted and led to tighter discipline within the Labour Party.

In the opinion of Max Westphal, of the German Social Democratic Party, young socialists did have some feminist ideals: 'They are in earnest as to the new relationship between the sexes. They despise those who think that woman is man's slave'. His evidence was that women were encouraged to take official positions in youth organisations. In Germany, Westphal wrote, it was a legacy of the revolution that young people intended to live out a new culture, in opposition to a Labour Movement which they perceived to have modified its principles. In other countries, Westphal reported different priorities: for instance, in Belgium, youth was anti-militarist; in Austria, where the youth movement was formed largely of apprentices, working conditions were the chief topic. In some countries, where membership was younger, social activities were the chief concern of socialist youth; in others, such as Sweden, Denmark, France, 'political education was predominant'. In the latter countries, the membership ceiling rose to 25 years of age. Westphal concluded: 'It is true that the main object of them all is to win over the young people to the cause of socialism ... There are, however, many differences in the execution of their task'.[62]

The objects of the Youth International were to keep the various groups in touch, through a youth journal, literature, art, exchanges, rallies and personal contacts. The groups would also collect statistics and information on legislation pertaining to youth. As with the LSI, there would be one affiliate per country unless there were multiple nationalities in the affiliated country, or more than one party in membership of the LSI. Britain was thus entitled to two representatives, one for the Labour Party and one for the ILP. Resolutions of the Youth International were binding on affiliates. 'Fundamental' tasks included encouraging young people's membership of trades unions, in order to improve labour conditions for youth. Child labour and night work was opposed, protection for apprentices demanded, a 44 hour week, and adequate education. The Youth International aimed to inculcate a sense of internationalism and a will to peace: 'active help in the struggle of the working class against the madness of another mutual murder of peoples'. The Youth International also took a stand against alcoholism and narcotics and, as Westphal had noted, for 'comradeship in unimposed relations between both sexes'.[63]

It is worth considering the Youth International's 'will to peace' in some detail, because it was distinct from the absolute pacifism of, for instance, the Cooperative Women's Guild. Ollenhauer explained Youth International anti-militarism:

> The proletarian youth is specially interested in this struggle because the greatest sacrifices of blood will be demanded of it first in case of war. Militarism also robs of the most robust and healthiest of them a few of the nicest years of their youth (sic), puts out of action their free will and manhood, tries to drive them in soul-killing discipline exacting from them unconditional obedience.[64]

However, the Youth International reserved 'the right to oppose ... the offensive might of reaction with the right of self-defence' and opposed 'anarchist individual refusal of service'. In part, this position rested on the liability of European youth to conscription and in part, on the desire to include socialists, 'revolutionary elements', in European armies. It was a position similar to that of the British Labour Party after 1934 but caused problems for ILPers whom, as we have seen, were pacifist.

In Britain, the international division of the youth movements into cultural and political bodies was reflected in recreational Labour Party youth sections and the politically concerned ILP Guild of Youth. There was also a Young Communist League and other organisations such as Socialist Sunday Schools. Egerton Wake, Labour Party national agent, in 1924 encouraged the formation of young people's sections in each constituency. Young people aged 14 to 21 were to be recruited and the sections managed by a directly elected committee plus two representatives from the constituency general committee. Two people from the youth section would, in turn, serve on the general committee. For those under 14 years, junior sections were to be organised. When the young people reached 16, they were entitled to join the Labour Party as individual members. Egerton Wake advised that 'care should be taken not to over-emphasise the political side' and that women would help with the youth sections.[65] The *Daily Herald* (7 January 1925) reported that the object of creating youth sections was 'to collect and disseminate news concerning all national and international youth movements'. In 1926 youth sections were renamed branches of the League of Youth.

At this stage, there was no attempt to affiliate to the Socialist Youth International, on the grounds that child labour was already prohibited in Britain and young workers were protected, so that Britain could not endorse demands for conditions which were worse than those its young workers enjoyed.[66] Some League of Youth members were reported by the *Worker's Life* (8 April 1927) to have broken reformist ranks by accompanying Young Communist League and ILP Youth delegates to the USSR in 1927. However, by 1929 youth organisation was developing and Gillies showed signs of interest in international contacts, writing to Ollenhauer for the addresses of Youth International affiliates in order to send them the League of Youth bulletin. The latter was produced monthly; there was a League of Youth badge, conferences were to be held annually and a National Advisory Youth Committee was formed, on the same lines as the Women's Advisory Committee. There was also a change in emphasis in that instead of recruiting young people to youth sections, with the option of Labour Party membership, Young Labour Party members aged 16 to 25 'who desire to function as League Members' were to be channelled into the League. The latter's function remained recreational and educational.[67]

Gillies now asked Ollenhauer for full information about the Youth International; the latter replied that the English (sic) were the only 'big party' not in membership and that the aims were the protection of young workers and acting as 'an instrument for peace'. There remained some procrastination on both sides; League of Youth conferences in 1930 and 1931 requested affiliation. Ollenhauer was keen to welcome the British section, but Youth International Bureau and Executive Committee acceptance had to be obtained. League of Youth delegates, John Huddleston, from Leeds, and Paul Williams, from London, attended the Youth International Conference in 1932 and affiliation was finally granted on 3 November 1932. R. T. Windle, secretary to the League of Youth Advisory Committee, affiliated on 3,000 members; branches could receive international membership cards on payment of two pence. One interesting point of the negotiations was that William Gillies seems to have taken one of his rare likings to Ollenhauer, sending cordial greetings to his wife and making an almost unique personal request, for information to help with a walking tour.[68]

Meanwhile, the ILP Guild of Youth had been making the running, although it changed international secretaries too frequently, was too poor and two pacifist to achieve much influence. The Guild of Youth membership was aged 14 to 25 and prioritised political education. Young people could join the ILP when they reached the age of 21, but the Guild of Youth was self-directed. Branches sent delegates to federations, which in turn sent delegates to the National Committee. Dorothy Jewson represented the ILP National Administration Committee on the Youth National Committee.[69] The youth journal was *Flame*. Between 1924 and 1932 youth international secretaries were Frank Rouse, Tetley (Christian name unknown), J. Irving, John Nixon, Peter Dockerty, H. G. Green.

Frank Rouse made the first enquiries of the Youth International and affiliated the Guild of Youth on 2,000 members in July 1924.[70] Tetley almost immediately took over. From South Shields, he was the international correspondent of *Flame* and an Esperanto fanatic. He tried several times to persuade Ollenhauer to adopt Esperanto, insisting that he would speak Esperanto at international conferences and that the Guild of Youth had resolved that at all meetings of people from two or more countries, Esperanto should be the chosen language. In common with most youth secretaries, Tetley had problems writing in Ollenhauer's language, German; Irving later told Ollenhauer that German had not been taught in British schools during the war. Tetley wrote to Ollenhauer that: 'The various national movements are linked up internationally but that is not sufficient because only the leaders meet each other'. However, he caused problems for Ollenhauer by not accepting the difference between Youth International anti-militarist and the ILP pacifist position. He wrote that the ILP could not change its position, as many of its members were also in pacifist organisations. He amplified ILP politics by writing that ILP youth would not work with the Young Communist League but would cooperate with the Labour Party: 'although we know that the officials of the National Labour Party are jealous of the success of our Guild of Youth'.[71]

In fact, Tetley's plans to visit Europe were upset by the general strike, which resulted in the imprisonment of some Guild of Youth members and a drop in membership. The Guild of Youth was unable to pay its Youth International subscription. According to Doris Sharp, Guild of Youth correspondence secretary, Tetley 'severed his connections' for business reasons.[72] J. Irving from Norfolk succeeded him and maintained the ILP stance on pacifism. He informed Ollenhauer that the Guild of Youth had advised members to refuse military service and that it was pacifist 'in the sense of refusal to bear arms'. This was in 1926, the same year as Fenner Brockway's Labour Party resolution on the strike-for-peace. The following year, Irving again raised with Ollenhauer amendment of the anti-militarist policy. Ollenhauer replied that refusing conscription would merely remove 'revolutionary elements' from the army. He said that the Guild of Youth policy would be discussed, but reminded Irving that resolutions of the Youth International were binding on affiliates. Guild of Youth members now consisted of 3,500 'boys' and 1,500 'girls' (Irving's terminology). The Guild now favoured work with the Young Communist League. However, the Guild's influence was limited because of continued financial difficulties, which meant that its national executive was disbanded.[73] Irving himself resigned the international secretaryship in 1928.

The next international secretary, John Dixon of Newcastle, concentrated on recommending united front work to the Youth International.[74] The Guild of Youth, which had fallen back to 4,000 members, was now reported to be up to 5,000 members and one hundred guilds.[75] Ollenhauer told Nixon that united front work had been abandoned because the Young Communists were not willing to share work, only 'to agitate in favour of their own ideas' and that the Communist Youth Congress had declined cooperation with the Socialist Youth International. Ollenhauer now made a spirited attempt to get the Guild of Youth to pay its affiliation fees, offering to discount debts up to 1928: 'The Bureau's opinion is that an organisation, the delegation of which has so energetically tried to influence the content and direction of the international work at the International Congress, ought to be quite willing to meet the financial obligations'. The Guild of Youth paid half its fees, but complained that meetings were conducted in German. Nixon resigned on reaching the upper limit of the Guild membership age.[76]

Peter Dockerty, seemingly a more colourful figure, took over in 1930 from Nixon. Both Irving and Nixon wrote formally correct missives, asked for detailed instructions to reach conference venues, whereas Dockerty's letters have a more lively tone, his reports were reasonably frequent and he seemed more excited by continental trips. The Guild of Youth still owed half its affiliation fees, but Dockerty explained that as membership had fallen to two thousand, the debt was, in effect, wiped out. Dockerty made the important step of recognising the rationale of Youth International anti-militarism; he wrote that 'a negative pacifist attitude to war acts as a smoke screen behind which the preparations for war are being carried on'. Dockerty, however, resigned in October 1931 on gaining a place at Fircroft College; regrettably, he left outstanding a personal debt of 50 marks owed to his German colleagues.[77] H. G. Green succeeded Dockerty, but reported that the political situation following the fall of the 1931 Labour government made organisation difficult. In 1932 the Annual Conference of the Guild of Youth 'decided to sever its connection with the Young Socialist International' because of an irreconcilable policy difference.[78] This policy was, presumably, that of anti-militarism. However, by 1932 the ILP had disaffiliated from the Labour Party and begun steps to create the Revolutionary Policy Committee at the LSI; this may also have affected the Guild of Youth decision to withdraw from the Youth International.

The field at the Youth International was left clear to Labour Party Youth who now numbered around five thousand.[79] These narrowly avoided imitating a militarist image when a suggestion of the Southgate branch was put to the 1933 youth conference, that the League of Youth adopt a uniform of shirt or blazer. After much discussion, this was rejected: the conference report noted that 'opposition came mainly from the delegates from the country districts who referred to the dangers of victimisation if their members wore any distinctive uniform'.[80] If this indicated political naïvety, so did League of Youth contacts with the Youth International headquarters, which were in Berlin. There was irritation about lost letters, rather than commiseration. Bureau meetings were transferred to Amsterdam; the British paid their affiliation fees, but by cheque drawn on a bank in Berlin. Ollenhauer moved the secretariat to Prague.[81] Henderson wanted to develop the League of Youth and appointed Maurice Webb, League organiser.[82]

Reflecting events at the LSI, some groups in the Youth International started to discuss a united front. The 'Latin' countries (France, Spain, Italy, Belgium) met in Basle in December 1934 to form a revolutionary programme. The French delegate, Pierre Bloch, spoke out in favour of the united front: 'nous n'avons rien abandonné, ni notre unité dans le Parti, ni notre socialisme'. ('We have not abandoned anything, neither our unity within the Party, nor our socialism'.) Godefroid, the Belgian delegate, who had organised the radicals' meeting, proposed a policy of revolutionary defeatism in case of war, civil war that would exploit the chaos in favour of a workers' revolution.[83]

In contradiction to Labour Party Policy, British youth were represented in this conference by a delegate from the group *Advance* which had begun to organise within the League of Youth. Ted Willis was a member of *Advance*; he joined the League of Youth in 1934 and was elected to the London League. Almost immediately, he found himself at odds with members of the National Advisory Committee, particularly Alice Bacon and George Brown (committee chair).[84] *Advance* was again represented when the radicals next met at Toulouse in July 1935.[85] Communist delegates arrived from Paris for this meeting but were not given a hearing; the radicals' intention was to reform the Socialist Youth programme, so that the offensive against fascism became the prime object, achieved through revolutionary dictatorship, with the unity of revolutionary forces as the first step.

Both the 'Latin' group and the moderates, led by Ollenhauer, wrote to the British Labour Party for support. The moderates held the 'Latin' proposals to be divisive and probably communist inspired and demanded attention be paid rather to youth unemployment, raising the school leaving age, setting up labour exchanges, lowering the pension age and creating public works' programmes. In Godefroid's opinion:

> hair-raising statements were made. A delegate said socialism could not be the product of a revolution, but could only be the fruits of a progressive development.

The 'Latin' delegates constituted themselves as 'L'Amicale des Jeunes Socialistes' and were joined by the Swiss and German 'left' socialists. Theirs was not to be a Fourth or Fifth International, but a distinct group working for reform within the Socialist Youth International. Meanwhile, in Paris at Easter 1935, the first International Youth Conference open to all youth federations had been held. This had decided to declare itself a permanent organisation and to call a World Youth Conference in 1936 to form a World Union of Youth.[86] This organisation did have communist representatives, in addition to pacifist and League of Nations youth organisations. Each affiliate was to be politically and organisationally independent. To settle the future of the Youth International, Godefroid proposed division into political and cultural groups. Rather than accept this division, it was decided to ask the Youth International Bureau to consider Ollenhauer's proposal that special departments could be formed for specific work, for instance, campaigns against war and for youth protection from unemployment.

The League of Youth was represented at the Bureau meeting due to its 1935 success in persuading the Labour Party to pay youth delegates' fees and expenses to meetings abroad; previously, delegates had travelled at their own expense; once, Henderson had paid.[87] The national executive arranged to recoup its expenditure by raising the League of Youth affiliation fees (from 2d to 2s per member) and chose Alice Bacon as delegate. She voted with the majority, which almost unanimously passed Ollenhauer's proposal, Godefroid abstaining. Adler, who was present, commented: 'the views held in the Labour Movement are widely divergent' and that the debate reflected that in the Labour and Socialist International. It was also decided not to send delegates to the Young Communist Conference, nor to the World Union of Youth (on the casting vote of the chair). De Brouckère was to attend the World Conference in a personal capacity. The one 'Latin' group victory was that the executive 'acclaimed with joy' the consolidation of the trade union movement in France and sent congratulations to Spanish comrades. The preamble to the final resolution indicated that a degree of hegemony had been reached within the Youth International:

> the war danger in Europe can only be dispelled when the workers have achieved power in the most important countries and are thereby placed in a position to exert an influence on the League of Nations. The struggle for peace is bound up with the struggle of the working class for political power.

Although Alice Bacon had voted as instructed, the outcome was not entirely in line with the Labour Party's decisive rejection of united front activity. To reinforce its control of the League of Youth, the National Executive sent a memorandum to the subsequent (April 1936) League conference, which condemned young people's desire for independence and the freedom to register opinion hostile to the Labour Party, reminding the League of its 'real object ... to enrol members and enjoy a social life'.[88]

The National Executive therefore proposed reducing the representation of the Youth conference and lowering the age limit to 21. On all the conference seats were two circulars, one signed by Ted Willis entitled 'The League Must Act' (against the NEC memorandum) and the second, 'A Programme at Last' which summarised Youth conference resolutions. Notice was given of an unofficial session which would consider how to defeat the NEC proposals and decide the LoY programme.[89] *Advance* was on sale outside the conference, as was *Youth Militant* ('as I understand' wrote Gillies, 'known as "Trotskyists"') and the *Bulletin* of the Socialist Youth Committee. The official Labour Party newspaper, *New Nation*, appears to have been less attractive as resolutions on its behalf were defeated by conference. In fact, the League of Youth exceeded the Youth International position, resolving to join the united front nationally and internationally, being of the optimistic opinion 'the traditional leadership in Britain in foreign affairs gave us a splendid opportunity for socialist world leadership'. A full-time officer was also demanded, while National Executive proposals for reorganisation were rejected. Resolutions were taken against sporting participation in countries where racial, political and religious minorities were suffering persecution. Opposition was registered against obedience to military authorities and air-raid drill. Telegrams were received from the European youth movements and from the National Council of the Communist Youth Movement. The national organiser and other members of the Young Communist Party sat in the gallery. A telegram was sent to the Independent Labour Party Guild of Youth. At the close of the conference a document was distributed signed by the Executive of the Young Communist Party and entitled 'From the Gallery ... to You'.[90]

Official Labour, in the shape of William Gillies, blamed *Advance* in general and Willis in particular for this rebellion. Willis, nominated by Stafford Cripps, was elected to the National Youth Advisory Council. To counter his influence, a national youth organiser was appointed, John Huddleston, who had attended the 1932 Youth International conference. Having received Gillies's report, the National Executive took to itself full control of the League of Youth. United and popular fronts in the youth movement were temporarily brought to a halt. The National Advisory Committee, however, asked for an international secretary to be appointed to keep in touch with European socialist youth.[91]

At the 1937 Labour Party Conference the University Labour Federation successfully called for the League's annual meeting to be again convened and for representatives to be elected to its Advisory Committee. *Youth for Socialism* was published in 1938 by this committee, a statement in favour of collective security, accusing the capitalist government of wrecking peace and calling for a world commonwealth of socialist states. It also reiterated the Cooperative position that promotion in the forces should be on merit alone.[92]

Meanwhile, *Advance* had proved a great success.[93] From five hundred duplicated copies in December 1935, its circulation had grown to two thousand in June 1936 (the first printed edition) and 10 to 15,000 in March

173

1938; one month in that summer, circulation peaked at 100,000. All this was managed by a voluntary, part-time editorial committee, chaired by Willis, with an advisory board including Alex Bernstein, that met monthly and held its own conferences. The Labour Party was manoeuvered into accepting *Advance* as the official Labour Party youth paper; the editor was paid £2.10s.0d per week, *Advance* organisers were sanctioned, a budget fixed and the League of Youth deemed responsible for finances. The League of Youth National Advisory Committee appointed the editor and editorial committee. This coup, although impressive, meant that the Labour Party could exert some control; the National Executive, the Publications Department and the Youth Organiser had seats on the editorial committee.

Willis remembered the editorial committee as a 'marriage that couldn't last. No one altered their views'.[94] The *Advance* group swept the board in the election for the National Advisory Committee at the 1938 League conference; the Youth Organiser was already complaining about stewarding and that Advance supporters invited delegates to unofficial conference sessions. She complained of a constant struggle to make *Advance* worthy of the title of 'official journal of the Labour Party League of Youth' and that it was too sensational. Willis pressed for the age limit for youth members to be raised again to 25 years.

The popular front now became the chief concern of the League of Youth. Willis told the organisers he had always made it clear that the League of Youth should merge with the Young Communist League. He now wanted to send a delegation to the new British Youth Peace assembly, which contained not only communists but conservatives. This was part of the World Youth Movement which was (rightly) perceived as a communist front. A National Youth Campaign was formed, with Willis as a member, to press for a Parliament of British Youth in 1939; the organiser accused him of being an employee of the British Youth Peace Assembly. Leagues of Youth in many constituencies worked for this organisation.[96]

Gillies intercepted a report by Godefroid, the Belgian delegate to the World Youth Movement, and underlined in pencil the following:

> In Great Britain a Young People's Peace Committee was formed, supported among others by the Liberal, Socialist, Conservative and Communist Party Youth, the league of Nations Union, the Boy Scouts, the Young Men's Christian Association, the National Students' Federation, etc.

Godefroid continued:

> Since this movement has originated from a purely English initiative but is working in the same direction as the Bureau of the World Union, we are trying to get this movement to co-operate in the movement for peace, freedom and progress. We are already in touch with it and are supporting its efforts.[97]

This was all the proof Gillies needed of a Willis plot to assist the communists in infiltrating the Labour Party.

Evidence against Willis was collected.[98] This amounted to his work for the Peace Assembly, travelling around the League of Youth branches to disseminate its propaganda, and to Prague (twice), Paris (eleven times) and Spain, where the Socialist and Communist Youth Movement had merged in 1930, (many times), attending the Socialist Youth International when the National Executive Council had decided not to send a delegate, and producing a report.[99] The Youth Organiser had sent an official report, only to find that it was preceded by one and a half foolscap pages from Willis on the British Youth Movement. Willis recommended Cecil Thomson and James Mortimer to the League of Youth school; these could be reached by telephone at the Communist Youth offices. Willis criticised the party for not doing enough for Spain. Moreover, there was a photograph in *Tribune* of Willis with Stafford Cripps, who had, of course, recently been expelled from the Labour Party.

Willis was interviewed by Middleton about his trip to Prague, where he had distributed leaflets about Chamberlain's policy. Neither his explanations, nor the Youth Advisory Committee request for permission to join the Youth Parliament, listing the affiliated organisations impressed the Labour Party Executive. Willis was asked to leave, the National Advisory Committee disbanded and the League of Youth Conference arranged for Easter cancelled. French delegates were to have come, but the Youth Organiser warned that these tended to be pacifists. Gillies instructed that *Advance* should not receive a press ticket for Labour conferences, as it could not be regarded as part of the socialist press; and Mrs Gould (the National Executive Council nominee on the National Youth Advisory Committee) agreed to inform the TUC Secretary that the Youth Committee had been disbanded. An application for affiliation, if it were received, should, of course, be rejected.[100] In contrast, Winston Churchill entertained Willis and his committee to lunch and thanked them for preparing British youth for a war that was inevitable. The leadership had succeeded in ousting the rebels and banning popular or united front activity, but the price of discipline was high. League of Youth numbers dwindled, so that, with the additional disruption of war, it would prove extremely difficult to resurrect youth sections in 1945. Willis joined the Young Communist League; although others of his associates were also assimilated into the YCL, Willis remembered that, remarkably, the communist organisation never seemed to grow.[101]

Young people's organisation had resembled that of women in being subordinate to the LSI internationally and to Labour Party interests nationally. However, young people were committed celebrants of the international faith; as Ollenhauer wrote, 'the greatest sacrifice of blood will be demanded of (youth) first in case of war'. After 1932, British Youth was represented abroad not by the pacifist ILP, but by the anti-militarist Labour Party, whose policy fitted more comfortably with that of the Youth International.

Churchill's commendation of Willis was not, in this context, bizarre: Willis was one of the many voices in the Labour Party calling for determined resistance to fascism, including 'the right to oppose ... the offensive might of reaction with the right of self-defence'. Internationally, the division between socialist and communist groups was overcome by some national parties, notably French and Spanish, but not by the Youth International. The British League of Youth was at the heart of this debate, as Gillies was at the centre of LSI discussions. Choosing the united front approach led to Willis's expulsion from the Labour Party and showed that the Labour Party Managers were determined to control the activities of all its affiliates.

Conclusion

Women and young people were vigorous participants in international organisations. However, in all cases, the attitude of the Labour Movement leadership at home was instrumental in determining the extent of the contact: youth contacts were consistent only from the 1932 Labour Party decision to approve affiliation and resolutions on women trades unionists severely limited their international input. Where the International Secretary, notably Adler at the LSI, was sympathetic to the creation and maintenance of separate bodies, British hesitation could, in part, be overcome. A committed individual - Marion Phillips, Margaret Bondfield, Eleanor Barton, Ted Willis - could also be influential in maintaining contact. Both women's and young people's leaders wanted to extend contact into the membership of their organisations. While their experience of international contact was largely much the same as that of Labour Party and trades union men, formal committee meetings and conferences, women did organise the 1936 Study Week which allowed a more relaxed approach, while young people, in particular Ted Willis and the *Advance* group, were energetic about travelling abroad. Both women and youth collected and exchanged statistics, while women used the innovative qualitative approach of collecting details about the day in the life of a woman in each country, to broaden their international understanding.

Fascism hit particularly hard at women. The stereotype of domestic femininity was translated into legislation that banned married women's work and the loss of the big German women's membership after 1933 was keenly felt. However, social democratic countries also banned married women's work, refused them the franchise (France and Belgium) and suspected their political participation was damaging to the balance of power in coalition governments (Weimar Germany). Both women and youth fought fascism within mixed, male led organisations, rather than presenting a gender or age - based response.

There were particular women's and youth philosophies of internationalism. That of women was to privilege peace and was centred in the Women's

176

Cooperative Guild, that of Youth was in supporting united and popular front work. Cooperative women promoted pacifism throughout the inter-war years and never reneged on this position. Youth were particularly conscious of the physical reality of war and its probable effect on their generation, but were anti - militarist rather than pacifist. This caused problems for the Independent Labour Party, but not for Labour Party Youth. Both women and youth were less dogmatic about work with communists than male-led organisations. Women, however, were willing to renounce united front cooperation when so directed. Ted Willis and William Gillies acted out a Machiavellian plot around the issue, until Willis was forced into the Communist Party: Gillies had the luck, as Ollenhauer, with whom he had already formed amicable relations, did not favour the united front.

Naomi Black questioned whether Cooperative women were feminist and we may apply this question to all Labour Movement internationalist women. Feminism is as difficult to define as socialism and means different things to different critics. A modern (1990s) definition of feminism, would include resistance to gender typification, and might not be applicable to the women's groups discussed here: one group unashamedly called itself 'the Mother's International'. However, LSI, IFTU, Cooperative women did run organisations for women, even if they were content to subdue their voice to that of male organisers. Labour Movement women were conscious of women's particular needs; for instance, the impact of women's family position on their labour market position. This was shown in the ICWW 1919 Congress, the IFTU 1927 Congress which debated domestic service and the resolutions to LSI Women's Congress in 1928 and 1931. Women also discussed birth control, at the LSI in 1928, and some progress was made on women's enfranchisement at the LSI in 1931. However, their concern for women's needs led internationalist women to seek *protection* for women. This has been seen as abandoning equal rights demands. Trade union women's 1936 debate showed how sensitive women were to the paradox of claiming both protection and equality.

It remains to say that internationalism was not confined to adult men. Women and youth did make their contribution and did form their own contacts. That their insights - on peace, and on the united front - were not welcome, does not diminish their commitment to the International Faith.

Notes

1. Collette, Christine (1989), *For Labour and For Women: The Women's Labour League 1906-1918*, Manchester University Press, p. 19.
2. Ibid., p. 69 ff. Collette, Christine (1993), 'Gender and Class in the Labour and Socialist International' in Hausch, G. (ed.), *Geschecht Klasse - Ethnizitat*, Linz.

3.   Liddington, Jill (1989), *The Long Road to Greenham Common: Feminism and Anti-Militarism in Britain since 1820*, London, p. 95 ff, p. 131. Reinalda, Bob and Collette, Christine, 'The ITF and women during the inter-war period' in Bob Reinalda (ed.), *The International Transport Workers Federation, 1914-1945: The Edo Fimmen Era*, (Amsterdam, 1997). Margaret Bondfield was elected to parliament in 1923 and later became Britain's first woman Cabinet Minister. Both Agnes Dollan and Helen Crawfurd worked with the Glasgow Women's Housing Association. Agnes Dollan became a Glasgow Councillor in 1921. Helen Crawfurd became a member of Workers' International Relief.

4.   Collette, Christine (1989), op.cit., pp. 118-19. Susan Lawrence became a Member of Parliament in 1924.

5.   *International Federation of Trades Union Papers*, International Institute of Social History, Amsterdam, report of International Congress of Working Women, 1920, IFTU 124.

6.   Ibid., report of International Congress of Working Women, 1921, IFTU 124. Labour Party Conference *Report,* 1922, p. 72 ff.

7.   *Labour Party Conference Report,* 1922, p. 72 ff. Trade Union Notes (1923), *Labour Magazine*, vol.ii, no.1, May, vol.2, no.3, July.

8.   Phillips, Marion (1923), *Labour Magazine*, vol.ii, no.3, July.

9.   Trade Union Notes (1923), *Labour Magazine*, vol.ii, no.1, May and vol.ii, no.3, July. *International Federation of Trades Union papers*, report of International Congress of Working Women, 1923, IFTU 125.

10.   Labour Party Conference *Report,* 1924, p. 80.

11.   *Soviet Russia: An Investigation by Women Trades Unionists*, London, p. 18, p. 27.

12.   *International Federation of Trades Unions*, op.cit., resolutions from Paris conference, 1927, IFTU 130.

13.   Ibid., International Committee of Women Trades Unionists, London, 1936, IFTU 132.

14.   Ibid., International Committee of Women Trades Unionists Conference reports, 1927, 1933, 1936, IFTU 127-34.

15.   Labour Party Conference *Report,* 1923, pp. 83-84. Labour Party Conference *Report* 1924, p. 80.

16.   *Sozialistische Arbeiter-Internationale Papers*, International Institute of Social History, Amsterdam, notice of International Women's Conference August 1925, SAI 4333. Dorothy Jewson was elected to parliament in 1923.

17.   *Labour and Socialist International Congress Reports*, 1925, p. 252, 1928, p. 3.

18.   *Sozialistische Arbeiter-Internationale Papers*, Adler to all affiliates, 10 March 1926, SAI 4359, Adler to all affiliates, executive committee meeting 25 August 1926.

19.   *Labour Party International Sub-Committee Minutes*, 8 October 1926.

20.   *Sozialistische Arbeiter-Internationale Papers,* Edith Kemiss, provisional agenda for conference, 23 July 1928, SAI 4336.

21.   Graves, Pamela (1994), *Labour Women: Women in British Working Class Politics 1918-1939*, Cambridge University Press, chapter three.

22.   *Sozialstische Arbeiter-Internationale Papers*, SAI 4336 op.cit., Ibid.,

unsigned to Edith Kemiss, 13 September 1928, presumably from Britain because the complaint is that the translation from English of Susan Lawrence's speech is particularly bad. SAI 4337.

23. Ibid., Gillies to Adler, 3 July 1931, SAI 4345.
24. Boak, Helen (1990), 'Women in Weimer Politics', *European History Quarterly*, 20 (3) July.
25. Huysmans, Sara (1927), 'Women's Suffrage in Belgium', *Labour Magazine,* vol.iii, no. 7, November 1927.
26. 'Labour Abroad' (1923), *Labour Magazine*, vol.ii, no. 1, May.
27. Polasky, Janet (1995), *The Democratic Socialism of Emile Vandervelde*, Berg, Oxford, p. 169. *Labour and Socialist International Congress Report* 1931, p. 3.
28. *Sozialistische Arbeiter-Internationale Papers*, Alice Pels, correspondence secretary of the International Women's Committee to Dear Comrade, 14 December 1931, SAI 4360. Ibid., report for Committee meeting, Prague 1931, SAI 4364.
29. Alberti, Johanna (1994), 'British Feminists and Anti-Fascism in the 1930s' in Oldfield, Sybil, *This Working Day World*, Taylor & Francis, London.
30. *International Women*, Labour Party Archives, Manchester, International Study Week *Report*, 1936, p. 4. p. 48.
31. *Sozialistische Arbeiter-Internationale Papers*, Mary Sutherland for International Women's Committee, August 1936, SAI 4367.
32. Ibid., International Women's Committee report, September 1937, SAI 4368.
33. Ibid., International Women's Committee Meeting report, Brussels 1938, SAI 4369.
34. Ibid., International Women's Committee report, June 1939, SAI 4370.
35. *Labour and Socialist International Papers*, Labour Party Archives, Manchester, International Women's Committee report, 16-18 September 1939.
36. *New Leader*, 8 February 1926.
37. Black, Naomi, 'The Mother's International: The Women's Cooperative Guild and Feminist Pacifism', *Women's Studies International Forum*, 7 (6) 1984, p. 471.
38. International Cooperative Alliance (1925), *Eleventh Congress Report*, London.
39. 'Cooperative Activities' (1924), *Labour Magazine*, vol. iii, no. 5, September.
40. 'Cooperative Activities' (1924), *Labour Magazine*, vol. iii, no. 6, October.
41. International Cooperative Alliance (1927), *Twelfth Congress Report*, London.
42. International Cooperative *Bulletin*, (January 1928), pp. 7-10; International Cooperative Alliance (1925), Eleventh Congress *Report*, London, p. 77, p. 119.
43. *Trades Union Congress Papers*, Modern Records Centre, Warwick University, details of Cooperative/trades unions relations, MSS 292 760 (1).
44. International Cooperative Alliance (1925), *Eleventh Congress Report*, pp. 112-128.
45. Krassin, Leonard (1927), 'The Problems of Anglo-Russian Trade', *Labour Magazine*, vol. iv, no. 3, July.

179

46.   'Cooperative Activities' (1927), *Labour Magazine*, vol. iv no. 3.

47.   International Cooperative Alliance (1927), *Twelfth Congress Report*, p. 116.

48.   Watkins, W. P. (1986), *Cooperative Principal Today and Tomorrow*, Holyoake Books, p. 6 ff.

49.   *William Gillies Correspondence*, Labour Party Archives, Manchester, Blum to Gillies, 11 February 1923, WG/LAB.

50.   Liddington, Jill (1989), op.cit., p. 88.

51.   Black, Naomi (1984), op.cit., pp. 467-76. (Black's opinion, p. 467: 'The Women's Cooperative Guild defined itself as a cooperative, a women's and a workers' organisation, but not a feminist one').

52.   Caedel, Martin (1980), *Pacificism in Great Britain: the Defining of a Faith*, Cambridge, 1980, *passim.*

53.   Black, Naomi (1984), op.cit., p. 471.

54.   Labour Party Conference *Report*, 1923, p. 83.

55.   Lansbury, George (1923), *Labour Magazine*, vol. ii, no. 2, June.

56   Bussey, G. and Timms, M. (1965), *Pioneers for Peace: the Women's International League for Peace and Freedom*, Allen & Unwin, London. *International Federation of Trades Union Papers*, op.cit., Tom Shaw to Catherine Masshall, 9 January 1924, IFTU 3057/3; LSI Women's Praesidium to WILPF, 331 March 1931, IFTU 3057/19.

57.   Liddington, Jill (1989), op.cit., p. 143, p.161, Black, Naomi (1984), op.cit., pp. 471-472.

58.   *James and Lucy Middleton Papers*, Ruskin College, Oxford, Middleton to R. A. Palmer, 17 November 1933, MID 30/38.

59.   *Ernest Bevin Papers*, Churchill College, Cambridge, NJC Statement. 28 July 1934, I6.

60.   *Pioneer,* October 1937. *William Gillies Correspondence*, Gillies to de Brouckère, 5 January 1937, WG/LAB.

61.   Black, Naomi (1984), op.cit., p. 473.

62.   Westphal, Max (1924), 'Youth tales the Helm', *Labour Magazine*, vol.iii no.7, November.

63.   *Sozialistische Arbeiter-Internationale Papers*, International Institute of Social History, Amsterdam, Ollenhauer (Secretary) to LSI, n.d., SAI 2974/9, Ollenhauer to LSI, n.d., SAI 2974/10: *Report of Brussels Conference on Education Questions*, 6 August 1928.

64.   Ibid., Ollenhauer to LSI, n.d., 2974/19.

65.   *Sozialistiche Jugend Internationale Papers*, International Institute of Social History, Amsterdam, memo from Egerton P. Wake to constituencies, August 1925, SJI 738/S; Gillies to Ollenhauer, 13 February 1925 advising creation of youth section, SJI 761/4.

66.   *Sozialistische Arbeiter-Internationale Papers*, Adler to all parties, 17 February 1927, SAI 2978/2, Henderson to Adler, 1 March 1927, SAI 2978/9.

67.   *Sozialistische Jugend Internationale Papers*, Gillies to Ollenhauer, 19 February 1929, SJI 764/20. G. R. Shepherd, National Agent to Labour Party branches, 1 November 1929, SJI 740/1.

68.   Ibid., Gillies to Ollenhauer, 12 December 1929, SJI 764/27; Ollenhauer to Gillies, 21 December 1929, SJI 764/34. Ollenhauer to R. J. Windle,

secretary League of Youth Advisory Committee, 30 November 1931, SJI 742/12; 14 March 1932, SJI 742/18; Windle to Ollenhauer, 24 September 1932, SJI 742/22; 28 September 1932, SJI 742/23; Ollenhauer to Labour Party League of Youth, 3 November 1932, SJI 742/28; Gillies to Ollenhauer, 26 May 1930, SJI 764/30.

69.   Ibid., Tetley's report, 1926, SJI 745/20; Tetley to Ollenhauer, 5 December 1925, SJI 745/17.

70.   Ibid., Rouse to Winter and Ollenhauer, n.d., 19 May 1924, 29 May 1924, 29 July 1924. Ollenhauer's acceptance, 6 February 1925, SJI 741-745.

71.   Ibid., Tetley to Ollenhauer, 6 March 1926, SJI 745/55, 9 March 1926, SJI 745/50, 24 April 1926, SJI 745/44; Irving to Dear Comrade, n.d., SJI 748/30; Tetley to Ollenhauer, 13 October 1925, SJI 745/12; Tetley to Ollenhauer, 29 April 1926, SJI 745/49; Tetley's memorandum, n.d., SJI 745/55.

72.   Ibid., Tetley to Ollenhauer, 17 May 1926, SJI 745/52; David Sharp to Secretary, 22 July 1926, SJI 746/1; Sharp to Ollenhauer, 23 June 1926, SJI 746/12; Irving to Dear Comrade, 26 October 1926, SJI 748/4.

73.   Ibid., Irving to Ollenhauer, 18 October 1926, SJI 746/17; Ollenhauer to Irving, 15 February 1927, SJI 748/48; Irving to Dear Comrade, 21 January 1927, SJI 748/14; Irving to Ollenhauer, 26 October 1927, SJI 748/57.

74.   Ibid., Nixon to Dear Comrade, 18 September 1928, 25 September 1928, SJI 749/1-4.

75.   Ibid., Nixon to Dear Comrade, 5 November 1928, SJI 749/18.

76.   Ibid., Nixon to Dear Comrade, 5 November 1928, SJI 749/18. SJI to Dear Comrade, 20 March 1930, SJI 749/77; Nixon to Dear Comrade, 1 June 1930, SJI 749/79.

77.   Ibid., Dockerty to Ollenhauer, 15 June 1930, SJI 750/1; Dockerty's report n.d., SJI 750/7; report 31 October 1930, SJI 750/12; Dockerty to Ollenhauer n.d., SJI 750/17; Dockerty to Ollenhauer, 6 February 1931, SJI 750/28; Dockerty to Secretary SJI, 30 June 1931, SJI 750/40; Dockerty to Ollenhauer, 5 October 1931, SJI 750/45; H. E. Green to Ollenhauer, 25 October 1931, SJI 751/1; Ollenhauer to Guild of Youth, 10 December 1932, SJI 751/42.

78.   Ibid., H. G. Green to Dear Comrade, 6 November 1931, SJI 751/5; Guild of Youth to Dear Comrade, 20 May 1932, SJI 751/39.

79.   Ibid., Windle to Ollenhauer, 9 February 1933, SJI 742/38.

80.   Ibid., League of Youth conference report, January 1933, SJI 740/54.

81.   Ibid., Windle to Ollenhauer, 26 January 1933, 6 February 1933, SJI 742/33; Windle to Roos Vorrinck (SYI treasurer), 12 March 1933, 742/39, Amsterdam League of Youth to Labour Party League of Youth, 29 June 1933, n.d., SJI 742/41, SJI 742/43; Windle to Ollenhauer in Prague, 10 May 1933, SJI 742/34.

82.   Ibid., Henderson to Dear Comrade, 10 July 1933, SJI 740/65.

83.   *William Gillies Correspondence, Le Populaire* Report, 16 August 1934, WG/ISU/2.

84.   Interview with Lord Willis, 19 July 1988. Baroness Alice Bacon won her parliamentary seat in 1945, as did Lord George Brown. The latter, 'born in the Labour Movement', began his ministerial career as parliamentary

private secretary to Hugh Dalton in 1946. See Lord Wigg (1972), *George Wigg*, London, p.254 for appraisal.

85. *William Gillies Correspondence*, Socialist Youth Executive report 1935, WG/ISY7.

86. *William Gillies Correspondence*, Report of Socialist Youth Conference, August 1935, WG/ISY/9, letter from Godefroid to Ollenhauer, 20 December 1935, WG/ISY/9; report by Godefroid 1935, WG/ISY/9.

87. Ibid., NEC *Memorandum* to League of Youth, April 1936, WG/LOY/57.

88. Ibid., Minutes of Socialist Youth Bureau, 30 March 1936, WG/ISY/8. League of Youth Conference *Report,* 20 March 1936, WG/ISY/8. League of Youth Conference *Report*, 11-13 April 1936, WG/LOY/9.

89. Ibid., League of Youth Conference *Report*, 11-13 April 1936, WG/LOY/9.

90. Ibid., C. G. Lacey (Chair, National Advisory Committee), WG/LOY/8, *Report* on 1936 LOY Conference.

91. Ibid., League of Youth Advisory Committee *Minutes*, 29 May 1936, WG/LOY/10.

92. The University Labour Federation admitted socialists and communists. Greenwood was first president of the ULF, followed by D. N. Pritt. See Pritt, D. N. (1963), *The Autobiography of D. N. Pritt, Part One, From Right to Left*, Lawrence and Wishart, London, p. 221. *William Gillies Correspondence, Youth for Socialism* (1938), WG/LOY/19.

93. Ibid., Report on *Advance*, March 1938, WG/LOY/20; interview with Lord Willis, 19 July 1988.

94. Interview with Lord Willis, 19 July 1988.

95. *William Gillies Correspondence,* Memorandum on the reconstitution of the League, 1938, WG/LOY/22.

96. Interview with Lord Willis, 19 July 1988: Lord Willis stated he was not an employee of the Peace Assembly, but of the Spanish foodship committee.

97. *William Gillies Correspondence*, Godefroid's report to Socialist Youth International, 1936, WG/ISY/10 ii.

98. Ibid., Memorandum of the reconstitution of the League, 1938, WG/LOY/22.

99. The merger of the Spanish Youth Movement illustrated the fears of the Labour leadership. Alvarez del Voyo, probably a covert communist but Foreign Minister under Caballero, masterminded the merger just before the outbreak of the Spanish Civil War and Caballero used the amalgamation as an example of how an alliance between the socialists and communists could be beneficial. Braunthal, Julius, *History of the International*, op.cit., pp. 454-59.

100. *William Gillies Correspondence*, National Advisory Committee *Minutes,* 25 January 1939, WG/LOY/32. Youth Parliament affiliates were listed as British University League of Nations Society, Central Youth Council of the Church of England, Federation of Zionist Youth, Girls' Friendly Society, League of Nations Youth Groups, National Council of Girls' Clubs, National Union of Students, Order of Woodcraft Chivalry, University Labour Federation. *William Gillies Correspondence*, Gillies to Youth Organiser, 20 July 1939, WG/ISY/16.

101. Interview with Lord Willis, 16 July 1988.

Table 6.1 Women's representation at the LSI

Countries	Politically organised women		% women in political party	Women organised in trade unions	% women in trade unions	Women's Suffrage	Women's poll for parties in LSI (where known)	Total number of women of all parties in:-		Number of Socialist women in:-		Women parliamentary candidates	Women's Press
	1928	1931						(a) Lower House	(b) Upper House	(a) Lower House	(b) Upper House		
Great Britain (Labour Party)	300,000	700,000 (1)(2)	23.3	430,532 (3)	11.5	yes	not counted separately	15	-	9	-	30	1 monthly, not obligatory
Great Britain (Independent Labour Party)	14,000	12,000 (1)	30	0(9)		yes	"			2(10)	-	4(11)	1 monthly obligatory
Germany	181,541	228,278	22	800,000 (1)	18 (1)	yes	not counted separately everywhere	41	-	17	-	not reported	1 monthly free of charge for officers, 1 fortnightly
Austria	221,500	228,179	33	161,314 (4)	21.88	yes	765,588	10	-	9	-	43	1 monthly, obligatory, 1 weekly, not obligatory
Belgium	20,000	143,478 (3)	23.9	57,191(4)	11.1	restricted	not counted separately	1	1	1	1	5	2 weeklies, obligatory in certain districts (1 French, 1 Flemish)
Denmark	48,469	57,610	33.6	49,723	6.6	yes	"	3	5	1	2	4	none
Sweden	26,018	38,171 (5)	13.8	57,807(6)	10.4	yes	"	3	1	2	-	5	1 monthly
Czechoslovakia (Czechs)	18,822	26,279	16.8	115,532	20.5	yes	"	10	4	1	1	41	1 weekly
Czechoslovakia (Germans)	24,000	25,712	38.8	53,560	26.2	yes	"	10	3	2 (7)		35	1 monthly, obligatory, 1 weekly, not obligatory
Hungary	20,000	24,135	16.1	16,635	16	yes restricted	"	1	-	1	-	5	1 monthly, obligatory in certain districts

Holland	9,600 / 8,000	21,577	29	16,106	6.08	yes	".."	7	1	2	1	7	1 weekly & 1 circular
Poland		9,200 (1)	20	24,941	10	yes	-	14	4	-	1	12	1 monthly
Finland		8,850 (4)	26	3,000(1)	12	yes	not counted separately	11		7		19	1 monthly
Switzerland	2,000	3,200	6.9	19,451	10.4	no	-	-		-		-	1 monthly, not obligatory
Palestine		1,500	6.7	11,771	39	yes	not counted separately	8		5		8	-
Rumania		1,000(1)	8.2			restricted							1 monthly circular in 3 languages
Russia (SDLP)	1,490	illegal		2,835,200	26.8	yes							
Bulgaria	1,000	not counted separately		not counted separately		no							
France						no							
Danzig	950	2,620	29	6,547	25.6	yes	not counted separately	-		-		3	1 (does not appear regularly)
Latvia	858					yes							
Esthonia	800	828	16.1	-	-	yes	".."	1		-		20	1 weekly supplem. in Party paper
Luxembourg	280	114	9.3			yes	".."	-		-		1	1 monthly
Greece	200	300(1)	10(1)	100		restricted	500	-		-		-	1 women's supplem. in Party paper
Lithuania		250(1)	8(1)	1,500(1)	10(1)	yes	not counted separately	4		-		5	

(1) Approximate. (2) Individually organised women in the Party *circa* 250,000, women organised collectively *circa* 450,000; some are counted twice. (3) Of whom 410,032 are affiliated to the Trades Union Congress. (4) Position in 1929. (5) Some affiliated as individual members, some affiliated collectively through trade unions. (6) Affiliated to the National Centre. In addition *circa* 20,000 not affiliated to the National Centre. (7) Out of a total of three German women MPs. (8) 86,327 individual members, the remainder collectively affiliated through sickness funds and trade unions. (9) See other parties in the country concerned. (10) Included in the figure for the Labour Party. (11) The ILP paid election expenses for 4.

Source: Labour and Socialist International Congress Reports

Conclusion

The British Labour Party and trades unions were of the first importance in recreating international organisation after 1918 and continued to play a prominent international role until 1939. Then, Britain became a haven for emigré socialists, a repository for the relics of the International Faith. Britain held the presidency of the International Federation of Trades Unions throughout the inter-war period, provided the Labour and Socialist International secretariat in its early years and was consistently represented on the LSI Bureau and Executive. Given the size and speed of advance of the forces of reaction in Europe, British Labour Movement connections with European socialist parties were remarkably resilient. Britain was represented in women's and youth organisations and at peripheral internationals devoted to specific subjects, such as education and sport. Britons participated in international travel, in the use of an international language, in internationalist music and art. The British Labour Movement believed in internationalism.

Just what British Labour Movement figures meant by internationalism was rarely defined. To many of the British leadership, including Ramsay MacDonald, Arthur Henderson and later, Hugh Dalton, internationalism meant, in part, helping to form and maintain organisations that were fora for discussion. More idealistic goals were indicated by 1918 rhetoric about 'a workers' peace', 'a League of Peoples', or Ramsay MacDonald's claim: 'For our foreign policy we shall create and use an international platform'.[1] Such statements seemed to promise the construction of a model for supra-national government. Small steps towards this ideal were the inclusion of German and Italian parties in socialist international meetings, a considerable achievement in the hostile 'squeeze the Kaiser till the pips squeak' climate at the end of the First World War. When IFTU/LSI were formed, peace and disarmament were their main policies and continued so throughout the 1920s. As was the case with the Youth International, this position was anti-militarist rather than pacifist. From 1933, resistance to fascism became the main cause. Henderson's 1933 statement of the International Faith, which won general approval throughout the British Labour movement included all the forms of internationalism. Demanding discussion at international level, Henderson spoke also of a socialist world community that would organise economic and social justice and freedom: 'a living reality of the international solidarity of the workers'.[2] He added also the goal of collective security. In 1939, Adler, LSI secretary, reiterated his belief in this international socialist solidarity: 'the final triumph of the International of the fighting proletariat'.[3] This vision was implicit, often explicit in many internationalist songs, in the writings of Esperantists, educators, sports people, travellers. The International Faith may be summarised as belief in the eventual creation of a socialist commonwealth and, meanwhile, assertion of the need to live together in harmony, respecting other cultures and joining to give protection against aggressors.

Commenting on past instances of failure, Anthony Smith has noted that National governments are incapable of creating true international organisations: instead they merely construct world organisations which demand and maintain the persistence of nationhood.[4] It follows that, to be successful, international bodies should be created by organisations whose ambitions extend beyond the maintenance of nation. That is why Labour Party, trades unions, Cooperative Movement perceptions of themselves as parts of international bodies were so important. These perceptions empowered the vision of supra-national government referred to by MacDonald, Henderson and Adler. LSI/IFTU did not evolve into such a supra-national body, partly because of the nationalist constraints of their affiliates. There was always tension between the position held by the British, despite their ideals, that international bodies were advisory and the position of Adler and the IFTU Executive, that international resolutions were binding. Political parties seek election at home, claiming to represent the national interest. Trades unions seek national bargaining power. This was illustrated by TUC reluctance to accept help in the 1926 general strike; its resistance to the 'strike-for-peace', bound up in fears that the 1927 Trades Union and Trades Disputes Act would be used to attack its finances and restrict its powers. In addition, the leadership of any organisation - TUC, Labour Party, LSI - is necessarily concerned with protecting the stability of its own hierarchy.

These nationalist constraints were not powerful enough to cause the British Labour movement to withdraw from international organisation. They do, however, explain Labour Party and, as the TUC identified closely with Labour electoral success, trades union refusal to cooperate with Communists in united front work. The Labour Party had chosen to follow the parliamentary road. This was a political policy arrived at and maintained through debate. It did not prevent 'Russophilism'. At home, where both the Communist Party of Great Britain and fascist parties were noisy but small, non-cooperation with communists was of relatively minor importance. It caused little discord between the Labour Party and the TUC. Although the trades unions reneged on a joint International Department and were free to explore Soviet connections from 1924 to 1927, they renounced the Anglo-Russian Council of their own accord. After 1931, when trades union influence on the National Joint Committee/Labour Party was strongest, there was no substantial policy difference between the Labour Party and trades unions. Lack of cooperation with communists did pose problems for the Independent Labour Party, which was consistently engaged in the search for international socialist unity from the Vienna Union experiment to that of the London Bureau. Fenner Brockway's account of the ILP 'drifting' into a united front was disingenuous. However, ILP disaffiliation prevented it influencing the Labour Party. The Socialist League, also favouring Communist cooperation, disbanded itself. League of Youth and major Labour Party rebels, such as Stafford Cripps, were expelled.

Abroad, where many people organised in communist, communist front or united front groups, Britain's attitude was of major importance in dividing socialist resistance to fascism. Understandable in men who had been denounced as 'lickspittle' and 'traitor', rejecting socialist unity demanded another policy which was never found. In addition, British policy was harmful to the LSI itself, which fractured between the 'Scandinavian' (anti) and 'Latin' (pro-united front) groups. Adler and Vandervelde were fairly skilful at managing this fracture, succeeding in holding the LSI together. At the Youth International, the 'Scandinavian' and 'Latin' split was repeated. The Sports and Education International suffered from this split, as did Esperantists.

For the Labour Party and TUC, the international experience largely became one of committees, agendas, reports. LSI/IFTU were councils where patronage and place were important. This can be seen in the way that the ILP tried to better its position by participation in LSI commissions and by holding an LSI executive committee seat, and in the Labour Party's equal eagerness to guard against LSI encroachment. It was, therefore, appropriate that William Gillies, a Labour Party Officer, came to the fore. Gillies reduced emigré representation at the LSI (1934) to enhance Britain's position. Similarly, the TUC sought to centralise authority at IFTU, insisted on a single secretary and captured the presidency. The British preferred to deal with recognised people and organisations; for instance, at the height of the Spanish Civil War, James Middleton (Labour Party Secretary) complained about the 'unrepresentative' nature of some of his European visitors.[5] Even Gillies's *Communist Solar System* was an account of the Communist organisational plan.

This bureaucratic type of international contact differed from that of MacDonald, whose international excursions were more like those of a Victorian traveller, engaged, curious, seeking atmosphere. Nevertheless, MacDonald admired Lenin as an administrator. Henderson had some of MacDonald's cosmopolitan approach. However, Henderson's administrative abilities were beyond question. With regard to the Labour Party he has been called 'the single figure capable of reconciling factions and binding up wounds'.[6] Both Henderson and MacDonald were capable of inspirational vision, rhetoric. These were, obviously, not qualities which William Gillies was expected to show. Gillies was, nevertheless, extremely influential from 1925 to 1935. He reported directly to the Labour Party Secretary and the sub-committee of the National Executive and his supervision was minimal. He had a good relationship with the Labour Party leadership generally, although he irritated Hugh Dalton. The yearly report of the International sub-committee, including lists of proscribed organisations from 1937, is evidence of Gillies's influence. Gillies did empower mass membership internationalism. He arranged trips abroad, gave advice, wrote articles for *Labour Magazine* and his own notes for constituencies and provided a translation service. He explained the socialist 'international platform' to Chatham House. Labour's 'new men' from 1935, in particular Hugh Dalton at the LSI, built on Gillies's work by playing international politics almost as if at the court of a European emperor.

The mass membership were less concerned than the leadership with dogma, political correctness, hierarchy. Its internationalism was participative, active. Bowen, of the Workers' Travel Association, gave a positive answer to his own question 'Have we reached the workers?'[7] Fritz Wildung, of the Sports International, wrote: 'Our International differs from the political and trade union international in that it brings its members together in action'.[8] Sports people, students and socialist lawyers were particularly active in 1936, on behalf of the Spanish government. It is generally accepted that building a socialist culture empowers a Labour movement, translating into local electoral success.[9] The international socialist culture similarly empowered the International Labour Movement, as Adler's files testify. Especially before 1933, when the threat of fascism was yet to be fully felt, the sheer volume and diversity of international activity is impressive.

This international activity was politically conscious, containing the vision of a new world order. The travellers rescued from Spain and Czechoslovakia, Felicia Browne journeying to paint in Spain, the singers around the Spanish camp fires engaged in activity because they envisaged political change. Its lack of dogma liberated the mass membership to dream of a new type of internationalism, sharing leisure, enhancing understanding of other people. To travel was to dream, to imagine alternative locations, to make an effort to communicate. To speak Esperanto was to express a vision of international communication. Emotion and information were conveyed by music and art, which enriched the imagination. The mass membership's vision of internationalism was implicitly a critique of militarism, imperialism, conservatism in government and a hope for a socialist future. Such a socialist consciousness has been claimed, for instance by Hobsbawm, to be at a higher level than the construction of class organisations.[10]

How far this socialist consciousness was influential within the Labour Party and trades unions at home is difficult to establish. The rank and file voice was heard at meetings, conferences, demonstrations, education classes, in the Labour press. On the issue of Spain, in particular, rank and file opinion was expressed forcefully and frequently. For instance, the National Emergency Conference in Spain, April 1938, was attended by 1,806 delegates representing 1,205 organisations.[11] However, the rank and file did not always speak with one voice. For example, while the demand for intervention in Spain was vociferous, Bevin felt the need to respond to Roman Catholic anti-Republican opinion, especially in the Irish Transport and General Workers' Union. Division between communists, anarchists and socialists, apparent in the Spanish Republic, had some impact at home. Henderson, Bevin and Citrine, were clever managers of Labour Party Conference and it was rare for the leadership to be embarrassed on such occasions. The sting was speedily drawn from occasional rank and file victories, such as Fenner Brockway's 1926 'strike-for-peace' resolution, or the 1933 Socialist League package of measures. On the other hand, Party managers won support for international ventures because they drew on broad rank and file support for internationalism. Working for peace, collective security, rearmament were in turn supported. Expenditure on international contacts was not questioned. Britain paid its international affiliation fees. Labour was, of course, in government merely for three years in the inter-war period, and then reliant on its allies. The rank and file thus rarely tilted at Labour government policy; but it could usually contribute to forming the policy of the Labour opposition.

It was the very vitality of its international activities before 1933 that prevented the British Labour movement from understanding the strength of reaction in Europe. Quite simply, the British expected international organisations to carry on operating and had a mistaken belief in the strength of German socialists and trades unionists. The British were aware of Nazi atrocities, but they sent a cheque drawn on a German Bank to the Youth International at Amsterdam. Indeed, the German and Austrian coups went largely unchallenged by LSI/IFTU. A sense of defeat was not fully realised in Britain until civil war in Spain finally revealed the importance of LSI/IFTU. There was neither mechanism, power, nor plan with which to resist fascism. In this context, the British had solid grounds for standing somewhat aloof, in addition to the disinterest of the British electorate, the sensitivities of the Roman Catholic trades union membership and worries about working with communists.

As the British Labour Movement's refusal to work with communists was so divisive, Vandervelde blamed the British with some justice for 'the funeral of the Second International'. Yet possibly more damaging to the LSI than its rejection of the united front was Gillies's 'inauguration of a vigorous debate' on neutrality.[12] British Labour, however, had rejected neutrality and resolved on rearmament step-by-step from 1934 in the *international* interest. It was the Spanish Civil War that converted the doubters. As Ted Willis wrote: 'Our enemy had a face - the face of Hitler, Mussolini and Franco'.[13] In 1937 Gillies wanted to send arms to Spain; it was Blum, the French Premier, and Dalton who urged restraint.[14] Gillies and Dalton were both keen to help Czechoslovakia. It was not until the invasion of Czechoslovakia that a *'sauve qui peut'* approach emerged and British rearmament was perceived by neutrals at the LSI to be activity in the national interest. It was difficult for national rearmament to co-exist with the unfocused war-resistance which characterised the LSI. Gillies refused to supply Adler with theses on the British position. He made no attempt to find common ground with the neutrals; but some of the Scandinavian parties who supported him participated in government. This possibility of LSI-induced partial collective security was not pursued. Overpowered by war, international organisation collapsed. IFTU's offices fell into Nazi hands, the LSI secretary emigrated to America. Van Roosbroeck, LSI treasurer, in Paris at the outbreak of war, hid LSI funds in an American account and one at the London National Westminster bank. He was arrested by the Gestapo on his return to Belgium and although he was later released from prison, was banned from approaching the LSI offices for the duration of the war.[15]

After war and cold war, the idea of nation remains powerful but causes as much bloodshed at the end of the twentieth century as it did at the beginning. The jigsaw puzzle of national states is being recast and, when completed, promises to reveal as barbarous a picture as its pre-war counterpart. Some of this barbarity is justified by its perpetrators by calling on national history, an imaginary construct, a vision and a dream. Nationalism thrives on the story-telling of national history. The alternative is to rediscover the dream, the vision, the narrative of internationalism, to legitimate present day and postulate future organising principles for social and political life. Some commentators, Anthony Giddens and Steven Lukes among them, have been cited as doubting whether the working class can be the agent of change; and have questioned whether socialism might, in future, find expression only in relation to a more dominant capitalism. But it is a very poor socialism that can exist only in fluctuating and bellicose nation states. To conclude with the words of Julius Braunthal, who became secretary when the LSI was reformed after the Second World War, and who wrote its history:

> For socialism ... is in essence an international gospel of humanism, a vision of the world made alive by a sense of human fellowship, a faith in social equality, not only of one's own countrymen but of the whole of mankind.[16]

Notes

1. MacDonald, James Ramsay (1925), *Wanderings and Excursions,* London, p. 228.

2. Henderson, Arthur (1933), Labour Party Conference *Report*, p. 188 ff.

3. *Labour and Socialist International Papers,* Labour Party Archives, Manchester, Adler's report 1939, LSI 22/4/64.

4. Smith, Anthony (1979), *Nationalism in the Twentieth Century*, Martin Robertson.

5. *Sozialistische Arbeiter-Internationale Papers,* International Institute of Social History, Amsterdam, Middleton to Adler, Jouhaux, Schevenels, 18 December 1936, SAI 27/51/52/63.

6. Leventhal, F. (1989) *Arthur Henderson,* Manchester University Press, p. 168.

7. Bowen, J. W. (1933), *Address to the WTA National Council* (typescript).

8. Steinberg, David A., 'The Workers' Sports International, 1920-1928', *Journal of Contemporary History*, 13, 1978, p. 236.

9. Williams, Chris (1995), 'Britain' in Berger, Stefan and Broughton, David (eds), *The Force of Labour*, Berg, Oxford.

10. Hobsbawm E. J. (1971), 'Class Consciousness' and Bottomore, Tom (1971), 'Class Structure and National Consciousness' in Istvan Mezaros (ed.), *Aspects of History and Class Consciousness*, Routledge, London

11. National Emergency Conference on Spain, *Report*, April 1938.

12. *Labour and Socialist International Papers*, Gillies to Dalton, May 1938, LSI 22/2/7.

13. Willis, Ted (1970), *Whatever Happened to Tom Mix?*, Cassell, London, p. 150.

14. Dalton papers, British Library of Political and Economic Science, London, *Diary*, 13 September 1937, I 18.14.

15. *Sozialistische Arbeiter-Internationale Papers*, 1945, 1946, SAI 4137-4139. Van Roosbroeck and Adler faced huge difficulties in reclaiming the LSI money, which they needed to pay the LSI landlord who insisted on his rent for the war years. Adler succeeded in negotiating an agreement to pay fifty per cent. Morgan Phillips, to whom the National Westminster bank referred the issue was of little help and Gillies, as signatory to the account, was called out of retirement to release the funds. Denis Healey finally wound up the LSI account in 1946.

16. Braunthal, Julius (1960), introduction to Cole, G. D. H., *A History of Socialist Thought: Socialism and Fascism 1931-1938*, vol. v, Macmillan, London, p. xiii. Braunthal, Julius (1967), *History of the International, 1914-1943*, vol. ii, London.

Bibliography

Bibliographical note

The Second International archives were at the Maison du Peuple, Brussels, until 1914. A part was transferred for safe keeping in the war to the Workers' College Library at Uccle, while Camille Huysmans took a second part home and deposited a third part at Antwerp Library. All the first International archives had been handed to Anton Menger; most of these were found in Vienna in 1918 and were deposited in the Marx Engels' Institute at Moscow. Some were lost altogether, for instance, the Minutes of the Copenhagen Congress, 1920, and the report of the Stockholm Conference, 1917. Adler, in 1927, transferred the Uccle Library Papers to Zurich in a furniture van. He obtained the Huysmans and Antwerp collections and managed to retrieve some Papers from the Marx Engels' Institute. All these were also deposited at Zurich. Writing 'there is no need to describe ... in detail the wanderings of these archives',[1] Adler proposed their transfer to Vienna, but the defeat of the Socialists under Dolfuss obviously made this ineligible.

Meanwhile, the records of the Labour and Socialist International at its London headquarters were deposited in the International Institute of Social History, Amsterdam when this was founded in the 1930s. Some of the records of the LSI at Zurich were also deposited in Amsterdam. The rest, plus the Second International archives, were moved to Brussels in 1935 when the LSI again changed offices. Adler suggested to Gillies that the records should be kept for safety in London; Gillies replied: 'if they would be safer elsewhere than in Brussels, they should be removed at your discretion'[2] and discussed the matter with Adler in March 1938. Owing to their disagreement, the records remained at Brussels until Camille Huysmans brought the bulk to London when war broke out. They remained in the Labour Party Headquarters' Archives, London and some were exhibited at Brussels in 1964, on the 100th anniversary of the first International, when Harold Wilson was vice-president of the exhibition committee.[3] While this book was being written, these archives resumed their wanderings, in company with those of the Labour Party. The collection was finally transferred to the National Museum of Labour History in Manchester.

Trades Union Congress records were not to be left standing by all this movement. The International Committee Minutes were available at Trades Union Congress headquarters, London, but have now been transferred, with the bulk of the TUC records, to the Modern Records Centre, Warwick University. These records were cross-referenced and indexed by Citrine and it is his references which are given in this book; the collection is now being refiled and properly indexed.

Ramsay MacDonald's diaries are cited briefly on several occasions. It should be noted that the contents of these diaries were, in Ramsay MacDonald's words, 'meant as notes to guide and revive memory as regards happenings and must on no account be published as they are'.

Notes

1.   Labour and Socialist International, *Third Congress Report*, 1928, pp. ii. 37-41.
2.   *Labour and Socialist International Papers*, letter from Gillies to Adler, 22 February 1938, LSI/22/2/7.
3.   100th Anniversary of International Socialism, 5-20 September 1964, *Exhibition Catalogue* (Brussels, 1964).

Manuscript Sources

Labour Party Archives, National Museum of Labour History, Manchester

Ancillary Organisations of the Socialist International
Arthur Henderson Papers
Germany: Correspondence, Reports and Memoranda
International Advisory Committee Minutes
International Sub-Committee of the Labour Party Minutes
International Women
James Middleton Papers
Joint International Committee of the Labour Party and Trades Union
    Congress Minutes
Labour and Socialist International Papers
Spanish Children's books
William Gillies Correspondence

International Institute of Social History, Amsterdam

International Committee of Women Trades Unionists Conference Reports,
    1927, 1933, 1936
Labour and Socialist International in London, 1921-23
International Federation of Trades Union Papers
Sozialistische Arbeiter-Internationale Papers
Sozialistische Jugend Internationale Papers

Churchill College, Cambridge

Attlee Papers
Bevin Papers
Philip Noel Baker Papers

British Library of Political and Economic Science

Dalton Papers

Ruskin College, Oxford

James and Lucy Middleton Papers

Public Record Office, London

Ramsay MacDonald Papers

Modern Records Centre, Warwick

Trades Union Congress Papers

Trades Union Congress, London

TUC International Committee Minutes and Papers (microfiche)
Workers' Travel Association Papers

Esperanto Centre, London

Esperanto Archives

Tate Gallery, London

Artists' International Papers

Bodleian Library, Oxford

Independent Labour Party Archives (microfiche)

Printed sources

(i) Primary

Bowen, J.W. (1933), *Address to the WTA National Council,* WTA, London
British Committee for Refugees from Spain (n.d.), *A Nation in Retreat*, London
Brown, Felicia (1936), *Drawings by Felicia Browne,* Lawrence and Wishart, London
Lord Citrine (1964), *Men and Work: The Autobiography of Lord Citrine*, London
Sir Walter Citrine (1936), *I Search for Truth in Russia*, London
Cramp, C.T. (1925), *Labour's Creative Task,* Labour Party, London
Cusson, Stanley (1933), *Artists at Work,* Harrap, London
Dalton, Hugh (1953), *Call Back Yesterday,* London
Dalton, Hugh (1957), *The Fateful Years,* Muller, London
Duff, Charles (1938), *Spain Against the Invaders,* London
Henderson, Arthur (1923), *Labour and Foreign Affairs*, London
MacDonald, Ramsay (1928), *Labour and the Nation*, Labour Party, London
MacDonald, Ramsay (1925), *Wanderings and Excursions*, London
Lord Morrison of Lambeth (1960), *Herbert Morrison: An Autobiography*, Odhams, London

O'Neill, F. R. (1931), *The Social Value of Art*, Psyche Monograph no. 12, Kegan Paul, Trench, Turnbull, London

Phelan, E. J. (1939), *Yes and Albert Thomas*, London

Pollitt, Harry (1937), *Pollitt Visits Spain*, International Brigade Dependants' Committee, London

Pollitt, Harry (n.d.), *Spain: What Next?*, Communist Party, London

Read, Herbert (1935), *Five on Revolutionary Art,* Lawrence and Wishart, London

Seven Members of the Labour Party (1923), *The Labour Party's Aims: A Criticism and Restatement*, Allen & Unwin, London

Phillip Viscount Snowden (1934), *An Autobiography, vol. 2, 1919-1934*, London

Spanish State Tourism Information Service (n.d.), *Nine Works of Art,* Spain

Stewart, Margaret (1938), *Reform Under Fire: Social Progress in Spain, 1931-1938,* Gollancz, London

Thomas, J. H. (1920), *When Labour Rules,* Collins, London

Trade Union and Labour Party Delegates (1938), *Spain 1938*, International Brigade Wounded and Dependants' Aid Committee, London

Willis, T. (1970), *Whatever Happened to Tom Mix?,* Cassell, London

Reports

Council of Action: *Report of a Special Conference on Labour and the Russo-Polish War, 13 August 1920*, London

Emergency Conference of the Labour Party, *Report: Labour and Spain,* October 1938

International Cooperative Alliance, *Congress Reports*

Labour International Handbook, Labour Publishing Co, London

Labour International Yearbook, Labour Publishing Co, London

Labour and Socialist International Congress *Reports*

Labour Party Conference *Reports*

National Emergency Conference on Spain, *Report*, April 1938

Soviet Russia: An Investigation by Women Trades Unionists, 1924, London

Trades Union Congress *Reports*

NewsPapers, periodicals

British Esperantist
Clarion
Contact
Cooperative Citizen
Daily Herald
Highway
International Cooperative Bulletin

Labour Bulletin
Labour Magazine
Labour Woman
Left Review
New Leader
Pilgrim
Pioneer
The Travel Log
Workers' Life

Songsheets

Barrett, Rowland (n.d.), *The Rookvale Collection of Twenty Socialist Songs,* Devon
Bush, Alan and Swingler, Randall, (1938), *The Left Song Book,* Gollancz, London
Cooperative Education Committee, (n.d.), *Pioneer Song Book,* Watford
Elsbury, A.E.(n.d.), *Proletarian Parodies: Labour Songs for the Street, Work and Home*, Proletarian Press, London
General and Municipal Workers (n.d.), *Anniversary Songbook*
Hill, Joe and Anderson, Tom (1920), *Songs of Your Class,* The Proletarian School Movement
Hogg, Rufus (1932), *Peoples' Parodies,* London
International Workers of the World (1928), *Songs*, 23rd edition, United States
Labour Party (n.d.), *Everyday Songs for Labour Festivals,* Labour Publishing Co., London
New Songs for Cooperators, (1923), Birmingham
Proletarian School (1919), *Proletarian Song Book* ,Glasgow
Sixteen Songs for Sixpence (n.d.), Lansbury's Labour Weekly, London
University Labour Federation (n.d.), *Songs of the People,* Cambridge
Woodcraft Folk (n.d.), *Songs for All,* Manchester
Workers' Music League (n.d.), *Workers' Songs*, WML, London
Workers' Theatre Movement (n.d.), *Workers' Song Book,* WTM, London

(ii) Secondary

Alberti, Johanna (1994), 'British Feminists and Anti-Fascism in the 1930s' in Oldfield, Sybil, *This Working Day World*, Taylor & Francis, London
Anderson, Benedict (1991), *Imagined Communities: Reflections on the Origin and Spread of Nationalisms,* Verso, London
Berger, Stefan and Broughton, David, (eds), (1995), *The Force of Labour:*

The Western European Labour Movement and the Working Class in the Twentieth Century, Berg, Oxford

Bernstein, S. and Richards, A. (1982), *Two Steps Back: Communism and the Wider Labour Movement 1935-45*, Socialist Platform, London

Bourke, Joanna (1994), *Working Class Culture in Britain 1890-1960*, Routledge, London

Boxer, J. M. and Quataert, J. H. (eds), (1978), *Socialist Women: European Socialist Feminism in the Nineteenth and Early Twentieth Centuries*, New York

Braunthal J. (1967), *History of the International, 1914-1943, vol. ii*, London

Breuilly, John (1993), *Nationalism and the State*, Manchester University Press

Briggs, A. and Saville, J. (eds), (1967), *Essays in Labour History, 1914-1943*, London

Brockway, F. (1942), *Inside the Left*, Allen & Unwin, London

Buchanan, Tom (1991), *The Spanish Civil War and the Labour Movement*, Cambridge

Bullock, A. (1960), *The Life and Times of Ernest Bevin, vol. I, Trades Union Leader, 1881-1940*, Heinemann, London

Cahm, E. and Fisera, V.C. (eds), (1986), *Socialism and Nationalism*, Spokesman, London

Calhoun, D.F. (1976), *The United Front: The TUC and the Russians 1923-1928*, Cambridge

Carlton, D. (1970), *MacDonald Versus Henderson: The Foreign Policy of the Second Labour Government*, MacMillan, London

Ceadel, M. (1980), *Pacifism in Great Britain 1914-1945: The Defining of a Faith*, Cambridge

Chambers, Colin (1989), *The Story of Unity Theatre*, Lawrence and Wishart, London

Cline, C.A. (1963), *Recruits to Labour: the British Labour Party, 1914-1931*, Syracuse University Press

Clinton, A. (1977), *The Trade Union Rank and File, Trades Councils in Britain 1700-1940*, Manchester University Press

Cole, G.D.H. (1958), *A History Of Socialist Thought: Communism and Social Democracy 1914-1931, vol. iv*, MacMillan, London

Cole, G.D.H. (1960), *A History of Socialist Thought: Socialism and Fascism 1931-1939, vol. v*, MacMillan, London

Collette, Christine (1989), *For Labour and For Women: The Women's Labour League 1906-1918*, Manchester University Press

Collette, Christine (1993), 'Gender and Class in the Labour and Socialist International, 1923-1939' in Hauch, Gabriella (ed.), *Geschlecht, Klasse, Ethnizität*, Vienna

Donoghue, B. and Jones, G. W. (1973), *Herbert Morrison, Portrait of a Politician*, Weidenfeld & Nicolson, London

Dowse, R. E. (1965), *Left in the Centre: The Independent Labour Party 1893-1940*, Longmans, London

Eley, Geoff (1992), 'Researching the Socialist Tradition' in Lensky, C. and Marks, G. (eds), *The Crisis of Socialism in Europe*, Duke University Press

Finkelstein, Sidney (1960), *Composer and Nation: Folk Heritage in Music*, Lawrence and Wishart, London

Foot, M.R. (1975), *Aneurin Bevin, 1897-1942, vol. 1*, Paladin, London

Francis, H. (1984), *Miners and Fascism: Wales and the Spanish Civil War*, Lawrence and Wishart, London

Fryer, Peter (1984), *Staying Power: The History of Black People in Britain*, Pluto, London

Fyrth, Jim (1985), *Britain, Fascism and the Popular Front*, Lawrence and Wishart, London

Gilroy, Paul (1987), *There Ain't No Black in the Union Jack*, Hutchinson

Gloversmith, Frank (ed.), (1980), *Class, Culture and Social Change*, Harvester, Sussex

Gordon, M. R. (1969), *Conflict and Consensus in Labour's Foreign Policy*, Stanford University Press

Graves, Pamela (1994), *Labour Women: Women in British Working Class Politics 1918-1939*, Cambridge University Press

Greene, Archie (1993), *Wobblies, Pile Butts and Other Heroes: Laborlore Explorations*, University of Illinois, Chicago

Greene, N. (ed.), (1971), *European Socialism Since World War One*, Chicago

Halèvy, Élie (1967), *The Era of Tyrannies*, Allen Lane, London

Hamilton, Mary Agnes (1938), *Arthur Henderson, A Biography*, Heinemann, Oxford

Haupt, Georges (1972), *Socialism and the Great War*

Healey, Denis (1990), *The Time of My Life*, Penguin, London

Heller, Wendy (1985), *Lidia: the Life of Lidia Zamenhof, Daughter of Esperanto*, George Roland

Hobsbawm, E.J. (1971), 'Class Consciousness' and Bottomore, Tom (1971), 'Class Structure and National Consciousness' in Istvan Mezaros (ed.), *Aspects of History and Class Consciousness*, Routledge, London

Hobsbawm, E.J. (1991), *Nations and Nationalisms*, Cambridge

Holthoon, F. van and Linder, Marcel van der (eds), (1988), *Internationalism and the Labour Movement 1830-1940*, IISG, Amsterdam

Hyams, Edward (1963), *The New Statesman: The History of the First Fifty Years, 1913-63*, Longmans, London

Jones, Stephen (1988), *Sport, Politics and the Working Class*, Manchester University Press

Kapp, Yvonne (1979), *Eleanor Marx: The Crowded Years, 1884-1898*, Virago, London

Kirk, Neville (1994), *Labour and Society in Britain and the USA, vol. 2*, Scolar Press, Hampshire

Kitchen, M. (1980), *The Coming of Austrian Fascism*, Croom Helm, London

Kofosky Sedgwick, Eve (1992), 'Nationalisms and Sexualities in the Age of Wilde' in Parker, Andrew et al. (eds), *Nationalisms and Sexualities*, Routledge, London

Levanthal, F.M. (1989), *Arthur Henderson*, Manchester University Press.

Libmann, Brigitte (1994), 'British Women Surrealists - Deviants from Deviance?' in Oldfield, Sybil, *This Working Day World,* Taylor and Francis, London.

Liddington, Jill (1989), *The Long Road to Greenham Common, Feminism and Anti-Militarism in Britain since 1820*, Virago, London

Lorwin, Lewis L. (1929), *Labour and Internationalism*, New York

MacKenzie, Norman and Jean (eds), (1984), *The Diary of Beatrice Webb*, Virago, London

McKibbin, R. (1974), *The Evolution of the Labour Party 1910-1924,* Oxford University Press

McShane, Harry (1978), *No Mean Fighter,* Pluto Press, London

Martin, R. (1969), *Communism and the British Trades Unions, 1924-1933: A Study of the National Minority Movement*, Clarendon Press, Oxford

Miller, K. E. (1967), *Socialism and Foreign Policy: Theory and Practice in Great Britain to 1931,* The Hague

Montague, C.E. (1922), *Disenchantment,* Chatto and Windus

Morris, Lynda and Radford, Robert (1983), *The Story of the AIA*, Museum of Modern Art, Oxford

Naylor, J. F. (1969), *Labour's International Policy: The Labour Party in the 1930s*, Weidenfeld and Nicolson, London

Noltenius, Rainer (1993), *Ilustrita Historio de la Laborista Esperanto - Movado*, Dortmund

Oliver, Paul (ed.) (1990), *Black Music in Britain*, Open University Press, Milton Keynes

Philips, Eileen (1983), *The Left and the Erotic*, Lawrence and Wishart, London

Pimlott, B. (1977), *Labour and the Left in the 1930s*, Cambridge University Press

Pimlott, B. (1985), *Hugh Dalton*, MacMillan, London

Polasky, Janet (1995), *The Democratic Socialism of Emile Vandervelde*, Berg, Oxford

Postgate, R. (1951), *The Life of George Lansbury,* London

Pritt, D.N. (1965), *An Autobiography of D.N. Pritt, Part One, From Left to Right,* Lawrence and Wishart, London

Ramdin, Ron (1987), *The Making of the Black Working Class in Britain*, Wildwood House, Oxford

Reinalda, Bob (1997), *The International Transport Federation (IFT) 1914-1945: The Edo Fimmen Era*, IISH, Amsterdam

Saville, John (1977), 'May Day 1937' in Asa Briggs and John Saville (eds), *Essays in Labour History 1918-1939*, Croom Helm, London

Seton, Marie (1988), *Paul Robeson*, Dobson, London

Shreeves, Rosamund (1992), 'Sexual Revolution or Sexploitation' in Rai, Shirin et al. (eds), *Women in the Face of Change*, Routledge, London

Smith, Anthony (1979), *Nationalism in the Twentieth Century*, Martin Robertson, London

Smith, Anthony (1986), *The Ethnic Origins of Nations*, Blackwell, Oxford

Southern, Eileen (1982), *Biographical Details of Afro-American and African Musicians*, Greenwood, London

Southern, Eileen (1983), *The Music of Black Americans*, Norton, London

Taylor, A.J.P. (1980), *Politicians, Socialists and Historians*, Hamish Hamilton, London

Thane, Pat (1990), 'The Feminism of Women in the British Labour Party' in Smith, H. (ed.), *Twentieth Century British Feminism*, Elgar Press, London

Tonkin, Humphrey et al. (eds) (1993), Pierre Janton, *Esperanto: Language, Literature and Community*, New York

Watkins, K.W. (1963), *Britain Divided: The Effect of the Spanish Civil War on British Political Opinion*, Nelson, London

Watkins, W.P. (1986), *Cooperative Principles Today and Tomorrow*, Holyoake Books

Williams, A. J. (1989), *Labour and Russia: The Attitude of the Labour Party to the USSR, 1924-34*, Manchester University Press

Williams, Chris (1995), 'Britain' in Berger, Stefan and Broughton, David (eds), *The Force of Labour: The Western European Labour Movement and the Working Class in the Twentieth Century*, Berg, Oxford

Wrigley, Chris (1990), *Arthur Henderson*, Wales

Journals

Berger, Stefan (1992), 'The British and German Labour Movements before the Second World War: the *Sonderweg* Revisited', *Twentieth Century British History* 3, (3)

Black, Naomi, 'The Mother's International: the Women's Cooperative Guild and Feminist Pacifism', *Women's Studies International Forum*, 7 (6) 1984

Boak, Helen (1990), 'Women in Weimer Politics', *European History Quarterly*, 20 (3) July

Buchanan, Tom (1988), 'The Role of the Labour Movement in the Origin and Work of the Basque Children's Committee 1937-39', *European History Quarterly*, vol. 18, no. 2, April

Collette, C (1991), 'New Realism, Old Traditions', *Labour History Review*, 56 (1)

Fyrth, Jim (1993), 'The Aid Spain Movement', *History Workshop*, 35, Spring

Jones, S. G. (1988), 'The European Workers' Sports Movement and Organised Labour in Britain Between the Wars', *European History Quarterly,* vol. 18, no. 1, January

Lewis, J. (1983), 'Red Vienna: Socialism in One City, 1918-1927', *European Studies Review,* vol. 13, no. 3

McKibbin, R. (1978), 'Arthur Henderson as Labour Leader', *International Review of Labour History,* xxiii

Parker, R.A.C. (1981), 'British Rearmament 1936-39: Treasury, Trades Unions and Skilled Labour', *English Historical Review,* 96

Richards, Sam (1983), 'Joe Hill: a Labour Legend in Song', *Folk Music Journal,* 4 (4)

Rickaby, T. (1978), 'Artists' International', *History Workshop,* 6

Rose, Sonia (1993), 'Gender and Labour History', *International Review of Social History,* 38, Supplement 1

Silverman, Victor (1993), 'Popular Bases of the International Labour Movement in the US and Britain, 1939-1945', *International Review of Social History,* 38 (3)

Steinberg, David A., 'The Workers' Sports International, 1920-1928', *Journal of Contemporary History,* 13, 1978, p. 236

Tabili, Laura (1994), 'The construction of Racial Difference in 20C Britain: the Special Restrictions (Coloured and Alien Seamen) Order 1925', *Journal of British Studies,* 33 (1) January

Thane, Pat (1990), 'Women and Labour Politics', *Labour History Review,* 55 (3)

Thomas, T. (1977), 'The Workers' Theatre Movement: Memoirs and Documents', *History Workshop,* 4

Tuckett, A. (n.d.), 'The People's Theatre in Bristol', *Our History,* no. 72

Winkler, H. J. (1956), 'The Emergence of a Labour Foreign Policy in Great Britain', *Journal of Modern History,* xviii, 2

Young, J. (1985), 'Idealism and Realism in Labour's Foreign Policy', Society for the Study of Labour History *Bulletin,* no. 50

Theses

Dare, R. E. (1972), 'The Socialist League, 1932-1937', Oxford University D. Phil. Thesis

Deepwell, C. N. (1991), 'Women Artists in Britain between the Two World Wars', London University, Ph.D. Thesis

Eatwell, R. (1975), 'The Labour Party and the Popular Front Movement in Britain in the 1930s', Oxford University, D. Phil. Thesis

Rose, R. L. (1959), 'The Relation of Socialist Principles to British Labour and Foreign Policy', Oxford University, D. Phil. Thesis

Shepherd, G. W. (1952), 'The Theory and Practice of Internationalism in the

British Labour Party with Special Reference to the Inter-War Period',
London University, Ph D. Thesis

Tombs, I. (1989), 'Socialist Policy and the Future of Europe: the Distinction
between British Labour and Continental Socialists in London, 1939-45',
Cambridge University, Ph D. Thesis

Interviews

I am indebted to many people, particularly members of Labour Heritage for
talking to me about the period 1918-39. I would especially like to record my
gratitude to the following, all active socialists of the period: Joan Davis,
Florence Davy, Annie Leff, Theo Pinkus, Angela Tuckett, George Wagner,
Irene Wagner, Lord Willis.

Index

Adler, Friedrich 47, 51-56, 58, 60, 62, 64 66-68,7 8-80, 85, 87-93, 99-101, 113, 114, 118, 120, 121, 128, 159, 160, 182, 185-187, 290
Adler, Kathia 46
Adler, Victor 51
Advance 176, 178, 179, 181
Aids for Study in International Relations 57
Albarda, W.J. (LSI, Netherlands) 79, 80, 89, 91
Alberti, Joanna 162
Aliens Act, 1905 4
All-In Conference (on Spain) 32
Allen, Clifford 54
American Federation of Labour 12, 13, 15, 33
L'Amicale des Jeunes Socialistes 176
Anglo-Russian Committee 18, 20
Anglo-Soviet Cooperative Wheat Exporting Company 166
Anti-Alcohol Alliance 99
Anti-Nazi Council 34
Anti-Nazi League Council 8
Appleton, William 15
Arbeiter Radio International 137, 138
Arendt, Hannah 109
Art and Power Exhibition (1995/6) 139
Artists' International (Association) 139-145
Artists Against Fascism and War Exhibition (1935) 141
Associated Society of Locomotive Engineers and Firemen 24, 25, 68
Atherton, A. (Railway Workers) 126
Attlee, Clement R. 31, 81, 85, 86, 88, 92, 131

Bacon, Alice 176, 177
Baker, Alfred 100
Baker, Philip Noel 50, 58, 138
Bandiera Rossa 135
Barbusse, Henri 67, 125
Barmat scandal (1925) 57
Barton, Eleanor (Women's Cooperatve Guild) 169, 170, 182
Bauer, Otto 54, 55, 66, 67, 80, 87
Bauhaus workshop 109, 139
Bell, Graham 140
Bell, Vanessa 140
Bentham, Ethel 159, 160
Berger, Stefan 3, 106
Berne Conference (1919) 47, 153
Bernstein, Alec 179
Bernstein, Eduard 5
Bevin, Ernest 16, 20, 23, 24, 26, 28, 29, 31, 32, 35, 51, 56, 63, 81-83, 104, 105, 144, 189
Billig, Michael 145
Binder, Pearl 140
Binet, Tom (Sports' International) 117, 118
Biro, Michael 142
Black, Naomi 168, 183
Blum, Leon 57, 66, 80, 84, 167, 190
Bolton, William (TUC) 23, 28, 56, 82
Bondfield, Margaret 152, 153, 160, 182
Boswell, James 140, 142
Boughton, Rutland 130, 133
Bowen, J.W. (Postal Workers' Union, WTA) 104, 106, 118, 126
Bramley, Frederick (TUC) 19, 56
Branting, Hjalmar 13, 14, 47, 48, 51, 53
Braunthal, Julius 190
British Bureau (RILU) 19

British Committee for Refugees from Spain 8
British Labour Esperanto Society 127-129
British League of Esperantist Socialists 125-127
The British Labour Movement and Communism (1936) 83
British Socialist Party 14
British Workers' Sports Federation 115-118
British Workers' Temperance Federation 99
Brockway, Fenner 25, 64, 65, 67, 77, 85, 167, 174, 187, 189
Bromley, J. (ASLEF) 25
Brown, George 176
Browne, Felicia 144, 145, 188
Brown, John W. (IFTU) 15, 20, 24, 109, 119
Burra, Edward 139
Bush, Alan 130, 134
Buxton, Charles Roden 50
Buxton, Noel 50

Cachin, Marcel 79, 80
Canciones de las Brigadas Internationalas 134
Carlin, Mary 160
Ceadel, Martin 168
Chamberlain, Neville 12, 85, 91, 181
Chatham House see Royal Institute for International Affairs
Chevenard, Jeanne 159, 160
Churchill, Sir Winston 181, 182
Citrine, Sir Walter 18, 20, 21, 23-35, 55, 56, 67, 81, 129, 189
Clarion Cycling Club 6, 115, 116, 118
Clarion 115
'Class Against Class' 62
Clynes, J.R. 52
Coe, Mrs (LSI) 49
Cole, G.D.H. 50, 67, 115

Collick, P. (ASLEF) 67, 76
Commissariat de Propaganda 141
Communist Party of Great Britain 2, 3, 7, 19, 21, 30, 60-62, 67, 68, 77, 79, 83, 84, 88, 118, 119, 128, 186
Communist Solar System 63, 68, 187
Contact 127, 129
Cooperative Ladies' Football Team 115
Cooperative Party 7, 111
Cooperative Party Citizen 170
Cooperative Wholesale Society 103
Cornford, John 6, 113
Court, Sidney 130-132
Crawfurd, Helen 152
Creech Jones, Arthur (TGWU) 104
Cripps, Stafford 77, 81-83, 88, 89, 100, 178, 181, 187
Crossman, R.H. 84
Cullen, C.K. (ILP) 65
Cusson, Stanley 139

Daily Herald 54, 78, 85, 127, 136, 172
Dalton, Hugh 32, 34, 50, 60, 80-89, 91, 92, 105, 169, 185, 188, 190
Davison, E. (Railworker) 139
De Brouckere, Louis 177
Deepwell, Katy 139, 140
DeMan, Hendrik 89
Deutsch, Julius 65, 86, 116
Devlieger, Jules (Sports International) 116
Dictatorship and the Trade Union Movement 27
Disarmament and Fascism (1933) 169
Dockerty, Peter (ILP) 103, 173, 175
Dollan, Agnes 152, 160, 168

Dollan, Patrick Joseph 58, 64, 66, 152
Durr, Karl 18

Ecoles Marxienne 110
Education Workers' International 110, 111
Esperanto 110, 112, 124-129, 145, 169, 173, 188
L'Etudiante Socialiste 113

Fabian Society 53, 160
Fimmen, Edo (ITWF) 15, 16, 23, 24, 153
Fitton, James 143
Flame 173
Foster, Lizzie Glasier 136
Friedlander, Otto 113
Furniss, Henry Sanderson (Principal, Ruskin College) 113
Fyffe, Hamilton (*Daily Herald*) 54

Gabriel 140, 142
Gaster, Jack (ILP) 65
General Federation of Trades Unions 15
General Strike (1926) 23, 25
George, Reuben, Fund 112
Gillies, William 6, 13, 19, 20, 27, 31-33, 48-51, 53-60, 62, 63, 65-68, 76, 78-80, 82-85, 87-89, 91, 92, 105. 110, 114, 120, 124, 137, 138, 145, 164, 167, 169, 170, 172, 173, 178-183, 187-190
Glasier, Katharine Bruce 35
Gloeckel, Otto 114
Godefroid (Socialist Youth) 175-177, 179
Gompers, Sam (AFofL) 15
Gossip, Alex (Furnishing Trades) 16

Gosling, Harry (TGWU) 14, 53, 101, 125
Gould, Barbara Ayrton 181
Gradwell, Angela Tuckett 129-131, 134
Graves, Pamela 161
Green, Archie 132, 144
Green, H.G. (ILP) 173, 175
Greene, Ben (parliamentary candidate) 114
Greenwood, Arthur 49, 65, 91, 93
Greenwood, Ernest (WEA) 105
Groom, Tom (Sports International) 6, 115-117
Guild of Youth (ILP) 103, 127, 172-175, 178

Haldane Society 100
Halevy, Elie 5
Hamilton, Mary 49, 54
Hannington, Walter 29
Hansen, Anton 142
Happold, Margaret 103, 107
Harrison Bell, Florence 152, 160
Haupt, Georges 5
Hauser, Arnold 138, 144
Hayday, Arthur (Garment Workers' Union) 24
Healey, Denis 49
Henderson, Arthur 1, 8, 12-14, 17, 19, 25, 28, 35, 46, 48-50, 52-56, 58, 60, 65, 68, 77, 81, 83, 85, 92, 93, 99, 124, 175, 176, 185-187, 189
Henderson, Arthur Jnr 100
Hicks, George (Building Trades Federation) 21, 24
Highway 109, 112, 134
Hill(strom), Joe 132, 144
Hobsbawm, E.J. 5, 188
Hodges, Frank (Miners' Federation) 16
Howie, Christine 50, 124

Huddleston, John 173, 178
Huysmans, Camille 141
Huysmans, Sarah 162

Independent Labour Party 2, 3, 5,
7, 14, 25, 32, 51, 52, 54, 58, 60,
63-68, 77, 84, 85, 103, 107,
115, 126, 127, 150, 152, 160,
162, 170-175, 178, 182, 183,
186
Independent Labour Party Artists'
Guild 139
Informa Bulteno 129
Inprecorr 63
International Advisory Committee
32, 50, 84
International Brigade 30, 86, 87,
117, 118, 131, 134
International Bureau of
Revolutionary Socialist Parties
64, 66
International Committee of
Women for Permanent Peace
152
International Committee of
Women Trades Unionists 157
International Congress of Labour
and Socialist Women 159
International Congress of
Working Women 150, 152,
153
International Cooperative
Alliance 3, 112, 165, 166, 169
International Cooperative
Wholesale Society 165
International Cooperative
Women's Guild 165, 169
International Department (Labour
Party) 62, 63, 77, 105, 124,
144, 186
International Federation of
Christian Unions 15
International Friendship Holidays
103

International Institute of Social
History 113
International Labour Community
64, 65
International Miners' Federation
23
International(e) 126, 134
International Labour Office 116,
128
International Policy and Defence
32
International of Proletarian
Esperantists 126-128
International of Proletarian
Freethinkers 62
International Red Aid 62
International Service 56
International Socialist Federation
for Sport and Physical
Education 114
International of Socialist Youth
170
International Solidarity Fund 34,
85, 91, 142
International Tramping Tours
103
International Transport Workers'
Federation 15, 24, 27
International Workers of the
World 101, 132
Interparliamentary Union 101
Irving, J. (ILP) 173-175

Jalkotzy (Socialist Education
International) 102
Jaures, Jean 4, 15, 125
Jay, Douglas 84
Jewson, Dorothy 160, 161
Joe Hill 132
John, Augustus 140
Joint International Committee 16,
18, 21, 48, 50
Jones, Joseph (Miners'
Federation) 99

Jouhaux, Leon (IFTU) 16, 25, 33, 34, 112, 153

Kemiss, Dorothy 160
Kuomintang 110

Labour Bulletin 107
Labour Campaign for Public Control and Ownership of the Liquor Trade 100
Labour Esperanto Society 111
Labour International Year Book 61
Labour Magazine 15, 19, 54, 56, 85, 107, 139, 141, 144, 162, 188
Labour Research 127
Labour Research Department 62
Labour Spain Committee 31, 186, 187
Labour Woman 152
Lansbury, George 28, 65, 67, 81, 92, 112, 167, 168
Laski, Harold 113
Lawrence, Susan 50, 153, 159, 160
Lawther, Will 30
League of Nations 13, 14, 28, 33, 47, 50, 59, 60, 77, 82, 83, 93, 128, 135, 144, 159, 164, 168-170, 176, 177
Lees Smith, Hastings 17, 53
Liberal Party 17, 65, 47
Libmann, Brigitte 142
Liddington, Jill 168
Lindsay, Hugh Scott 101
Living Art in England Exhibition (1939) 142
Llewellyn Davies, Margaret 168
London Bureau 2, 7, 66, 187
Lowenstein, Kurt 114
Lucerne International (Sports) 116, 117

MacArthur, Mary 153
MacDonald, James Ramsay 14, 17-19, 26, 35, 46-54, 57, 58, 61, 64, 65, 68, 92, 104, 130, 185-187
MacDonald, Sheila 57
McGovern, John 66
McNab, Clarice 136
McShane, Harry 65, 66
Mahler, Maria 163
Maisky, Ivan 82-84, 86
Mallon, J.J. 100
Manifesto of Anationalistes 125
Marconi 136
Martin, Kingsley 83, 84
Marwick, W.H. 110
Marx Memorial Library 63
Matteotti Fund 26
Maxton, James 77, 130
May, H.J. 165
Mellor, David 138
Middleton, James 5, 31, 53, 56, 81, 82, 85, 86, 88, 92, 137, 169, 181, 187
Middleton, Lucy 84
Milk for Spain Campaign 169
Miller, Lee 142
Mitchison, Naomi 107
Montague, C.E 4
Morrison, Herbert 63, 68, 78, 81, 82, 86, 105, 119
Mortimer, James 181
The Mothers' International 135
Munzenberg, Willi 62, 63, 78, 100
Mussolini, Benito 30, 80, 81, 85, 109, 190

Nash, Paul 139
National Council for the Prevention of War 18
National Council of Labour Colleges 111, 128
National Emergency Conference

on Spain (1938) 86, 189
National Federation of Working
  Women 150, 153
National Minority Movement 19-
  21, 29
National Unemployed Workers'
  Movement 3, 29, 66
National Union of Teachers 111
National Workers' Committee
  Movement 19
National Workers' Sports
  Association 117
New Leader 5, 8, 32, 107, 115,
  124, 125, 137, 139, 142
New Nation 178
New Statesman 83, 84
Nixon, John (ILP) 173-175
No Conscription Fellowship 47
No More War Exhibition (1934)
  142
No More War Movement 15, 18
Novotny, Julius (Arbeiter Radio)
  137

O'Neill, F.R. 139
Ollenhauer, Erich 103, 170-177,
  181, 183
Orwell, George 30
Oudegeest (IFTU) 15, 21, 24,
  153

Pallister, Minnie 107, 160
Paton, John (ILP) 64
Peace Alliance 7, 170
Pels, Alice 160
People's Parodies 135
Phillips, Marion 128, 152, 153,
  155, 159, 160, 163, 168, 182
Pilgrim 103
Plant in the Sun 131
Plebs 127
Plebs League 110, 111
Pioneer 170
Polasky, Janet 66
Pollitt, Harry 85

Ponsonby, Arthur 50
Popp, Adelheid 160, 165
Posthumus, Prof. N.W. 113
Practical Socialism for Britain
  (1935) 81
Pravda 78
Price, John 84
Pritt, D.N. 100
Proletarian Parodies 135
Protection of Animals 100
Public Order Act (1936) 114
Purcell, Albert 16, 19, 20, 24,
  156

Quaile, Mary 155

Radical Workers' Esperanto
  Movement 126
Ramdin, Ron 8
Rank and File Movement
  (London Busmen) 29
Read, Herbert 141, 142
Red Falcon Youth 114
Red Flag 131, 132, 134, 145
Red International of Labour
  Unions 19, 20
Red Triangle Tours 103
Reichstag Trial 100, 130
Relief Committee for the Victims
  of German Fascism 78
Revolutionary Policy Committee
  7, 65, 175
Richards, Mary Bell 160
Robeson, Paul 130-132, 143, 144
Robins, Mrs Raymond 153
Rogerson, Cecil (WTA) 103
Rolland, Romain 124, 125
Rouse, Frank (ILP) 173
Royal Institute for International
  Affairs (Chatham House) 57,
  68, 78, 188
Ruskin College 1, 110, 111, 113,
  128
Russian Famine Relief 62

Salter, Arthur 99
Sassenbach (IFTU) 15, 25
Samuel, H. Walter 100
Scott Lindsay 101
Scottish Labour Football
    Federation 111
Senior, Clarence 79
Sennacieca Asocio Tutmonda
    126
Sennaciulo 126
Seton, Marie 130
Shaw, Tom (Textile Workers)
    16, 19, 48, 52, 53, 55, 101, 160,
    168
Siaba, Rudolf (Sports'
    International) 116
Silverman, Sidney 57
Six Point Group 162
Slater, Montague 141
Smith-Rose, Rose 160
Snowden, Philip 26, 49, 51, 52,
    58, 65
The Social Scene Exhibition
    (1934) 142
Socialist Education International
    110, 114
Socialist League 3, 7, 66, 76, 77,
    83, 85, 187, 189
Socialist Workers' Sports
    International 188
La Socialista 125
Spanish Campaign Committee 31
Spiller, C.W. (Postal Workers'
    Union) 126, 128
Spoor, Ben 4
Sports' International, see Socialist
    Workers' Sports International
Standing Joint Committee of
    Industrial Women's
    Organisations 152, 153, 155
Starr, Mark (Builders' Union)
    126, 128
Stuart-Bunning, George Harold
    14
Sutherland, Mary 163, 164

Swales, Alonso Beaumont 19
Syndicalist International 15
Szorbel, Geza 142

Tapsell, Walter (CPGB) 117, 118
Teachers' International 110
Teachers' International 142
Teachers' Labour Committee 111
Thomas, Albert (ILO) 13, 128
Thomas, J.H. 15, 17 25, 26, 47,
    48, 53, 54, 65
Thomas, Tom (Workers' Theatre
    Movement) 131
Thompson, Fred (TGWU) 29
Thorez, Marcel 79-81
Tillett, Ben 19, 25
Tolpuddle Martyrs 117
Tracey, Herbert 19, 21, 28, 33,
    56, 67
Transk, Martha 160
Transport and General Workers'
    Union 1, 14, 16, 20, 29, 101,
    104, 155, 160
Transport House 26, 31, 56, 57,
    63, 101, 143
Trades Disputes and Trades
    Union Act (1927) 21, 186
The Travel Log 103
Trevelyan, Sir Charles 83, 86
Tuckwell, Gertrude 153
Turner, John 19

Union of Democratic Control 47
Union Internationale des Villes et
    Pouvoirs Locales 101

Van Roosbroeck (LSI) 55, 85,
    190
Vandervelde, Emile 6, 52, 56, 58,
    59, 66, 67, 79, 80, 82, 92, 100,
    113, 116, 162, 187, 189
Vienna Sports' Festival (1926)
    117
Vienna workshop 139

Wake, Egerton (Labour Party
National Agent) 172
Wallhead, R.C. (ILP) 54
War Emergency: Workers'
National Committee 152
Webb, Beatrice 47, 48, 50, 150,
159
Webb, Maurice (League of
Youth) 175
Webb, Sidney 50, 53
Wels, Otto 48, 55, 78
West, Alick 141
Westphal, Max 171
Wheatley, John 161
Wilkinson, Ellen 58, 67, 130, 150
Willis, Lord (Ted) 170, 176, 178-
183, 190
Windle, R.T. 173
Winter, Max (Socialist Education
International) 110
Wintringham, Tom 142
Wireless International, see
Arbeiter Radio
Women's International Council
152
Women's International League
for Peace and Freedom 168,
169
Women's Labour League 106,
115, 150, 152, 153, 155, 159
Women's Peace Crusade 152
Women's Social and Political
Union 150

Women's Trade Union League
150, 152, 153
Woodcraft Folk 114, 118
Woodcraft Lodges 114
Woolf, Leonard 50
Workers' Dreadnought 127
Workers' Education Association
103, 107, 111, 112
Workers' Esperanto Club 126
The Worker Esperantist 127
Workers' International Relief 62,
78
Workers' Life 21, 128
Workers' Music League 130, 134
Workers' Olympiad
(Frankfurt,1925; Vienna, 1931;
Barcelona,1936; Antwerp,1937)
117, 118
Workers' Travel Association
125, 188
Workers' Weekly 61
World Congress on Disarmament
(1922) 17, 18

Young Communist League 114,
172, 174, 179, 181
Youngman, Nan 140
Youth for Socialism (1938) 178
Youth Militant 178

Zamenhof, Lidia 126
Zamenhof, Ludovic Lazar 126
Zinoviev letter (1924) 61

211